WALL STREET'S BULL AND HOW TO BEAR IT

By Robert A. Isbitts and Ian Lohr

PREFACE

Investment books are a dime a dozen—look at Borders or Barnes & Noble and you'll see hundreds of titles. Titles like: "Get Rich Quick," "Investing for Idiots," "How to Make a Killing in the Market," "The Best Investment Product," "10 Stocks You Must Own," and so on.

Furthermore, the media purports to offer a plethora of investment advice. News shows feature analysts touting sectors or securities. "Gene, we've seen the absolute rock bottom trough in [fill in sector, stock, bond, etc.]. The time to buy is now!" or "Phyllis, [fill in sector, stock, bond] has seen a dramatic run up the past [week, month, year, decade]. Every investor should hop on the bandwagon now."

Newspapers showcase the returns of mutual funds for yesterday, or this week. And the ads—if you believe every mutual fund ad, there isn't a fund on the face of the earth which hasn't beaten the S&P 500 by 700% over the past [year, five years, to the beginning of time and so on . . .]

Magazines like *Rich*, *Investing*, *Affluent*, actually every magazine which MAY be read by the potentially affluent from *Golf Digest* to *Money* to *Forbes* are rife with ads for investment products—funds, managers, ETFs—and you know, ALL of them are entirely appropriate for every investor!

So why another investment book and what's different about this one? Well, the current crop of the above have very little information content, and nothing to help mom and pop investor make sense of their financial prospects. Most of the sources of investment "Help" have an ulterior motive—to tout a particular investment product, and guess who wrote the source. Rob Isbitts' book doesn't try to sell you anything and would NEVER profess to claim any investment is right for all investors.

Responsible investing isn't about blindly picking yesterday's winners; it is about developing investment objectives, which are appropriate for the specific goals you have for the assets you've accumulated. Isbitts encourages all investors to begin their investment search by developing well thought out investment objectives.

Responsible investing isn't about the search for astronomical returns—it is about undergoing a sophisticated process to develop a well thought out investment strategy, which matches your investment objectives. Isbitts' book explains such a process.

Responsible investing doesn't mean dumping all your hard earned assets into one particular fund or funds; it is about asset allocation and investment style allocation that fits the investment strategy. Isbitts discusses developing an asset allocation methodology.

So, life is full of self-serving investment books which offer very little benefit to investors. The authors, purported experts all, are seldom neutral in their recommendations. Generally, in the investment game, one thing investors need to be aware of—it's all about sales. Investment sales people get paid for selling product.

Once in a while, though, a real professional comes along—one with no axe to grind and no product to push. A financial advisor who so fervently believes in doing what's right for the client that he'll forego a client relationship rather than risk having the client select something inappropriate. Rob Isbitts is one such professional.

This book is for investors frustrated with the lack of personalized investment advice who want an objective unconflicted plan to develop suitable investment strategies. I hope someday you have an opportunity to meet Isbitts and discuss investing with him. I trust you will be as impressed with his caring integrity as I was.

John Lohr, Esq.
Owner, Howling Wolf Enterprises
Investment Education Experts

Ian Lohr
President, Islepress
Co-Author

Orlando, FL
January 14, 2006

INTRODUCTION

Today's investors have a lot on their mind. They are constantly bombarded with sales information created by the tens of thousands of investment firms and financial advisors out there. Virtually every magazine, newspaper and financial web site claims to offer investment advice which is appropriate for everyone.

But, there are fatal flaws in this system. Not every investment is appropriate for everyone although national and local media would lead you to believe that everyone should chase today's hottest dot.

I've been in the investment business since 1986, and what I have seen as the greatest need among today's investors is quality, easy to understand basic education about the workings of today's global economies and the investment opportunities within them.

Given all the bad advice I have seen, the one thing I can say is, "If it sounds too good to be true, it is".

There is no one prescription for success; no simple black box which everyone can access which will give them a good shot at investment success; no guarantees. Rather, investing is a methodical process—a process which requires introspection, analysis, a balancing of goals and desires, and good old fashioned hard work. Unless you have money to throw away, investing should not be undertaken lightly. Stocks and bonds, hedge funds and commodities, futures and ETFs are not for everybody. Despite what proponents of Social Security reform say, the stock market is not for everybody. After all, Woody Allen hit fairly close to the mark when he defined a stock broker as, "Somebody who invests your money until it's gone".

So, if there are no sure things, what do we offer you in this book? We offer you a process: Education, discipline and a plan. Successful investing does not mean getting the highest return possible. It is not about beating the S & P 500, nor is it about owning last week's hot stock.

Successful investing requires a process. It begins with carefully examining your current financial situation—liquid assets, real estate, liabilities, income, potential for growth, and other relevant factors. There are some basic questions to address, and we will go over them in this book so that you will be familiar with them. The answers to these questions need to be set down in writing. Once you have a clear grasp of what your current financial health is, you have to consider your future liabilities. These are reflected in your investing goal. Maybe you want to send your kids to great private colleges. Maybe you want to retire early, buy a Winnebago and head for Alaska. Maybe you want to leave a legacy to your favorite charity. Once you have considered your goals, you can create a series of liabilities, which have to be funded. Matching your financials to your goals, the question to ask is, "Can I get there from here, based on my direction?" This is the process of investment strategy setting. It often is erroneously referred to in some circles as "financial planning". It is so much more than that, as you will see.

The process involves give and take, fine-tuning and adjusting, balancing and rebalancing. It may require some sacrifice on your part. Maybe you really won't be able to retire when you want, or live exactly the retirement lifestyle you want, or the kids will have to go to Tier 2 schools.

We encourage everyone to engage in this dialogue with a financial advisor, but, it should be the right financial advisor—one who exudes trust, who listens and who can render objective, unconflicted investment advice for a reasonable fee. In this book, you will learn what it means to be "product neutral" and why you benefit from dealing with a product neutral financial advisor. There are so many investing opportunities available today, it is difficult to sort through the myriad of financial products. There are cost effective methods of using investment professionals to assist you. Use wisely.

We want you to understand investment basics in their simplest forms, so you can have a meaningful dialogue with your financial advisor. The core understanding is a study of how the various markets act and react with one another. Remember a term called **"low correlation"** as it becomes essential to the process later.

At our firm we have been helping investors since 1998. I have been writing this book in my head since 1986 when I entered the industry. I have developed a core investment philosophy, which I will share with you.

In the past few years, as markets have exploded and imploded, fraught with myriad "right" investment vehicles, we have developed a "Hybrid" approach to investing which, if utilized properly, can be a key to your portfolio success. While we have become known for this unique proprietary methodology, we are happy to share it with you as an educational tool to help you sort through the maze of financial products.

The most crucial component of your investment success is accurately and truthfully managing your own expectations within your comfort level. Far too many financial advisors are willing to let you purchase some investment opportunity that is totally unrealistic to either meet your financial expectations or, even worse, has too much downside possibility for real loss. These are *salespeople*, not advisors, and what an investor needs is expert advice, not personalized advertising. Others allow you to be artificially categorized according to some proprietary model: you are anointed a "6" or a "3", or "Conservative", "Aggressive," "Moderate". Your account gets shunted into a bucket with a bunch of other investors who may or may not have similar circumstances and goals, to receive only a pittance of individual attention. The mind boggles.

Your personal Investment Objectives aren't fit for a Black Box. They will be as unique as you are. This is not the stuff of cocktail parties—it is a methodology to gain control of your investment strategies and maximize your chances of reaching your goals.

The opinions I make in this book are original, but the observations I make are not. Wall Street's indiscretions have been public news for years, especially since the stock market "Tech" bubble burst in the year 2000. There are ways to stay clear of the shenanigans and pursue a strategy that allows you to get what you want out of your hard-earned wealth.

I plan to point out how you can identify Wall Street's "bull," and not only "bear it" but persevere through it.

I hope this book helps you.

Rob Isbitts
Chief Investment Officer
Emerald Asset Advisors
Weston, FL
January, 2006

TABLE OF CONTENTS

CHAPTER 1: BULLS, BEARS, PIGS AND ME

"Ah, Wall Street. High Finance. Bulls, bears, people from Connecticut"
– Jerry Seinfeld

The world of finance and investing is stereotyped in many ways. When you hear the term "Wall Street," what do you think of? What image first comes into your mind? Is it people in slick suits walking into skyscrapers in New York City? Is it a crowd of traders huddled around a trading pit at the stock exchange? Or perhaps it's one of the stockbroker movies: *Bonfire of the Vanities*, *Trading Places*, *Wall Street*, etc. Whatever the image is, it carries no more than a shred of truth for most individual investors. More likely, Wall Street to them is more about the reading and research they might have done for their own investments, or the investment advisor they have worked with. But all of the supposed glamour of the investment world has led, in my opinion, to a huge misconception about what it means to invest your hard-earned money and seek advice in doing so.

To start our journey to demystify some of the financial world's greatest stereotypes, and help you to separate reality from mythology, let's take a quick look at the history behind the terms, "bull" and "bear" which are commonly used in financial jargon.

A fellow named Cecil Adams wrote the following explanation on the website straightdope.com. Ironically, he wrote this back on July 11, 1986, which was right about the time I started my career in New York City:

"Bear" is thought to have originated in a proverb that goes along the lines of, "Don't sell the bearskin before you've caught the bear." This is roughly equivalent to "Don't count your chickens before they're hatched," which is precisely what stock market bears do. Anticipating declining market prices, they sell stock they don't own yet, gambling that the price will fall by the time they actually have to buy the stock and deliver it, netting them big bucks. The term had become popular among London stock traders by the early 1700s, when the bearishly inclined were called "bearskin jobbers."

The origin of "bull"--i.e., somebody who buys stock in the expectation that the price will rise--is not as clear. The term appears to have arrived on the scene a bit later than bear, and some believe it was suggested mostly by alliterative analogy to the earlier expression. The usual explanation for the choice is that bulls habitually toss their heads upward, but you could just as easily make the case that bulls get their way by bulling their way ahead--they create a stampede of optimism that prices will rise, and the inevitable result, the laws of supply and demand being what they are, is that prices do rise. However, this theory could be a load of you know what.

So, this is the common wisdom about the bull-bear thing. But it could be inaccurate. I've also heard that the symbols were so named because a bull attacks upward with his horns, and a bear attacks with his claws moving downward. This is a good warm up for a lot of situations we'll encounter in this book and as investors. Certainly those who take a beating in the market may be left with the feeling they have been gored and mauled.

Investing and financial planning are not black and white. They are very gray. Yet a lot of advice is given to people every day that is based on what is presented as certainty. "Invest in stocks for a decade and you'll make a lot of money. Grow your assets by 7% a year and you'll be able to retire at age 60." I don't want to de-emphasize planning. It is important. I do want to de-emphasize treating the outcome of a projection as if it were reality.

With that in mind, let's examine the tale of the biggest investing generation ever to grace our planet…the Baby Boomers – those born from 1946-1964. I wrote this piece for a magazine story I was asked to write in 2005. This version was too long to publish in the magazine, but we have nearly 200 pages to go so it fits just fine here ☺

You've Learned, You've Earned, You've Partied…Now What?

(An Ode To The Baby Boomers)

The baby boom generation has had a significant impact on the world at every stage of their lives. This group, defined as those born from 1946-1964 (I just made it), will have a big influence on how the markets behave in the next 30-40 years at least. They will also determine how financial advice is delivered and what standards advisors are held to. This is my message to the Baby Boom generation, but if you are not a "boomer" this still applies to you because the way these people use their wealth will have a direct and significant impact on what happens to yours.

A while back, I learned an expression that stuck in my memory. "Learn in your twenties, earn in your thirties." You graduate high school or college, set out into the world to make your fortune, and hopefully make a difference, too. For many of us, the early years of the journey brought us to one level of schooling we may not have anticipated after finishing our college or graduate degrees: the school of hard knocks.

Many successful people I've met recall the struggles of their first decade on their own. The process of choosing a career, establishing oneself in an industry, perhaps building a company, and starting a family is a rigorous one as we all know.

By the time you reached your thirties, life seemed to be taking on more direction. In part, this is because you discovered who you were – as a person, as a companion, as a business leader. You developed a skill set that allowed you to really go out and get what you wanted out of the various parts of life. As part of this, you enjoyed the thrill of making "real" money for the first time. You discovered the pleasure of fine dining, exotic vacations, and a birds-eye view of your favorite sporting events. The sky was the limit for you – the good times were here.

For many from the baby-boom generation, the decade of their thirties ended between the late 1980's and mid-1990's. The timing could not have been better. Just when they were entering their peak earning years, the U.S. stock market went on its best run in history. From the beginning of 1988 through early 2000, the market, measured by the S&P 500 Index, gained about 15% per year over twelve years. The Nasdaq Composite gained 24% per year. That's pretty good for an "average" return! Home prices increased steadily, and interest rates dropped, and dropped and dropped some more. For those who wondered what would happen after learning in their twenties and earning in their thirties, the answer became quite apparent: they would earn more, invest it, earn a lot more, and spend like they had never spent before! It was our generation's version of the "Roaring 1920's."

And like that time, there came a thundering halt to the fun. Not in one day, as in the 1929 stock market crash, but over a three year period where all the investment rules many grew up with were rewritten. Remember "buy the dips" as the mantra of so many Wall Street pros, referring to how easy it was to make money in stocks by simply buying more Intel and JDS Uniphase and Sun Microsystems whenever they temporarily fell in price. Then, declines in one's monthly investment statement became more the rule than the exception. Fortunately, unlike in 1920's, you didn't have to "bootleg" to get a stiff drink. Let's face it, many investors needed it.

The fallout is not entirely what you would expect. Investors in the "Baby Boomer" generation have not, as a group, become more concerned about their wealth. A recent survey of 1000 boomers and retirees by Oppenheimer Funds found that most are uncomfortable with how much they've accumulated during their pre-retirement years. A whopping 97% said they regret how they spent their money, considering how much they could have accumulated. Despite this, they say they still overspend and many are not concerned about rising costs. In a very 21st Century way, this is a case of "live and learn…but only if you really want to".

So, where is our learner-earner-investor now? Forget about what the stock market and interest rates and all of that other Wall Street stuff are doing.

These are the questions you should be asking yourself and communicating to your advisor if you have one:

1. What is it I really want out of life?

2. What kind of retirement do I want (and if I am retired, am I getting what I want out of it)?

3. Do I want to work harder now to improve my chances of retiring earlier than most people do?

4. Is it more important to keep what I have or do I want to use my current wealth as a stepping-stone to pursuing a much larger fortune?

5. What sacrifices am I willing to make now in order to achieve a comfortable balance between how I live today, how long and how hard I will work, and when and how I will retire?

This last question is particularly important now that many people, especially entrepreneurs, say they don't want to retire in the traditional sense. What they want is, at a fairly early age, to have amassed sufficient assets such that if they manage it prudently, they don't have to work for financial reasons. They may still want to work, but on their own terms. They may want to freelance within their industries, or teach, or just take a lot more time off. I call this state of mind and wealth "financial retirement".

This concept does not only apply to the person in their early 50's with $1.5mm in liquid assets and a $200,000 annual income. It is also a very helpful process for the ultra-wealthy to go through. If you have a portfolio of $40mm, and you spend $2mm a year, that means you are spending 5% of your assets. While it may not sound like someone in this situation would have a financial care in the world, this is reality for many, particularly in luxurious So. Florida. Once you get used to a standard of living, it is very tough to take a step backwards. Just ask yourself what mental turmoil you'd create for yourself if you had to go back to living on the income you made when you were 25.

Bulls and bears have ways to reach their objectives. But those who turn into investment "pigs," always trying to make a quick buck or extrapolating their recent returns into the future ("I just made 50% on this last year, so I'm not going to sell it – I think it will go up even more this year"), are ultimately doomed to failure. Think about how many people you know that made a lot of money on tech stocks in the late 1990's. Now, how many of them retained anywhere near their peak value? Not many.

Keep this in mind as well. The bull and bear are Wall Street's long time symbols. The pig is also a symbol of the leanings of some investors. And as the expression goes, "Bulls Make Money, Bears Make Money, Pigs Get Slaughtered".

ABOUT ME

When I first told my wife Dana (pronounced Dahna, not Dayna) that I was writing a book, she responded with that basic human emotion…laughter. "After all," she said, "You haven't READ a book since I've known you (1990). How will you write one?" Dana has a great sense of humor, and her facts were not totally inaccurate. I have probably read a handful of books in the last decade or so, but there's a good reason. I have an obsession – I read constantly about investing: articles, newsletters, market reports, financial planning ideas, trends, market history, client service ideas, asset class studies, new investment vehicles, etc. Money management is a constantly evolving world, and getting caught in the clichés of the past can get you in trouble. The only way to stay ahead of the sea of change is to read, read, read…and think.

I started my career in 1986 as a portfolio assistant with Fuji Bank and Trust in New York City's World Trade Center. Working on the 97th floor right out of college was quite an experience. Part of my job was to read all of the research reports that the Wall Street brokers sent to us, and report any interesting ideas to the portfolio managers.

This was back when Japanese banks were on the verge of taking over the world. The Japanese economy had made incredible strides since the end of World War II, and Japanese companies were sending employees to the U.S. to bulk up operations here. They were an economic force, so naturally Fuji Bank was a prime target of the U.S. brokerage firms. While the portfolio managers were wined and dined, I read the research and built a spreadsheet tracking system for the bank's investment portfolio (they were using pencils and accounting paper to track positions and security prices before that).

I became what you might call a "serial learner" and my curiosity for what made markets work and what influenced market participants was overwhelming to me. I had found a career passion, and set out to learn everything I could about how this thing called Wall Street worked. When the Internet came around, with its endless supply of information and research capabilities, I was in "pig heaven". That passion and drive to learn is even stronger for me today than it was in 1986 because I have seen investing from so many different angles, and feel I have separated what is worth pursuing and what is not. Today, I focus on using the knowledge I have accumulated to help investors make the best choices for themselves.

I haven't read many books since then, but if you were to convert the number of pages and charts I've read and studied since 1986, I'd guess you could fill a mid-sized library. Just ask my wife, who on more than one occasion has had to repeat something to me because I was deeply involved in a report about merger arbitrage, a new system for tracking client communications, or an observation about investor behavior. It is an obsession for sure, but I assume that my clients prefer that to an advisor who feels that it is OK to stop learning.

I was born in Fair Lawn, New Jersey, a suburb of New York City, in 1964. I grew up in a middle class town that experienced solid growth during the 1970's and 1980's. I graduated with an undergraduate degree in Finance from SUNY Albany (1986) and subsequently earned an MBA at Rutgers University (1994). I received a Certified Fund Specialist (CFS) degree back in 1995. This involved successfully completing an extensive, 60-hour study program and exam on the analysis and use of mutual funds.

My parents were both a big inspiration and continue to be. My father taught me the basics of technical analysis (or "charting" securities prices), which he has practiced for 50 years. This helped drive my interest in the capital markets and investing. My mother made sure that my brother and I grew up in a caring environment, and I believe that is a big reason why I try so hard to provide that to my clients today.

My other great inspiration came from participating in team sports as a kid. Whether it was pick-up basketball or Little League baseball, the idea of being part of a team striving to make each other better and achieve a common goal is something I really enjoyed then and do now. As a kid, I probably didn't realize that -- as an A-type personality, I just liked anything that allowed me to run around a lot. As an adult, I get tremendous satisfaction out of what we as a team accomplish for our clients.

Based on the number of hours I have put in learning and practicing my craft, I could probably get credit for four decades of experience, not two. Just ask my lovely wife who has made many incredible meals over the years that I've unfortunately had to reheat in the microwave. In the past I have worked for other notable firms in the industry, including DLJ, Morgan Stanley, Fiduciary Trust, and the aforementioned Fuji Bank and Trust.

I pioneered the "Hybrid" investment strategy used by Emerald Asset Advisors, and this will be an important topic as the book goes on. I was named a "Heavy Hitter in Finance" by the South Florida Business Journal in 2004 and 2005. My published work includes more than 50 investment articles, commentaries and newsletters, and I regularly act as a source for several investment industry newspapers and magazines.

In 2005, I was named one of the Top 100 Wealth Managers in the United States by Robb Report Worth Magazine. I am most proud of this honor for three reasons:

1. It is not something you achieve because you have the right connections or pay a lot of money. There are a lot of "awards" in my industry and others that are based on that instead of who is truly operating at the highest level.

2. It is not based on how many assets you manage or how much money you have made for yourself. As Worth describes it, its about "dedication, vision and experience." Respondents must provide detail and insightful answers to a very long list of questions about how they approach and run their relationships with clients.

3. It puts an emphasis on the advisor's use of alternative, or non-traditional investment strategies. If you do not think "outside the box" and recommend alternative investments to clients, you do not qualify for the list. This was not always the case with the Worth 100 list but it is now. I believe that what distinguished me from the many qualified advisors who vied for the Top 100 was my creation and development of something called the "Hybrid Strategy" which I discuss in detail further along in this book.

I mentioned that I was born in 1964, long after the Great Depression ended. However, we cannot escape our genetics, and particularly from my father's influence, I am a child of a child of the Depression Era – my dad was born in 1931 so he grew up in it. I suspect that is where my innate concern for protecting one's rear-end from financial disaster came from. I think that has benefited my clients over the years and I hope it helps you to keep your thinking balanced when it comes to reading this book and assimilating the information within.

Outside the office, I am a Board member for the Daniel Cantor Center, a Member of the Nova Southeastern University Young Entrepreneurs Council. I have been an active member at my local temple, Bnai Aviv of Weston, Florida. I have been married to Dana since 1992, and am a father of three very special children – Jordann (born in 1996), Tyler (born in 1998) and Morgan (born in 2002). My interests include golf (decent short game, but by the time I get to use it, I've taken too many strokes to salvage par or bogie!) and coaching Little League baseball.

So this is the path I took to become an advisor to hundreds of millions of dollars of investors' wealth. Since I co-founded my firm, Emerald Asset Advisors with South Florida insurance veterans Bruce Levy and Scot Hunter in 1998, I have written over 50 articles, newsletters and commentaries on a wide variety of topics for my clients. This book was created to expand on those thoughts, and provide a more complete picture for an investor who wants the comfort of knowing that there IS a way to invest without looking over your shoulder, without worrying that your interests may at some point be secondary to those of your advisor or their superiors.

CHAPTER 2: THE BIRTH OF A FLEXIBLE INVESTMENT STRATEGY—AN INTRODUCTION TO HYBRIDS

"It's always in the last place you look" Old Proverb

During my time at DLJ (1995-1998), I started to realize that the days of 30% annual returns in the stock market would not last forever. I have always been a student of financial market history and realized that while I could not predict when the stock market bubble would collapse, it ultimately would. Bubbles always burst.

Several years ago, I started a research effort with the goal of identifying mutual funds with strategies that used the stock and bond markets, but with protective measures in place—some call them "hedged" mutual funds, we call them Hybrids. Since we started using that name before Hybrid automobiles and Hybrid golf clubs hit the mainstream, we feel like we were not copycats. Then, in 1999, with a lot of help from my partner Allan Budelman, I created the Emerald Hybrid Strategy as an educational tool to explain to clients how they could pursue investment returns that aimed to exceed the interest rate on their bonds, and spare them much of the volatility of the stock market—without using hedge funds.

I have advanced training and many years of experience using mutual funds, and consider myself to be very well aware of when they are effective and not. When the stock market fell over, we increased the use of these strategies for clients.

The Index started as an educational tool to explain to clients how they could pursue investment returns that had an excellent chance to exceed the interest rate on their bonds, while sparing them most of the volatility of the stock market. As the bear market got underway, we realized that hedge funds were becoming popular with investors. However, while we identified and used a small number of hedge funds we felt were helpful for some of our clients, we also realized that there was much about hedge funds in general that would not address the needs of our clients for the long-term. Their limited liquidity, potentially high fees and lack of transparency (i.e. what is going on inside my portfolio?) were a turn off to us, and by extension to our clients. While the advisory industry started to find every possible way to make hedge funds accessible to investors, we started to go in another direction.

Using our Hybrid Strategy as a guidepost, we started running diversified portfolios containing these specialized funds. I became convinced that we could deliver the kind of return that conservative hedge funds do, without some of the headaches that come with hedge funds. In addition, there seems to be much more focus in our industry on creating fancy-looking products to access hedge fund managers. One fellow I know referred to hedge funds as a "compensation scheme masquerading as an asset class". I think there's some truth to that because I have seen how well our Hybrid Strategy compares to the more conservative types of hedge funds, without a lot of the baggage that hedge funds carry in the eyes of investors.

The financial services industry thinks their clients want hedge funds. In my opinion and from my experience, what they really want is more consistently positive returns than they get from the broad stock market, while exceeding the low returns available on bonds.

To us, the proof is in the fact that we rarely if ever have had someone tell us that the Hybrid Strategy is a bad idea. I have presented it to several other advisors and asked them to poke holes in it to make sure we were not crazy - they have had little success in doing so, and in fact have asked us to sub-advise portfolios for their clients. Earlier this year, I realized that while over 1/3 of our clients' assets are currently invested in the Hybrid style, there would be many other investors and advisors who would want access to what we are doing. So, we have set up a way for that to happen. Most importantly, I think we've done so in a way that is quite beneficial to our existing clients. As our firm grows in part from our "exporting" our Hybrid Strategy to people outside our full-service client base, the services and service level we provide to our clients will continue to increase. It's a win for everyone. I think our clients really appreciate that we continuously look for ways to solve their financial issues, instead of doing what some in our industry have a reputation for: pushing products that are more beneficial to the advisor than the client. Sometimes, the solutions are already available, and we just have to learn and understand them. Other times, we need to be more creative and design something ourselves.

In fact, I have struggled over the years to appropriately describe what I do to people who are completely unfamiliar with the independent financial advisory business. I'm not a stockbroker, and I'm more than a portfolio manager. There are other people at Emerald who handle the sales and marketing, so I'm not that either. Recently, I decided that what I really am is a designer -- a designer of action plans to maximize the probability that you will be able to live a comfortable lifestyle, now and when you retire (if you are retired, they are one and the same). It started nearly twenty years ago as a learning experience. It later became a personal search to find what I was good at it, and now it has become a passion. I love what I do and I get a real thrill out of helping people get where they want to go. People don't come to us because they want to own stocks and bonds. They work with us because they want certain things out of life, and their portfolio is the currency that allows them to get those things. Our job is to make sure they take the best path to get there.

THE THREE RULES OF INVESTING

(A Recurring Theme For This Book)

Throughout this book, I keep coming back to a few key themes. One of these is what I consider to be the three most important rules of investing.

I'll list them here for you:

Number One: Keep what you have.

Number Two: Grow what you have as much as you can.

Number Three: Rule one is more important than rule two.

Not all investors would agree with that order. Young, confident people earning huge incomes may prefer to grow their money aggressively, knowing that if they lose it, they can always make more. They fashion themselves as some kind of family mint—"lose all the money you want, we'll print more."

But I'm not saying that one should simply hunker down, protect their nest egg and hope that somehow it still grows over time. I'm saying there are approaches to portfolio management that in my opinion offer a higher probability than most for you to have your investment cake and eat it too. That is, they offer reasons to expect that your money will grow most of the time, but you will be shielded from the worst the markets may offer. Over time, this approach may very well allow you to meet or exceed the returns of more aggressive investors. Why? Because a strategy that can successfully preserve capital in tough markets and simply tag along in strong markets often leads to greater success than trying to navigate the roller coaster ride that most investors experience when they pursue growth of their capital.

Over the past several years, I have tried to gradually familiarize my clients with the Hybrid approach. Since most people reading this book have not been down that educational road with me, I decided to present this series of essays (with some updated information), so that you can quickly acquire the background knowledge that it took me about a decade to develop.

I first presented the Hybrid strategy to our clients formally in a 2002 article, excerpted on the following pages.

When Growth and Income Aren't Enough:

Strategies That Seek Stock-Like Returns With Bond-Like Risk

Investors and their advisors have traditionally designed portfolios with a basic mixture of two widely divergent types of investments. On the one hand, Preservation/Income Investments—bonds and cash holdings designed to provide safe cash flow and stability of principal—and on the other, Growth Investments—a diversified portfolio of stocks and/or stock mutual funds to pursue long-term returns above those available in a "fixed income" investment. While there are many variations on these simple themes, the basic purposes for investment generally fall into on category or the other.

Advisors and their clients have devised an infinite number of "Asset Allocation models" in search of the right of mix of these investments. During the 1990's, strong returns were common, as the stock and bond markets performed well. It was tough to fail.

Then came the market downturn of late 2000, and the beginning of 2001. Many investors reacted with confusion and deep concern. Not knowing what the volatile stock market would bring next, some ran to the shelter of cash, hoping to ride out the rough patch and re-enter the market. Others tried to guess when the market would bottom, hoping to make maximum profit from an eventual recovery.

I believe that in down market periods, both of these pursuits have a low likelihood of success. We believe that most portfolios should have core investments in both preservation/income and growth. We also feel strongly that many investors can benefit from a third type of investment that can complement and enhance one's core portfolio. This collection of strategies, which we call "Hybrids" offer some or all of the following benefits:

1. Historical returns that have rivaled those of common stocks

2. Volatility that is more like bonds (low) than stocks (high)

3. Excellent performance relative to stocks during down stock markets

4. A risk-reduction feature that leads us to believe the strategy will continue its risk-reward characteristics in the future

The actual investments come in a variety of packages including mutual funds, individually managed accounts and limited partnerships. They each have slightly different features, but are all designed to accomplish the same goal: a lower-risk way to invest for growth. We have employed several Hybrid strategies for our clients, customized for their investment objectives. We are continually searching for others.

In addition to being core investments, there is another feature of Hybrids that goes beyond the mathematics of portfolio management: it focuses investors on the most important reason to invest in stocks – to exceed the return of bonds and increase your ability to outpace inflation. In the 1990's, beating the stock indexes (S&P, Dow Jones, etc.) became a national obsession. The sobering period that followed made people realize that they do not want their entire portfolio to grow like the market, because with that comes the market's downside risk. A generation ago, equity investing was about beating the return of bonds, and investing within your tolerance for risk. Now that many investors have learned (perhaps the hard way) what their risk tolerance is, we believe they will come to recognize Hybrid Strategies as an important piece of their long-term investment plan.

The following year, I sent this article to clients to continue the education process (again, updated for your benefit). It introduces you to why and how we build Hybrid Portfolios.

I always approached investing in general as a process of meeting life's financial obligations, as opposed to beating a standard stock or bond benchmark. This philosophy has led to the creation of an investment methodology that continuously seeks to grow assets in as consistent a path as possible. I seek out investment strategies and products that share this view, or that can be combined with others to pursue consistently positive returns with low correlation to the stock and bond markets.

This is how I define the Hybrid Strategy. Over the years, it has become the core of my clients' investment strategy and somewhat of an icon for our firm.

It is a customized portfolio of no-load mutual funds and balancing strategies specially chosen and managed. These funds are judged by us to have hedge fund-like qualities, seeking returns that approach those of stocks with far less expected volatility.

In summary, Hybrid investing is similar to the multi-manager approach used by market-neutral and opportunistic hedge fund of funds. However, by using mutual funds that employ hedge fund-like strategies, I can deliver to the investor a similar experience as hedge fund of funds in terms of absolute return, but absent many of the headaches of fund of funds. The advantages of this strategy include lower total cost, much greater liquidity, greater transparency, greater tax-efficiency and more overall flexibility in the process. I run the Hybird Strategy in Conservative, Moderate and Aggressive models (these terms are relative—even the "Aggressive Hybrid" is still far less volatile than the broad stock market). We also run a model that combines Hybrids with traditional equities.

In addition, working with my firm and other highly skilled professionals, we continue our dynamic research effort to identify additional investment vehicles to fit into the Hybrid strategy that we feel are not easily available to most investors.

The Hybrid investment process is fourfold: First, I screen the universe of all mutual funds to arrive at a list of those which pursue strategies that best represent our definition of the Hybrid approach. Many of these funds are components of the Emerald Hybrid Index, which we created in the 1990's as a way to educate our clients on what we define as Hybrids, a separate asset class from stocks, bonds and cash.

Second, I determine for each sub-sector of the Hybrid Universe (e.g. REITS, Long-Short, Arbitrage, etc.) whether we should be equal-weight, over-weight or under-weight the allocation of our Emerald Hybrid Index.

Third, I select for the portfolio a combination of funds that I feel offer the best prospects for competitive positive returns with low volatility and correlation compared to the broad stock market, in a tax-efficient manner. Again, this is a strategy for those investors who view investing as a tool to help achieve their desired lifestyle instead of relying on whatever the market provides to them as an outcome.

Finally, I continually monitor these holdings. Detailed analysis may reveal reasons to consider or execute changes to the model.

In early 2006, we were appointed as the sub-advisor (portfolio manager) of a private partnership in which we run the Hybrid Strategy. As an introduction to the limited partners that would be investing with us, I wrote the following piece, which provides a rationale for Hybrid investing:

The Rationale For Hybrid Investing

When investing the wealth you have worked so hard to achieve, you have many choices. It can be quite confusing. With all of the investment strategies out there, from the most simplistic to the utterly complex, why are we such believers in the approach we call "Hybrid Investing?"

During the course of my two decades in the investment advisory business, I have had the privilege of learning about so many different investment strategies. One conclusion I've reached is that there is something for everyone. The problem is, by the time many people find out what fits their investment "comfort zone," one of the following has occurred:

1. **They have lost a lot of money**

2. **They have not made enough money**

3. **They experienced something they didn't expect from the investment.**

Very often, it is a lack of flexibility in the investment approach that caused this comfort zone to be disrupted. Our hope in managing your assets using the Emerald Hybrid Strategy is that we can keep you in your comfort zone. While there is no guarantee that we will meet this objective, if you and your advisor have determined that our strategy is consistent with your risk profile, we like our chances of succeeding for you.

In the Emerald Hybrid Strategy, we are attempting to provide what many "hedge fund of funds" do, but deliver it in what we believe is a greater comfort zone for you. Specifically:

1. We use <u>a diversified, multi-manager approach</u>. We use multiple investment styles, run by several different money management firms. We select those firms for you and decide when to buy, hold and sell their portfolios. Over the years, we have identified many different Hybrid strategies, and we endeavor to keep searching for more.

2. We aim for <u>low market correlation</u>. That is, we try to generate long-term returns that are largely independent of what happens in the stock and bond markets.

3. We employ <u>alternative strategies to classic stock or bond portfolios</u>. We use styles that tend to have either a hedging mechanism in place and/or have not historically moved in tandem with the broad stock or bond indexes.

4. We typically use <u>no-load or load-waived mutual funds and Exchange-Traded Funds (ETFs)</u>, vehicles most experienced investors are familiar with. These vehicles are registered with the SEC under the Investment Act of 1940. This is different from a hedge fund of funds which may invest most of its assets in unregistered, private entities which are not subject to as stringent a level of regulatory due diligence.

5. <u>We do not charge an incentive fee</u> (i.e. a percentage of your profits) for our work, as hedge funds and fund of funds typically do.

6. We have <u>extensive experience</u> in using these types of investments for our clients.

<u>The bottom line for you</u>: Hybrid investing is a very FLEXIBLE approach to investing your hard-earned wealth. We will discuss the Hybrid strategy, and how I implement it, in Chapter 10.

CHAPTER 3: THE ECONOMY, MARKETS, AND CYCLES - A PRIMER

"There are two requirements for success in Wall Street. One, you have to think correctly; and secondly, you have to think independently." - Benjamin Graham

In this chapter, I present some background knowledge to help you better understand some of the investor issues we'll tackle in future chapters. Feel free to skim through as much of this as you like, depending on your level of investment experience. However, even if you have a strong grasp of some of the concepts, I still urge you to at least spend some time in this chapter so that you can get more familiar with some of the investment "mythology" I'm trying to steer you away from.

In addition, APPENDIX A at the end of this book is specifically designed to introduce you to the different types of investment styles, strategies, and products. Read it now if you are an investing rookie, or refer to it as you need to as you read the book.

I should also mention that a website I've found extremely helpful is www.investorwords.com. It's an easy to use online dictionary of investing. Feel free to use it or a similar site as a companion to this book as you seek to understand some of the terminology you might not be familiar with. In Chapter 3 we'll continue by discussing some mistakes that investors of all types have endured and how to learn from them. I am not an economist. Fortunately, my co-author Ian Lohr and his father, John, have written extensively on this subject, and have agreed to provide the relevant material.

The Federal Reserve Bank and the Domestic Economy

The economy of the United States is a seemingly complex (but actually simple) engine for continuous growth, driven by fluctuations in the amount of money that exists. Because of this deceptive, disguised simplicity, relatively few people actually understand how our economy operates. Inherent to an understanding of the American economy is an understanding of the Federal Reserve System. The Fed itself is often misunderstood, and there is a lot of misinformation about its powers and actions. Everyone seems to agree that the Fed is important and powerful, but how and why remains somewhat obscure.

The Federal Reserve System, created in 1913, is the central bank for the United States. The primary responsibility of the Fed is the regulation of the money supply (including all currency in circulation and the deposits and reserves held by banks). The amount of money in circulation in turn influences the rate of borrowing. This happens in the following way: When more money is available, it is easier to borrow money; when less money is available, the reverse is true. The rate of borrowing in turn has a significant effect on the rate of growth. Hence, the Fed regulates economic growth without actually regulating economic growth.

To summarize, the Fed regulates the money supply, and leaves the regulation of the rate of borrowing, and therefore of economic growth, to the forces of supply and demand. Before 1913, there was no real centralized control over the money supply, and bank "panics" and other minor financial crises were frequent. The Fed was designed to stabilize the banking system—a job it does admirably, and with considerable finesse.

If the Fed believes the rate of growth is too rapid, it will reduce, or "tighten", the money supply; if growth is stagnating, the Fed will increase, or "loosen" the money supply. To prevent the Fed from falling prey to partisan politics, it is distanced from the government—in it's day-to-day business, the Fed operates independently of any governmental authority.

The Fed is not a single institution. There are 12 Federal Reserve Banks in major cities and 25 additional branches in smaller cities, led by a seven-member "Board of Governors" headed by a Chairman, and a twelve-member Federal Open Market Committee (FOMC). Individual banks are also part of the Federal Reserve System—membership is required for all national banks, and state banks may also join. Members of the Board of Governors are appointed by the President—the only direct political control the Fed is subject to.

The primary function of the Fed is to maintain the health of the economy. This ideally means low inflation, high employment, moderate interest rates, strong financial markets, and a stable currency. This is a delicate balance, since high employment can lead to runaway wage hikes and inflation, undermining financial markets; however, ameliorating the effects of inflation may slow down the economy, weakening markets. Obviously, the ideal is seldom completely achieved. Some variation is normal; the Fed is responsible for preventing things from getting out of control.

The regulation of the money supply is known as "Monetary Policy". The primary tool used by the Fed in setting Monetary Policy is the careful manipulation of Short-Term Interest Rates. Banks typically adjust their interest rates in lockstep with short-term rates both in terms of loan rates and interest paid on deposits. Fed actions, or even *speculation* about future Fed actions, can also influence the pace of trading on securities markets, altering securities prices. In the long term, higher interest rates tend to curb growth and lower stock prices, while making bond and cash equivalent investments more attractive; alternatively, lower rates may boost securities prices, as growth makes more investors become comfortable accepting additional risk.

The FOMC holds regular meetings, at which it decides to loosen, tighten, or not change monetary policy, and issues a "Risk Statement" indicating current economic conditions. These Risk Statements are considered a reliable indicator of what the Fed plans to do in the future. As mentioned above, the relative tightness or looseness of Monetary Policy determines the rate of borrowing, which influences the rate of economic growth.

Changing Interest Rates...And The Ridiculous Speculation That Accompanies It

When the money supply is changed, interest rates also change. In fact, an increase or decrease in short-term rates is what the Fed is trying to achieve in authorizing its open market operations. This is done indirectly, through utilizing the market forces of supply and demand, rather than through direct control over the economy.

As reserves increase and the money supply expands, the interest rate known as the federal funds rate drops. That is the rate that banks charge each other for very short-term, overnight loans. A drop in the federal funds rate results in an immediate drop in the prime rate. That rate determines the interest rate banks charge on consumer and business loans. And when the cost of borrowing drops because the supply of money increases, demand for borrowing increases.

The opposite is true when reserves decrease and the federal funds rate increases. In this case, the prime rate increases, the price of borrowing increases, and demand for loans decreases. Reduced borrowing slows spending, which in turn slows economic expansion. While the federal funds rate may change in response to supply and demand without Fed action, it always changes when the Fed buys and sells.

The difference between the federal funds rate and the prime rate is known as the "spread". It is typically three percentage points, although not exactly and not always. For example, if the fed funds rate is 2.25%, the prime rate is 5.25%. If the Fed raises rates to 2.50%, the prime rate will rise in lockstep to 5.50%.

Moral suasion in the form of public statements by the Fed, especially by the Fed chairman, can have a substantial effect on economic activity. For example, if the Fed releases a report predicting economic growth in the near future, this may spur otherwise hesitant investors to action. In my opinion, investors today put way, way too much emphasis on guessing on what the Fed will do. The media fuels much of this by devoting endless hours of coverage to the subject of what the Fed will do.

What can't we control in this situation? The actions the Fed takes at their meetings. What can we control? We can control the way we prepare for the result of Fed actions. A big part of this preparation is very simple: the Fed's moves often mean absolutely nothing for most investors in the short-term. Not reacting to a single event whose true economic impact will not be known for several months is a good idea. What do I mean? It is typically assumed that a change in interest rates by the Fed will not be truly felt in the economy for 9-12 months. So, to engross oneself in speculation is largely a waste of time. Yet there is a great deal of time spent (perhaps unwisely so) micro-analyzing everything the Fed says and does.

Another misconception about the Fed is that when they change rates, they are changing many types of rates. In reality, they directly influence short-term rates only. But what impact does the Fed have on 5-year bonds, 10-year bonds, 30-year bonds? These rates actually have nothing to do with what the Fed is working on. They may be impacted indirectly though, as the bond market experiences a change in interest rate "spreads." For instance, if the 3-month Treasury Bill rate (which is highly impacted by Fed actions) moves up $x\%$ because the price of the Bills drop in anticipation of the Fed raising the Federal Funds rate, 10-year bond rates may move up $x\%$. However, depending on a variety of factors impacting the markets and the economy at the time, 10-year rates may go down or up by an amount other than the change in short term rates. Why? The bond market is constantly re-pricing the risk of owning a bond for 10 years (and typically getting a higher rate than a shorter-term bond) versus the lower yield but sooner maturity (less time before you get your money back) of a shorter bond.

Now, I just mentioned the "risk" of a 10-year bond. There are many different types of risks in investing, but to me, many of the so-called risks of bonds are not really risks. I would refer to them instead as "opportunity costs". You see, I believe that if you are investing solely for income and preservation of capital in a portion of your portfolio, you should own high-quality bonds and nothing else in that part of your account. And if you own high-quality bonds (such as U.S. Treasury Bonds, U.S. Agency Bonds, Corporate Bonds with high ratings (A or better), Certificates of Deposit (CDs) or Municipal Bonds (I typically stick to AAA-rated bonds here), one risk of bonds is virtually eliminated (the risk of losing your principal). Now, I'm sure that there are a very small number of examples in history when a high-quality bond ran into trouble and could not pay its interest or principal payments. Worldcom's bond rating was A before the company fell apart – that's A, which is less than AAA and AA. But I think you might have a better chance of winning the lottery than having, say a AAA Muni Bond go bust on you.

The other risk bond investors consider is "call risk". For bonds that have a call provision, the issuer can pay you back earlier than the final maturity. You get your principal back, so that part is fine; however, you don't get to enjoy the interest rate for as long as you originally expected. As I see it, this is like hearing that the restaurant you're eating dinner at ran out of dessert. Your biggest problem is finding another place to have dessert (as a self-confessed choco-holic, I'd find the nearest convenience store and grab a chocolate bar). The bond investor now realizes the "risk" of having to replace that bond income, but to me that is a much better problem than suffering a permanent loss of principal.

Market Cycles

As we have said before, in the changeable world of investment markets, one thing is certain: In some periods, prices of securities go up, and in other periods they go down. The pace of this recurrent cycle of gains and losses is not predictable. Furthermore, the peak of a rising market or the bottom of a falling market is difficult if not almost impossible to pinpoint until months after it has happened.

Two basic points to remember about market cycles are, first, that cyclical patterns recur in all asset class markets, and second, that the cyclical pattern in one asset class may work in opposition to what occurring at the same time in another asset class.

In practical terms for the investor, this means that there is no "bad time" to invest, no matter what the prevailing market conditions—the trick is in finding the appropriate investment. Furthermore, all market conditions are more or less temporary, and will change as the relevant cycle comes around again.

Cyclical Markets, Secular Markets

We touched on the bull/bear terminology earlier in the book. Now let's go beyond the words and examine them in practice. In an article in USA TODAY in 2004, "Is it a bull or a bear?", reporter Adam Shell said, *"The trend of the market is up now, but you can't say the long-term trend of the market is up anymore."* This article is further excerpted below.

> *The most simplistic definition of a bull market is when a major stock index such as the Dow Jones industrial average rallies 20% from a prior low. A bear market is a 20% decline from the most recent high. But there are various types of Bull and Bear markets.*
>
> *For instance, "Secular Market moves are those that occur over long periods of time." Shell points out that The nearly 18-year run that pushed the Dow Jones industrial average up 1,409% from August 1982 to its January 2000 peak is an example of a secular bull Market. Conversely from 1966 to 1982 when the Dow went nowhere basically is an example of a secular bear market. Different investment strategies may prove to be more effective in these differing conditions. Long bull runs favor the buy and hold mentality; while active portfolio management might be better in long bears. The problem for investors is that the type of market we are in can only be measured in hindsight—a practice most of us outside the world of the occult are not very adept at.*

33

Since 1900, there have been four secular bulls and four secular bears, Ned Davis Research says. By contrast, a cyclical move is a market trend that lasts several months to a couple of years. There have been 33 cyclical bulls and 33 cyclical bears since 1900, Ned Davis says (that's about 18 months per cycle).

Fig. 1: Secular Bull/Bear Cycles

Mr. A (Secular Bear Markets)			Mr.B (Secular Bull Markets)		
Period	Duration	Annual Rate Return	Period	Duration	Annual Rate Return
1802-1815	13	+2.8%	1815-1835	20	+9.6%
1835-1843	8	-1.1%	1843-1853	10	+12.5%
1853-1861	8	-2.8%	1861-1881	20	+11.5%
1881-1869	15	+3.7%	1896-1906	10	+11.5%
1906-1921	15	-1.9%	1921-1929	8	+24.8%
1929-1949	20	+1.2%	1949-1966	17	+14.1%
1966-1982	16	-1.5%	1982-2000	18	+14.1%
Overall	95	+0.3%	Overall	103	+13.2%

(Source: Mike Alexander's book "Stock Cycles: Why Stocks Won't Beat Money Markets Over the Next 20 Years")

Look at the table above. In our office, we simply call this "the scary chart". We show this information to clients and prospective clients as a standard part of the process of understanding how we think. Investors have been conditioned by their advisors that "stock market history" is about what happened in our adult lifetime. That certainly plays into the hands of the investment firm. They know that more than anything else, people pay attention to past performance when evaluating an investment. So, they might as well focus on a period that makes most investment performance look outstanding. One of the recurring themes I touch on throughout this book is "what's good for them is not always good for you".

Let's look at how to read this chart. The left side shows the periods classified as secular bear markets. The right side shows secular bull markets. Beside the annualized return of each period is the number of years the secular period lasted. This is important, as we are defining long (secular) trends here. This is different from a market move that lasts, say a few months or even a few years.

If you go from left to right and back to left again, down the chart, you cover 200 years of U.S. stock market history in seconds. As you do so, you get the idea that there are long periods of time in which stocks gain next to nothing, and others where they experience tremendous returns.

The secular cycles run anywhere from eight to twenty years. The last bull cycle, in the opinion of the fellow who put this together (I share that opinion) ended in 2000. If that's the case, you would expect that the secular bear that began in 2000 would run through 2008 at the earliest and 2020 at the latest, unless a record is broken.

Notice also that the secular bull market we all lived through, from 1982-2000 was the most powerful on record. While the "Roaring 1920's" produced the highest annual returns on record before the infamous Crash of '29 occurred, the secular bull market lasted only eight years, the shortest time period on record. The secular bull of our generation lasted much longer. Indeed, the compounded return in the 1920's bull was just about 500%. Not bad. But the 1980s-1990's bull produced returns well over 1000%!

But as we often say in my business, you can't eat past performance (you can't buy clothes, buy toys or give to charity with it either). We are likely in a new time zone when it comes to investing for our goals. This era doesn't give a hoot about the past twenty years. But it does have some older cousins we can check out to see if there are some clues about how to navigate our portfolios through the next many years. And while the Internet and other media have made our instant-gratification world a reality, basic human nature does not appear to have been altered. Wars still occur, people still lie, babies are still pampered (as they should be), and sex still sells in the advertising world. And following the greatest bull market in history, it seems only fair to consider that the greatest bear market could follow.

Now, I am not trying to put a negative spin on this. I'm simply saying that after the generation investors have been through, we should make ourselves aware of what variety of outcomes could follow. Simply expecting the recent past to extrapolate itself forward is not an investment plan; it's a gamble.

For a glimpse of what challenges could await us over the next many years, look back at the period from 1966 and 1982. People who watched the stock market during this time marveled at the Dow Jones Industrial Average reaching the 1000 level in 1965. They were equally surprised when, 16 years later, it still had not crossed 1000 for any significant period of time! Despite several attempts to burst through to new highs, the Dow could not sustain it. Instead, a series of alternating mini-booms and busts occurred. Importantly for those hooked on history, there were many professional investors that made annualized returns in the high single-digits to low teens during this period. Brandes Investment Partners, the outstanding San Diego-based money manager, conducted a study that identified a group of 47 mutual funds that as a group returned just over 10% during this period. Now, with many thousands of mutual funds in existence today, 47 sounds like a "needle in a haystack" kind of figure. But when you consider that in 1965, there were only 170 mutual funds, the fact that nearly 30% of them performed so well in a historically bad market is impressive. Given the relatively small number of traditional managers that produce that type of lifestyle-saving performance in the current era, it makes you wonder what happened to many of the great money managers. It also begs the question, are there any good ones left? The answer to that last question, fortunately, is yes. But for now, let's go back to our discussion of secular bear markets.

Minibulls during multiyear bear markets are not uncommon. These countertrend rallies can translate into spectacular gains for investors. For example, during the 1966 to 1982 secular bear, there were four cyclical bull markets that, on average, delivered gains of 44% and lasted nearly 29 months.

Corrections

Sometimes stock prices stabilize and don't move noticeably up or down for a period of time as brief as a few weeks or as long as several years. During these times, the market is said to be operating within a "Trading Range". At other times, prices drop rather suddenly before they recover and begin to move higher again. If the major market indexes drop 10%, the drop is considered a "Correction".

This term arises because such events typically occur when the market is overvalued, and ultimately restore equilibrium. Corrections tend to be cyclical, sometimes occurring as frequently as once a year or sometimes as infrequently as twice a decade.

According to economic experts, market corrections are healthy, despite the immediate concerns of investors about losing money when prices drop. The argument is that a correction resets over-valued stock prices to more reasonable levels, bringing them more in line with the company's earnings and growth potential. On the other hand, if prices continue to drop, a severe correction may threaten to turn into a bear market unless things turn around.

I know there are investors of all types, but the kind I have tended to work with over the years do not look at it this way. They do not look so casually upon a 10% drop in their portfolio's value. That does not mean it never happens. It just means that we and they don't take it in stride as much as many would.

The best way I have found to reduce your chances of getting hit by a market correction is not the typical advice of Wall Street. They'll tell you to allocate less money to stocks and more to bonds. For many reasons, that may not be enough. I'd prefer to use an investment style that has some built-in disaster protection. This is the Hybrid approach I introduced in Chapter 2, and will cover more extensively in Chapter 10.

Measuring the Markets

The familiar Dow Jones and S&P 500 are just two vehicles among many that continuously monitor various aspects of the securities markets. Such a monitor is called an "index" (pl. indices or indexes). There are indices for virtually every type of investment—stocks and bonds, domestic and international, broken down by asset class, style, and other categories. Different indices can convey different information about investment the economy depending on what they measure and how they measure it.

Some indices are very broad. The broadest index, the Wilshire 5000, tracks most publicly traded U.S. companies (there are currently more than 6,500). Broad indices may help by providing the big picture, however they are not as useful in evaluating specific investments or styles.

Some indexes are designed to measure a narrower and more specific range of investments. Some concentrate on securities within a single industry (for example the Dow Jones Utility Index, which follows 15 utility companies). Others are broken down into style specific categories, and are used by consultants in benchmarking and style analysis. These types of narrow indices provide more precise measures within a smaller range, but don't necessarily reflect the performance of the market. Morningstar tracks over 200 indexes and even they are only scratching the surface.

Regulators and Regulations

Because I deal primarily with securities, the main regulator I am familiar with is the Securities and Exchange Commission (SEC), however, because other investing practitioners include state and federally registered Investment Advisors (RIA's), accountants and financial planners, I also discuss a number of different agencies and statutes that serve to regulate aspects of the financial industry, including states and professional watchdogs of industries like the CPA Board, and the NASD

SEC

The Securities and Exchange Commission governs activities of advisors under the Securities Acts of 1933 and 1934, mutual funds under the Investment Company Act of 1940, and money managers under the Investment Advisors Act of 1940 (IA40). While brief, the IA40 sets down the rules and requirements, which apply to investment advisors.

To register with the SEC, an advisor must have at least $25 million under management and have some discretionary authority with respect to the assets. In the early stages of our business we held most of our assets under a broker-dealer firm, so the assets we managed were counted under their RIA's umbrella from an SEC standpoint. We later converted our status from what was technically an independent brokerage operation (NASD-regulated) to an independent Registered Investment Advisor (RIA). I believe this decision created a far better environment for our clients. Today we are not associated with a broker dealer; we are a Registered Investment Advisor in our own right, so all of our client assets come under our own firm. Since the late 1990's, there has been a clear trend of assets moving from brokerage firms to independent financial advisors. I am thrilled to be part of that trend.

Disclosure

Every IA is required to provide a complete disclosure in form ADV and Part II must be given to prospective clients prior to their entering into a contract for money management services. This is how you know that what an RIA is telling you about their business is reliable. An ADV is not a glamorous piece, and it is not exciting to read. But I think too many investors ignore the opportunity to see how an RIA firm presents itself to its regulators. Instead, they stop after they've read the firm's marketing material. It seems to me that the ADV is written with the detailed, curious investor in mind. Even if you are not detailed or curious, it is worth your while to spend the 10 minutes it takes to read most ADVs before you do business with an advisor. Heck, you may find a surprise that could change the way you approach your business with that firm.

NASD

The National Association of Securities Dealers is the self-regulating Broker/Dealer watchdog and it promulgates rules and audit function actions policing the more than 700,000 registered brokers.

How the NASD Operates

Created in 1938 by an act of Congress, the National Association of Securities Dealers is the largest self-regulating body in the world. The NASD:

- Sets professional standards, registers, monitors and disciplines the nation's 5,500 brokerage firms and 700,000 stockbrokers.

- Requires that all Wall Street firms and brokers belong to it and that they fund the association's $400 million annual budget.

- Runs the arbitration process to settle disputes between investors and brokers. Every investor who opens a brokerage account must sign an agreement to resolve any disagreement with their broker before one of these arbitration panels. A ruling by a three-person arbitration panel—usually one person from the securities industry and two from outside—is often the only way an investor can recover money lost because of broker misconduct.

ERISA

The Employee Retirement Income Security Act of 1974 is a Federal Statute, which applies to all private sector retirement and welfare benefit plans. It has specific provisions on Fiduciary Responsibility, standards of conduct of a Fiduciary and specific rules regarding the prudent investing of other people's money. The often-quoted "prudent man rule" demands that people in positions of fiduciary responsibility make decisions for clients that a prudent person would be expected to make. I do not interpret that to mean "always do what is popular." However, an advisor must exercise common sense. Investor-advisor clashes occur because the advisor does not do that. They feel more responsibility to themselves than to the client. That is never a formula for success.

State Regulators and Statutes

Each state has adopted rules and regulations to control investment activities within that state. These are enforced by various departments— Banking, Commerce, Securities, etc. All investment advisors not eligible to register under the Federal Statute (see above) are required to register with the State in which they reside, or which is their place of business. In addition, Federally registered advisors and their sales agents often have to file a "notice" filing as an Investment Advisor Representative (IAR) in at least their home state.

I look at regulation of my industry as serving two important purposes: to lay down guidelines and rules for advisors on what they need to do for clients, and to take away the option of doing nothing for their clients. The key word in "fiduciary responsibility" is the last one. Based on the many stories I have heard from our clients about how they were mistreated at other firms, I must conclude that many advisors are focused on the act of closing a sale and pushing products on their clients. I am confident that this is driven by their firm's upper management, and the selfish process works its way down to the local office. The advisor in this environment who wants to do right by his client can always find a way to do it, and most of them do. But as the years go on, the pressures of creating revenue for the firm overcome the ability to do what the advisor set out to do for clients. The result is that the advisor's ability to serve is compromised by their employer. Many in the brokerage industry complain that the firm really sees themselves as in control of the client, even though the client is probably with that firm because of their trust in the advisor. How else do you explain that so many clients will follow a broker from one firm to another (maybe more than once) as the broker moves within the industry?

Unfortunately for many clients of brokerage firms, this situation can potentially lead to the advisor compromising their belief system (e.g. "this is not great for my client, but it won't hurt them and I'll score points with my firm."). This may also lead to advisors taking shortcuts. Instead of thinking through decisions for clients, they do what is easiest. Now, I'm all for time-efficiency, but not at the expense of what a particular client needs. So much of our industry is moving toward cut and dried solutions to complicated client issues. Some of it is worthwhile, but a lot of it is moving our industry in the wrong direction. In the next chapter, I'll discuss some of the most common shortcuts I've observed, and suggest ways for the investor to avoid being subject to them.

Market Influences

Markets rise and fall for a variety of reasons. Some market factors serve to encourage investment while others serve to discourage it. And sometimes, markets simply fall under their own weight, and just following the financial news does not provide justification for the actions of the market. What do I mean by that? As I have no shortage of sports analogies, here's one.

Professional football teams play most of their games on Sundays. During the week, they practice at training camp. They work on drills, try out new plays, evaluate new players and determine what strategy they will use to defeat this week's opponent. They also decide which players will play and in what situations. In summary, they are doing their research in preparation for Sunday. But no matter how well they do in practice, and what strategy they employ, the only thing that matters is what happens on Sunday.

The investment markets have a lot in common with this. You have probably heard a media reporter or investment advisor summarize the market's activity for the day by saying something like "investors took profits today following unexpectedly poor economic news," or "stocks surged on news of XYZ Company's solid profit report".

OK, first of all, investors don't take profits based on one day's news...traders do. There are more characteristics of traders versus investors noted elsewhere in this book. Also, I find it hard to believe that true long-term investors make a decision about the entire stock market based on one company's latest announcement. Perhaps this is true in smaller economies where there are one or a few dominant companies, but not in the U.S. or other large markets. I just don't buy that. Again, traders may reinvent their strategy based on one piece of temporary news (as they should because they are short-term oriented), but investors don't.

So, what does all of this have to do with football? Just like teams prepare all week for the big game, so do investors. But the big game is not a game at all (it least it shouldn't be!). It's their participation in the financial markets on a daily basis. And no matter how much insightful, logical research you have done, the only thing that matters is what happens on the field. If your strategy pays off, you have won on "Sunday". If not, you go back to camp and see how to make things better, now and in the future. Of course, investment planning is done over a much longer period of time than a 16-week football season, but the principles are the same. So just as the best preparation helps the Giants, Dolphins, Rams and Patriots get an edge for Sunday, so too does investment research and analysis help you prepare for the many "Sundays" ahead in your investing life.

But despite all of the best efforts to succeed, an NFL football team may not win every game they are supposed to. Sometimes, the plans just don't work. Similarly, an investment approach that has worked before does not necessarily work all the time. The good news is that you have a lot more time for your strategy to succeed than does an NFL coach. You can be much more patient, and you should be.

I have always emphasized the importance of a team approach to managing money. I may be the lead investment thinker at our firm, but I know that no one has a monopoly on good ideas. However, there are plenty of bad ideas. Unfortunately, they often become very popular, engulfing millions of investors in terrible advice and awful results with their money. The next chapter is my effort to point some of these out to you.

CHAPTER 4: COMMON INVESTOR MISJUDGMENTS AND HOW TO AVOID THEM

In investing as in life, the "Five Ps" are critical: prior planning prevents poor performance - Allan Budelman

When a new investor enters the market, buying their first shares of stock or their first bond holdings, they typically have relatively little understanding of the complex and challenging process of investing. There is, of course, nothing wrong with being inexperienced. Everyone starts out that way. The important thing is to correct it.

Now how can anyone who works hard for a living in another career, or has retired to have fun just pick up a list of the best performing mutual funds, or simply ask a stockbroker to do it all for them, and expect to succeed? The answer is that some people will, but most won't. And many of the rules that many investors have been force-fed by Wall Street about how their money "must" be invested are in the process of becoming irrelevant.

Many investors are taken in by common misconceptions about the economy, the markets, and individual investments that they can make serious misjudgments, which adversely affect their prospects for realizing their financial goals. Knowing about these common investor misjudgments ahead of time can help keep you out of trouble. To start on our journey to re-educate you (or educate you if you are new to investing), let's examine some of the most common investor misjudgments in hopes that you will be able to recognize and avoid them.

Misjudgement 1—using price instead of valuation to judge the attractiveness of a stock.

It is easy to look up the literal dollar value of virtually any stock or bond on a daily basis, either in a newspaper, or on the Internet you can get nearly real time pricing scrolling across the bottom of your screen. Many investors check the "progress" of their investments fairly frequently. Some too frequently—like daily or hourly or continuously! The problem arises when inexperienced investors try to make what they believe are informed financial decisions based on a relatively small piece of information such as the listed trading price.

If the stock market is really an "Efficient" market, and stock prices reflect their perceived value to investors, then price may be an indicator of When a certain company should be bought or sold, but it still doesn't necessarily reflect the "Real" valuation of that company. A lot of emotional factors affect stock prices: Takeover rumors, earnings expectations, expected investor sentiments about a new product, bad publicity, and so on. Stock prices are a function of supply and demand. If there are more buyers than sellers, the price goes up; more sellers, and the price goes down. Institutional buyers like mutual funds and pension plans drive the supply and demand.

Believe me, the mom and pop investor doesn't drive prices. You can rest assured that by the time you read something in the media about a company, Wall Street institutions have already factored the event into their bids and offers. So don't get misled about price—it's a result, not a cause of events.

One example of how price misunderstanding is damaging is regarding stock splits. Investors seeking lower prices may buy into a recently split stock merely because it has split, without understanding the circumstances which caused it. A financial event such as a stock split is significant enough to demand investigation by an involved and informed investor.

In many investment circles, there is a prevailing idea that when a company splits its stock, it's a *great* thing. Part of the theory behind this idea is that since the price is now half of the previous figure (in the case of the usual two-for-one split, or otherwise lower than it was before, in the case of more complex splits), it will be more affordable and attract more investors. During the reckless 1990's, a stock split announcement was nearly always followed by a rise in the stock price.

I ask you in a world where billions of shares are traded each week does an $80 stock splitting to $40 a share *really* make your toes tingle? If it does, maybe you are unaware that those who own the stock will now own two shares at $40 instead of one share at $80—the same $80. The company has not created new value. They have only created more work for their accountants. The overall net dollar value change is *zero*.

The theory that a stock split allows hordes of smaller investors to buy into a stock seems more like an explanation for this self-fulfilling prophesy than something that really impacts the trading in a stock. Oh yes, in a stock that trades on very low volume, it may make a slight difference. But when a large or midsize company splits, do you think that all those 100-share buy orders from the people who allegedly can now afford to buy 100 shares carries weight in a world of multi-million share program trades and institutional investing? The answer, of course, is "No".

The corollary to this is when we hear someone say, "I wouldn't buy that stock, it's $120 a share". The dollar *price* of a stock is really meaningless in judging its investment worthiness. Its *valuation* is more important. For instance, if ABC and XYZ are two stocks in the same industry, and the price of ABC is $120 and XYZ is at $40, does that mean that ABC is a better company? No.

If ABC earned $10 a share last year and XYZ earned $2 a share, we learn more about these two firms. That gives ABC a price/earnings ratio of 12($120/10) while XYZ's is 20($40/2) The theory of PE Ratio is that lower ratios mean the company earns more proportionally for every dollar the shareholder spends. So, on the basis of one common valuation measure, ABC is actually the cheaper investment, despite having a higher dollar price.

A friend of mine who is a commercial real estate broker has told me that investment success in the real estate market is not achieved when you make a sale, but when you buy. If you have bought wisely, you need merely wait until market conditions are favorable, and sell to realize your investment. The same could be said of the securities market. One should "buy low and sell high". The real trick is in knowing when a given security is low enough to buy, and when it has reached a peak that makes it high enough to sell. While stock picking *per se* is not the best way to do business, it is always good to be on the lookout for undervalued core securities. These securities are generally trustworthy over the long haul— GM or IBM may be down, but both companies are essentially solid—and as more investors compete to buy shares, the value will inevitably rise.

Uninformed investors typically seek false predictors for their own sake, instead of considering investment options as a part of a coordinated financial strategy. With stocks, this usually means looking for low prices, "hot tickets", and high volatility (more about this later), yet in a vacuum, they're all relatively meaningless in predicting the possibility of a stock going up.

Misjudgement 2—buying the "sizzle" of advertised bonds: More is Better.

With fixed income, this phenomenon of investors jumping after the "hot ticket" usually means chasing bond yield. Higher bond yield does not signify a better bond. It means you will get a higher fixed return, but it may possibly expose you to more risk. If high quality companies are paying 4% on their 30 year bonds, a lower quality company will have to pay more than that to attract any investors. How much more depends on how inferior the company financials are to those of the quality company paying 4%. So, here, "More is not better". The low quality, higher yield bond is fine for an investor who is comfortable with taking the necessary chances, but may provide problems for an investor who thinks they can get high yield without risk.

Now, consider the bond you see advertised in the local newspaper. Let's say it's a municipal bond and somehow, its yield is 2% higher than anything your advisor has discussed. Is your advisor just not "with it"? That's probably not a good assumption.

Bond sales firms often advertise in a way that is somewhat misleading Here is the typical ad that I've seen for years. Assume that 10-year, AAA-rated (the highest rating) Municipal bonds are yielding 4% at the time. Matter of fact, to appreciate the context in which this sort of information is usually presented, let's see what it looks like in big block capitals.

INSURED MUNICIPAL BOND: YIELD 6.5%

Well, what yield-seeking investor wouldn't notice this? The sad part is, there is no free lunch on Wall Street. There's something not quite right here. How can a bond be yielding so much more than the benchmark 10-year AAA bond?

There are several possible explanations.

One possibility is that the bond has a very long maturity date – typically, ads of this nature feature bonds that mature a long time from now, for instance 30 years, because they often yield the most. This long period also means the bond has a large amount of inflation risk. While 6.5% may look good today, in a few years, the average rates may be 8%! This is a rule to keep in mind: bonds with longer periods of maturity are more susceptible to loss of value due to future changes in interest rates. In other words, in 10 or 15 years, if your cost of living has doubled and bonds are available at much higher rates, you're stuck with this bond whose yield is now uncompetitive. And you're stuck with it for a long time. The other thing to remember is that a bond is not a CD. The market value of that bond paying 6.5% in an 8% market will be less than what you paid for it. Bond prices go up and down inversely (opposite) to the yield. Sure, if you hold it for the full term (say 30 years), you get the face value back, but in the meantime, the price is going up and down all the time. So, you can't simply "trade it in" at face value along the way for something better. Bonds CAN BE risky. You should remember that.

A second possibility is that the bond has more credit risk than the word "insured" would imply. It's a common misconception that all Municipal bond insurers are the same. In truth, there is a considerable amount of variation. For instance, the backing of some well-known insurers gives a bond a "AAA" rating. Other insurers are not as financially sound, and their support of a bond garners only an "A" rating. Still other bonds may not be rated at all. Ratings are not automatically assigned to bonds. The issuer has to apply for them. If the issuer chooses not to, the bond is unrated. Furthermore, Rating Agencies raise and lower the ratings all the time depending on the current credit quality of the issuer. In other words, if you buy the bond, you'd better do your homework, and keep doing it.

A third possibility is that the bond could have an ugly feature that the ad does not mention. There can be many variations of this. For instance, the issuer may have the right to "call" the bond, which means that on a specified date, they can give you your money back. If this happens, your yield might be much lower than you expected. This is common in the market for Certificates of Deposit (CDs). In my home area of Southeast Florida, with its large senior citizen population, CDs are a staple in many portfolios. When rates dropped to generational lows just after the turn of the century, many banks started offering "callable CDs." They'd pay a nice return for, say 15 years, but the CDs could be "Called in" by the bank.

Why would the bank call them in? Here's an example that will show you how people may be misled: one year CDs are yielding 2%. Frank and Estelle Costanza, who have just recently relocated from New York City to the Del Boca Vista community in Florida, have a CD mature and want to reinvest it. But 3% seems so low, and they need the income to live on. Their stockbroker offers them a 5% CD. It matures in 15 years and has this thing called a "call feature." Frank and Estelle don't care what other features it has, they were sold on it as soon as they heard 5%. They buy it and congratulate themselves on buying a great 15 year investment.

Then, interest rates go down…a lot. The Costanza's receive a call from their broker 3 months later telling them that the CD has been called. The good news is that they earned a 5% annualized return for the three months (but that only comes to 1.25% for the three months). They also receive their initial investment back. The bad news is that they now have to find a way to earn a high return on their investment.

They ask the broker to put them into another 5% CD, but they are told that investments similar to the one they bought the last time have now dropped to a 4% yield. The Costanzas, with their fixed income needs, now realize they have gambled and lost. Rates have gone against them. You can't blame the bank for calling the CD in; they took their 5% debt off the market and replaced it with 4% debt. Good for them, bad for our investors. Once again, what's best for them isn't what's best for you.

The lesson here is not that the Costanzas were swindled. They were not. But they were probably not warned that this could happen. We hear so many stories of investors not being told what could happen if the expected or best-case scenario does not occur. Well, I guess they can always call their son George or his rich friend Jerry Seinfeld for some dough.

Bond ads sometimes offer issues that are deliberately priced very cheaply. What's that you say? There's nothing wrong with a bond broker luring you in with an inexpensive bond! That's true unless it's the old bait-and-switch. Yes, that happens in the investment business too.

I've heard numerous stories of the Bait-and-Switch. There are two typical versions. In the first, you buy this bond, and a month later, the broker calls with a "better" bond to sell you. This goes on for a while, until you figure out that they are making a lot more money than you are, by charging a commission or fee each time a transaction is placed.

The second variation on the Bait-and-Switch is when you call up to inquire about the bond in the ad and are told that it has been sold. The broker may have offered a very small amount of the bond knowing that it would generate phone calls. One client gets a great deal (and then is subject to variation #1 described in the preceding paragraph), and everyone else gets pitched some lesser offering.

When a client brings us a bond from a newspaper ad, we don't advise them on it until we enquire about that offering with one of the bond trading firms we access, firms that cover the whole market for independent advisors like us. They can tell us with great confidence what is going on, and how real or deceptive the offering is. They can also tell us how much "fat" is in the bond. In other words, if they can tell us that the bond offered in the ad at a price of 100 should really be offered at 96, there's a good chance that the broker will make an unreasonably high 4% commission. Then we bring that evidence to the client to educate them on what the reality of the situation is.

By the way, the one thing we find is common to all bond ads: somewhere along the line, the brokers behind it are positioning themselves for a big fat payday, at the investor's expense!

Misjudgement 3—Confusion About The Difference Between Realized And Unrealized Gains And Losses

If you buy a stock and its price drops, you have a loss. However, the IRS doesn't care until you actually sell it. The money isn't in your pocket— it's invested, and investments always have the potential to change in value. So, if you bought at $20 and it's selling for $15, all is not lost (literally and figuratively). You have a loss that is unrealized – you have not closed out your buy-sell combination, you still own it. When you finally do sell it (let's assume at $19), that transaction results in a realized loss.

The same logic applies to gains—a gain is realized only after you have sold something for a profit. Value on paper is one thing, but money in your pocket is something else entirely. The former may provide a sense of accomplishment when you see the price of your holdings increase (or a slow sinking feeling if prices go down), but only the latter provides the wherewithal to fund retirement or education or send a portion of it to the IRS as a taxable capital gain.

On more than one occasion, we have heard of advisors explaining how they have performed well and the client has made money because they have realized a lot of gains. For instance, they have bought and sold five stocks for a total gain of $50,000. They explain this to the client and the client is delighted. But this is like telling your wife that you got a nice check from your employer, but forgetting to tell them that it was a severance check. The bad news could be that there are another five stocks you are holding that were bought for you and they are down $100,000 from what you paid for them. Your overall performance is negative even though your realized gains are positive. That's no fun.

The bottom line: realized gains or losses are only part of the picture. Performance of the entire portfolio is what counts. Anything short of that is just bragging about your winners. This was very common just after the tech stock bubble burst. We'd hear bragging about the big gain on some stocks, yet the Lucent, Nortel and EMC positions were still in the portfolio…at a small fraction of the price paid for them.

Misjudgement 4—"Now Is Not A Good Time To Add Money To The Stock Market, I'll Wait Until It Looks Better."

So much of what investors ask about centers on what direction the stock market will take in the immediate future. No one has that crystal ball. If the market could be "Timed" correctly, and there were a money manager who could truly "time" the market with nearly perfect success, then he or she should have all your money (not to mention all of my money; I'll take a sure thing if I can find it). But market timing is a penguin—it just doesn't fly.

For most people, the portion of their portfolio devoted to stocks is the money they do not expect to spend for several years. The moment the market becomes a daily or weekly source of frustration, its time to reconsider whether equity investing should really play a significant role in your portfolio, and evaluate how much of a role you should actively participate in.

Misjudgement 5—"Right Now" Investing.

We watch in disbelief as short-term worries disrupt long-term plans. It seems that more and more investors give in to what is moving the markets "Right Now" instead of what will move them between now and the time their objectives must be met. The difference is a mile wide! Here's how the two crowds think and where they disagree:

The "Right Now" investor would think about:

1. Stock prices are falling and if they are falling now, they'll fall more. Headlines like "Indexes hit lowest points in years" are everywhere.

2. A company's CEO is on trial so it must be a bad time to invest.

3. We're at war with some other country.

4. Accounting gimmickry makes earnings figures released by companies unreliable.

5. Stock analysts have misguided motivations.

6. A company missed analysts' earnings targets by a penny or two this quarter.

7. Money market funds don't lose value, and my stocks have.

The investor's inaccurate conclusion: wait until the news is better before making any changes.

Bottom line: this type of thinking is dangerous. Don't do it.

Inexperienced people can get caught up in the complexity of the economy. Sometimes this results in an investor taking short-term events and thinking of them as events that will have long-term impact. For instance, consider the subject of the Federal Reserve Bank governors. As noted in Chapter Two, virtually every market commentator is infatuated with "will they or won't they" raise or lower interest rates at a given time. Fed meetings are watched so closely. Two years later, who remembers this, much less what happened and what impact it had? The Fed raised rates seven times in 1994. By the next year, many investors could not tell you how the market reacted. Good for them, since these actions by the Fed probably did not have much impact beyond a month after they were announced.

Was all the speculation and excitement worth it? No way. Investors' time is usually more productive if they focus their energy on how longer-term factors that impact their portfolio may be changing.

As opposed to the right-now investor, the objective-oriented investor is thinking about:

1. Bear markets are the pain that leads to the eventual gain.

2. Geopolitical concerns have existed in our country since they signed the Declaration of Independence. From the British in the 1700's to Al Queda today, there is always an enemy to contend with (apologies to today's citizens of the United Kingdom). It hasn't stopped the economy yet. Even when the United States was divided by Civil War, the markets continued to function, and there were good investments to be found.

3. Buying great businesses at favorable prices from panicked sellers has produced the greatest long-term gains in stocks. I want to be the buyer, not a seller in that transaction.

4. I will look at the stock market portion of my portfolio with realism, not perfectionism. That is, I know that if I keep my losses small in down markets and get most (not necessarily all) of the up markets, I'll be fine in the long run. Expecting to beat the market when its up and not lose money when its down is unrealistic. There will always be another bull (up) market after a bear (down) market, so I'll play "defense" when things are rough so I'm in a relatively strong position for the next bull (up) market, whenever it occurs.

5. Bonds will barely preserve my capital after the impact of taxes and inflation. They still play a role for me, but they're not a growth investment.

There are many ways to play it "halfway". Hybrid investment styles offer potential upside that can leave bond and cash returns behind and are less volatile than traditional stock market vehicles. You can also engage in a regular hedging program on your stock portfolio. We'll cover this extensively later in this book. The bottom line: Don't get caught up in "right now", and you will increase your chances of getting it right in the future. The future lasts much longer.

Misjudgement 6—Putting Investment Fees Above All Else.

People sometimes seek to have their money managed in the way that causes them to pay the lowest fee. They assume that all investment advisory services are essentially the same, so they should pay the lowest they can for this "commodity". They treat investment advice as they would treat any other product they might find on a shelf in a store, and devoted their time to "comparison shopping" to find the product they want at the lowest possible cost.

That often backfires in the investment world. You end up paying someone who has cut their fee to win your business, and then they don't watch your portfolio and don't service you, because their profit margin on your business is so low!

These investors do not pay enough attention to *quality*. They assume that many investment products are similar—and they are right. But some money managers are special, and should not be treated as commodities. Unfortunately, some of the good ones cost more. But they are worth it. The old adage "you get what you pay for" is very applicable in the investment management business.

The Vanguard funds have become synonymous with low-cost investing. Many of the funds directly track a specific market index. I often hear people say things like "I've done really well with Vanguard over the years". That is not really surprising when you consider what I just said.

If the stock market goes up by over twenty percent a year as it did each year from 1995-1999, simply tracking the market will be good enough to impress a lot of investors. But what happens when stocks hit a bear market, especially a long one? The answer is easy – the Vanguard funds that benefited from the up market follow the bear down.

So, is Vanguard a company that offers great funds or is it just a way to participate in whatever the stock market does? I'd say it's the latter, adding that the firm has done a terrific job of educating and marketing to individual investors. They have focused attention on mutual funds' expense ratios, so that investors understand what money management costs much better than before Vanguard came onto the scene. Vanguard provides a service and it does so in a cost effective manner--but index funds are most likely to underperform the market. Remember, the index IS the market, so once you take out the fee (even Vanguard's very low fee) you should expect to slightly underperform the benchmark!

This issue with Vanguard is actually part of a larger investor misconception. Remember earlier in this chapter, how I discussed the investor who chases after high return? Some investors are the opposite— infatuated with passive investing. They believe indexing is the best investment strategy, because the market always goes up if you stay in long enough, and most managers don't beat the index – I've written ad nauseum to my clients about this multi-part fallacy in the past, but two main points sum it up:

First, the indexes may give you full exposure to the stock market's upside, but the same is true on the downside – the latter is what freaks people out and leads to bad decisions when the going gets tough. Second, there have been many long periods of time when the broad stock market averages did not make much at all. Examples include the S&P earning a net increase of about nothing from 1966-82, and the Russell 2000 Small Cap Growth index returning less than 5% a year from 1988-03. Does that surprise you as much as it surprised us when we realized it?

We use indexing in our practice. In fact, a segment of many of our clients' portfolios is invested in a strategy that buys a group of indexes through Exchange-Traded Funds (ETFs). These are investments that trade on the stock exchange like stocks, but instead of representing companies, the shares replicate the performance of an index such as the Dow Jones, the Japan stock market, energy companies, etc. But to us this is simply one part of a well-diversified portfolio, and it's actively managed. Since we devote much of our practice to hiring private money management firms to invest in stocks for clients, the index portion of the portfolio might be thought of as "manager insurance". If the managers don't do very well in a rising stock market, at least the index portion should keep pace.

Misjudgement 7--Techfatuation

Many people crave volatility – how else do you explain the infatuation with tech stocks that drove investor behavior in the ninties? History has shown that tech stocks are usually more volatile than stocks in other sectors. However, they are not clearly better (or worse) investments. Despite this, the investing public and particularly the media still focuses more of its time on tech than is warranted. And investors at the turn of the century (from the 20th to the 21st) wondered how they missed "obvious" investments like Philip Morris and Allstate that more than doubled when techs were falling endlessly. Call it "Techfatuation".

Where does that leave the rational, long-term investor (our typical client)? We feel that technology should be a part of most equity portfolios, but for many of our clients, it should just be "one of the gang", and not an outsized percentage of assets relative to other sectors. In fact, in our portfolio construction work we often operate as if Tech is its own asset class. We think the historical data supports this.

So, next time your friends tell you about how their portfolio is positioned for the next bull market since their money manager owns many of the big tech stocks, remind them that there's more than one way to make money. And help them realize that "Techfatuation" is a dangerous way to approach your financial future.

Misjudgement 8—An Obsession With Risk Avoidance

Risk avoidance is generally good, but taken to any extreme, it is not often very helpful to your overall goals. In addition to indexing, many investors believe that staying clear of high-risk investments will protect them indefinitely. This is simply not true. "Conservative" investments such as utility stocks and low volatility hedge fund are also fallible. For example, utility stocks, once thought of as the "safe" money, have experienced some wild price swings in recent years. The lesson here: nearly every investment carries risk and will experience some volatility. The challenge is to offset the negative characteristics of certain parts of your portfolio with other styles that allow the entire portfolio to succeed most of the time, and to keep the losing periods to a minimum. We have shown clients over and over that you do not have to invest aggressively to earn solid, productive, long-term returns. However, you have to remove the money from under your mattress to have a chance.

Misjudgement 9—"I Could Have Done Better Having My Money In The Bank"

Investing is making an educated guess about what will perform most in line with your objectives over your time horizon. Either you make those educated guesses and follow them along, or you have an advisor do it for you. Do you want to do the educated guessing and the research that goes with it, or do you want to pay someone to do it for/with you?

We think that the reason many clients come to an independent firm like ours is that they feel that their broker did not take this "educated guess" role seriously. Instead, the client had a salesperson whose interests were more aligned with the firm than the client.

We have also seen many people come to our firm and to other independents from trust companies. In this case, it seems that the advisor there was unwilling to deviate from what the firm was doing for thousands of other clients – there was little regard for the particular issues in the investor's financial life.

To us, investing in the 21st century will be about grinding out return where and when it is available; opportunities may not be plentiful like in the 1990's. The key to achieving goals will be a <u>flexible</u> game plan using a wide variety of resources (i.e. several different investment strategies). Want to simply put all of your money in an S&P index fund and endure the ebbs and flows of the market, or sock it away in whatever asset class had the best year last year (a.k.a. the "hot dot")? That's an educated guess we don't agree with, yet many individual investors have done that. More power to them, but we think it will be much tougher than that to accomplish what you want.

Misjudgement 10—Focusing Too Much Mental Energy On Short-Term Market Predictions

Instead of educating themselves on the Long-Term tendencies of the investment styles they are using, some investors are driving by looking in the rear view mirror. They draw conclusions and reactions from looking at the price changes of stocks on their computer screens, instead of trying to understand what factors are causing that reaction. Most often, the dramatic moves we see are caused by temporary factors that are forgotten soon thereafter (for more information, see the article "Market Volatility in the Context of the Real World" included as an appendix).

Misjudgement 11—The "Seen One, Seen 'Em All" Rule

"I'm not investing in mutual funds anymore. Did you hear what those bums did at Putnam and Strong Funds?" If you are in the healthcare field and you are reading this, let's hope the same logic doesn't apply to your industries. Is every doctor guilty of malpractice, or is every dentist a clone of that dentist whose office was also his car? Or are those people who diluted the pills taken by cancer patients a symbol for all of you? I doubt it.

A similar roadblock to success is a general failure to recognize Déjà vu when it happens again. Heck, even the immortal Yogi Berra figured out when it was "Déjà vu all over again". Do you want a recent example? Let's flash back to 2003: Internet stocks lead the market and bad news is ignored. Terrorism is not a big concern because it is happening in some other country, not at home. Retailers are upbeat because Christmas season could be strong and we'll think about next year when it gets here, not now. As an investor, the more you live in the moment, the better the chances that your portfolio will suffer later (oh yeah, and when you least expect it).

Misjudgement 12—Shooting The Weak Performer.

When you invite your advisor to a performance contest, no one wins. One of the most popular yet unproductive memories of the 1990's was performance "contests". A client would tell an advisor that "I'll give you and another firm a year, and whoever makes more money will get the assets I gave to another firm". This is a lot like going to a top quality restaurant, having a meal you don't like and deciding never to go again.

Let's face it, everyone has a slump. In addition, the reasons that an investment may deliver mediocre performance over a short stretch of time (yes, a year is short) are not all bad ones. A quick look back at some recent U.S. stock market history will help you understand this point. For instance, the key to success in 2003's stock market was owning companies with poor fundamentals. This sounds strange but in this year "junk" was king.

2004 was a year in which some of the riskiest asset classes earned the highest returns. Small Cap and Emerging Market stock returns were notably higher than those of "Core" investment styles. Defensive styles did not fare well.

Now turn back the clock to the 2-year period that ended in late 2002. Those same defensive investments saved your portfolio. Hedge funds and hedged styles were far more likely to earn a positive return than the styles that dominated in the two years that followed. In some years hedged investing would win a lot of performance contests easily. In other years, they'd lose badly.

The bottom line is this: portfolio management is not a game, but it IS a team. Constructing a portfolio involves identifying investments that each play a role in your ultimate success. In some years, any one of those investments will be the hero, the next year it could be your only negative return in the bunch. If your goal, like many of our clients, is to earn more consistent, lower-volatility returns instead of simply tracking the ups and downs of the markets, your portfolio should have a mix of investments that in some ways offset or complement each other.

By the way, if the "winning" firm in that performance contest gets the other half of your money, what assurance do you have that they will be the superior firm next year? Answer: none. So next time you feel the urge to make your portfolio's return the subject of a contest or race, turn on the television and watch a ballgame. And when its time to analyze your portfolio, spend your energy on understanding more about what's in it, how it addresses your specific goals, and how prepared it is for a variety of market conditions.

Don't get me wrong—there is a time and a reason to pull the trigger on an investment firm, but it is NOT because of short-term underperformance.

Misjudgement 13—"Rear-View Mirror Investing"

This is one of the most blatant violations of the rules investors should beware of.

Maybe there should be a sticker on lists of recent top performing mutual funds: "Warning: you may be too late to enjoy any of this!" While recent performance may be attractive, the numbers alone do not tell the whole story. What drove the performance? Was it an overall tendency in the market, an indication of the success of the investing methodology of the fund, or the result of random events and blind luck? The most important question regarding performance is, are the conditions that led to such performance likely to continue? Is performance sustainable? This is where detailed, and professional, analysis comes into play.

Check *Money* Magazine's list of "hot" mutual funds, watch CNBC to hear about a trendy Internet Stock, act on a "tip" from a friend. For many investors, this has been their education, and is now their way of life. Earnings growth? Who needs it? Fundamental analysis? That's for old-timers. Wait a minute, is this the stock market or a Las Vegas casino?

"The Trend is Your Friend" is an old Wall Street saying, but it can also get you and your portfolio in trouble. Much of the stock market's trend in the late 1990's was to buy debt-ridden companies that bleed red ink, and profit handsomely. An Internet firm announces that they won't make a profit for years and the stock doubles; a stable growth company misses Wall Street's quarterly earnings estimate by a penny, and the stock drops 40%.

This century began with two markets: a tech boom and a non-tech bear market. The impact this had on investors' approach to the stock market is striking, yet worrisome. Those who rode the Internet bandwagon from the beginning profited handsomely. Others joined in later because they felt they had missed out. This is what we call "Rear-View Mirror Investing". A driver who looks only at what's behind is unprepared for what's on the road ahead.

This can be a dangerous game. The media, by focusing tremendous attention on what is popular, helps to create these emotions in us. As a friend once told me: if CNBC came on the air and said "buy quality stocks, hold them for the long-term, and have a nice day," they'd be off the air in a week!

What's the historical record of chasing what's hot? The table below shows how one would have fared by buying into an investment style immediately after it had a high-performing year. If the results don't scare you, they should.

The point is not that technology investing is a fad (it isn't); it is that diversification still has a place in everyone's portfolio. You may want to bet on yesterday's winner, but the stock market has shown time and again that things have a way of evening out. If and when that happens again, you'll want your portfolio to be ready for it.

For instance, look at the fifteen categories of stocks depicted in Figure 2, on the following page. They each had their "15 Minutes of Fame". But look at the data. You had a great short term return if you bought them on January 1 of the respective year, and sold them on December 31, but if you held them as investments, the picture wasn't quite as bright, was it? It may be trite, but my point is, don't focus on the Hot Dot!

So much of what investors are asking about centers on what direction the stock market will take in the immediate future. The portion of your portfolio devoted to stocks is for the money you do not expect to spend for several years. The moment the market becomes a daily or weekly source of frustration, it's time to reconsider whether equity investing should really play a significant role in your portfolio.

Fig. 2: The Hot Dot

Year	"Hot" Investment	Return	But Next Year...
1989	Japanese Stocks	+31%	-29%
1991	Healthcare Stocks	+64%	-5%
1993	Precious Metals	+82%	-12%
1993	Emerging Market Stocks	+73%	-10%
1993	Emerging Market Bonds	+51%	-16%
1994	Japanese Stocks (again)	+17%	-2%
1995	US Long Bonds	+26%	-1%
1997	Real Estate Investment Trusts	+23%	-16%
1999	Technology Stocks	+116%	-16%
2000	Utilities	+51%	-26%
2001	U.S. Small Cap Value	+20%	-15%
2002	U.S. Long Bonds (again)	+17%	+2%
2003	Technology Stocks (again)	+54%	+3%
2004	Telecom Stocks	+19%	-4%

Source for performance data: Morningstar; Chart: Lohr

Misjudgement 14—I'm going to wait until the market goes up

Another thing we hear when markets are down is, "My portfolio is so far-off its highs that I'm not going to do anything until I recover a bit. I appreciate the fact that you, my financial advisor, bring new ideas to my portfolio, but I'm going to sit tight for a while". This thought process will keep you on the sidelines when the market goes back up.

And make no mistake about it—markets always go up and down!

While most stocks do fluctuate from low to high and back again, and what goes down does usually go back up, not every loss can be ridden out. Some losses must be accepted as such to keep the overall portfolio in balance. On the other side of this is the possibility of "Buying down". If you buy according to valuations, not price, if a stock was a good value at $40, and the fundamentals have not changed, it should be a great buy at $27. Remember, stocks go up; stocks go down.

Gains can be just as much of a problem. It's dangerous to hold out for that little bit of extra profit – as with this series of thoughts an investor might have:

"That stock is up 40% in just over a year. Sure, it's trading for a sky-high p/e ratio. Yeah, I know I didn't expect to even go this high. But it just keeps going up, and I shouldn't sell something if it's going up right? What's that you say: it's down 7% today? Well, it'll come back. And when it gets back to where it was yesterday, I'll sell it...

"...(Fast forward to 6 months later): OK, so now that stock is back down below where I bought it. But I can't sell it now and take a loss, right? I'll just wait for it to come back."

What's the problem here? Very simply, the investor makes a sell decision based on the movement of the stock price, not on the basis of any discipline (fundamental analysis, technical analysis or any type of selling rule). Greed overruled all other emotions here.

Panic reactions to market behavior can also be a problem. There is no reason to sell out of stocks just because they are down. Professional managers will find out *why*, and sell if the reason they bought it is no longer valid, but hold otherwise. It is tough to learn to think this way, but the extra effort is worth it. This is where having a discipline, some method of investing you trust, is so important.

Some of the most disciplined professional investors I have met are "Contrarian Value" money managers. A stock they buy may fall initially because the manager is ahead of the market in seeing a positive future for a company. When the manager's idea goes from "contrarian" to popular, large gains can result for the investor – provided they didn't panic and give up too soon. Contrarian investing is an excellent example of a strategy that may fit part of your portfolio, but if you tend to get concerned about occasional large swings in the value of your investments, you must keep the amount you invest in such a strategy to a low percentage of your total portfolio.

The Pain Doctor

Dr. Bruce Mann is one of my best friends. He is a fellowship-trained pain management doctor and a darn good one. I admire his thorough approach to what he does and he thinks to same of me. He also does the best impression of Scooby-Doo I've ever heard. For years he worked as an anesthesiologist, and I imagine his sense of humor helped him put his patients at ease before they went to surgery. I did not expect him to contribute to this book, but while I was writing it, he said something I felt would fit in just fine.

Dr. Mann believes that people are often motivated more by negative behavior than positive. Crime is probably one of the most stable "growth" industries in the world. ARROGANCE is the downfall of so many investors (Do it yourselfers, the tech craze, etc.). Why is there such a lack of perspective? Probably because it's not their full time business. Most investors don't learn the nuances of the advisory business, and do not develop the perspective that is so critical to make appropriate decisions over a lifetime of wealth management. There is an instinct that can be developed. But like a golfer who only plays every couple of months, that instinct is hard to summon if you do not get the constant repetition that one gets from being immersed in the business of advising a wide variety of people every day.

I think that by listening to the words of Bruce the pain doc, investors can prevent a lot of pain in their portfolios.

Conclusion

Don't get caught up in the misconceptions.

Haphazard investing will yield haphazard results. Your investing horizon should have a goal on it, and the strategy you employ should have a roadmap of how to get there. If you have "play money", that's fine—play with it. Speculate, take risks or go to Vegas. But for your serious money think growth and preservation. Don't focus on yesterday's winners and don't try to "time" the market. Do be aware that markets and securities go up and down. Make some sense out of the investment environment, look at historical events to evaluate today's climate.

CHAPTER 5: THE MOST PRESSING ISSUES FOR INVESTORS TODAY

"Tachlis – that's Hebrew for what's the bottom line?!" – Bruce Levy

Now that we've discussed some of the investment moves to avoid, let's move on to the environment investors face today. If the decades of the 1980's and 1990's were about investing becoming more of a mainstream activity, the current decade may be about adjusting to an environment in which the mainstream was taken advantage of. From Wall Street scandals to new investment vehicles, a lot has changed and it changed quickly. If you are devoted to the idea of maintaining an investment plan for the long run, you have two choices. You can educate yourself about what is real and what is a myth at investment firms. Or, you can throw caution to the wind and hope you are placed in appropriate investments by qualified advisors. This chapter should help you size things up and make you aware of some critical issues going forward. Then, in Chapter 6, we'll discuss some of the things I believe you can do to make your investment experience from here a positive one.

Investing is a very different venture today than it was in the 1980's and 1990's. On the next few pages is my short list of reasons why, and explanations.

INVESTING TODAY VERSUS THE 1980's AND 1990's

1. **Absolute vs. Relative Return** – in the bull market decades, investors became index-trackers. If they used an active money manager instead of an index fund, that manager was considered dirt if they did not consistently exceed the return of the relevant index. People who considered a return of 25% from an active manager when the index made 30% a "failure" were missing an important point: 25% return is a lot of money! Yet the investor was not focused on the "absolute return" of 25%, but rather on that figure's shortfall "relative to" the index. This has also led to many misconceptions about indexing as a strategy. Below is a summary chart I've used with clients for years to help them think through this very critical decision about themselves.

WHAT'S YOUR OBJECTIVE?

Relative Returns -vs.- **Absolute Returns**

	Relative Returns	Absolute Returns
Annual Return Goal	Stay competitive with the market	Make money
Expected Return Path	More Volatile	Less Volatile
Correlation To Market	High	Low

In the Long Run: There is no guarantee that the more aggressive approach (Relative Returns) will outperform the more conservative (Absolute Returns) over a long period of time

Conclusion: Absolute Return Strategies have a role in many investors' portfolios

EMERALD
ASSET ADVISORS, LLC

Fig. 3: What's Your Objective?

Source: Emerald Asset Advisors

2. **Secular Bear Market Mentality** – the awareness of market cycles is more prevalent than in the past. However, many investors are still stuck in the past, believing that investing in stocks is some kind of automatic wealth-production system. It's hard for me to judge whether the advisory community is getting the word out to their clients that the secular trend may indeed have changed (or more importantly, that secular patterns exist at all). Based on investor behavior, however, I suspect that it is being downplayed. After all, secular bear markets are an enemy of Wall Street. Trading activity drops as investor fatigue sets in, clients get impatient and job cuts accelerate. You can understand why commercials for financial firms don't talk much about their strategies for tough speculative styles.

3. **Inflation/rising Interest Rates?** – Interest rates generally fell from 1980-2003. As a result, bond investments posted their best returns in history. Even if rates continue to fall over the next decade, they are now starting from a much lower rate level. That means that the bond gains many have seen as a birthright for over two decades will not be matched. It changes the whole way we look at bond investing.

4. **U.S. Deficits (Government and Consumer)** – the hefty tab run up by the U.S. government over the years is a cause for some concern, and the media covers this regularly. The plight of the consumer is potentially much worse. Credit card debt has become the currency of choice for many families. I marvel at how long people have stretched the proverbial rubber band of borrowed money. If the band breaks, this could have a ripple effect on the financial system. Again, I'm not trying to be gloomy or make precise predictions; I'm increasing your awareness of the potential for an environment change. It would be an environment change that would be very unfamiliar to most of today's investors. Rather than downplay it, advisors should be stirring up the conversation about it, and including their clients.

5. **Global Competitiveness** – very simply, it's a global marketplace. Just look at communication systems, most prominently the Internet. What took days to become world news now takes seconds. That necessarily changes the way financial markets work.

6. **The Retirement Boom** – I discussed "Boomers" earlier in this book. They have impacted our world at every phase of their lives. Now they are prepping for or entering the retirement phase. That has numerous implications for investing, but what they are is simply conjecture at this point.

7. **More styles to choose from** - my friends who read this book will know immediately that I am NOT talking about clothes or cars. I'm referring to Wall Street's ingenuity. Here is where I truly applaud financial firms, especially the larger ones. As time has gone by, they have found ways for investors to take a stand in their portfolio on nearly any investment style, sector or theme. Now, sometimes they charge an arm and a leg for it, and sometimes they sell it to clients as something beyond what it is. But for those of us that keep a close eye on the latest and greatest strategies and products, the freedom of choice that has developed is outstanding for investors. That is, as long as their advisors are looking out for the clients' best interests and not just their own.

8. **Terrorism Risk** – without going into too much detail, one can no longer ignore this in today's environment. It is something that did not exist in a similar form in the glory days of the 1980's and 1990's.

I've written to our clients on many occasions about this subject of "important issues for investors". Here are some of those articles.

This article, which follows, was originally written in 2002, but the culture it describes has been brewing for much longer than that.

Who Can We Trust?

- Enron and Anderson, in cahoots, fool everyone and destroy documents

- Other energy traders execute "sham" trades to pump up revenues

- Drug companies don't comply with manufacturing regulations, and take advantage of seniors

- Telecom CEOs run their firms into the ground while margining their stock

- Brokerage firms' conflicts of interest are brought into plain view

- Certain mutual funds "favor" some institutional investors with preferential trading

- Companies announce earnings and investors wonder if they are real or fabricated

What the heck is going on? Corporate leaders, doctors and priests are creating headlines normally reserved for the tabloids. Politicians and evangelists are beginning to look comparatively genuine. **Is there anyone left we can trust?**

YES! **Trust history.** History tells us that crises of confidence are common. As this relates to the financial markets, the good news is that there is a lot of bad news. It's about evolution. Mutations can enable organisms to adapt to changes in their environment, and cause plants and animals to evolve. That's what has been happening in our Corporate and Financial world.

None of the problems I listed above are likely to be permanent. In fact, the indiscretions of today's corporations are already leading to positive change. Change is a painful process, and investors and shareholders will be better off for it.

Think about what it was like being an investor in the 1980's and 1990's. It was so easy. Too easy. Many new investors took short cuts to making money, did not understand why they made decisions, and lacked perspective in their investing. It was all a game.

Now, things have changed. Try telling someone that investing today is as "fun" as it was in the 1990's. Not only is it tougher to make money, we don't know if we can trust the companies we are investing in.

Now, here's some perspective. If history repeats itself as it always has, the excesses of the 1990's will eventually be wrung out. Companies will be more forthcoming. Security analysts will write what they mean and do it with clarity. Independent investment research will gain greater popularity. People in influential positions will be more responsible in their roles. In short, a "cleaner" financial world will replace the tarnished one that exists today. It's already happening.

Does this mean that a wonderful new bull market is here? Not necessarily. Does it mean that the excessive investor optimism of the late 1990's has been replaced by excessive pessimism? In some circles, the answer is "Yes".

But history repeats itself because human behavior does not change much over time. That means a disciplined investor has opportunities to capitalize on the madness of masses and to keep pursuing their ultimate objective for wealth while others are confused and changing their plans without really knowing why. If you continue to focus on what you are investing for, and not follow the media noise of the moment, you will be better off for it. However, I'm NOT telling you what you've heard many a pundit or broker say about long-term, buy and hold investing. Simply doing nothing and hoping the problem of low or negative returns on your money goes away is not a strategy. What is a strategy is realizing that the environment may have changed for a half a generation or longer, and revising your approach to the financial markets accordingly.

So how does your financial advisor or investment consultant fit into this picture? Investment advisors are trusted by their clients to provide unconflicted, unbiased recommendations and advice. They too have a fiduciary debt to the client and accordingly are considered "special skills persons" by the courts. As such, they are held to higher standards of behavior than a non-skilled party. Investment Advisors have an obligation to adhere to only the highest ethical standards. There is no place for an investment advisor to recommend--or allow—a client to continue to invest in a firm which has perpetrated ethical fraud upon its client.

The investment advisor's charge is to provide full disclosure and adequate education to their clients, while ensuring that the information the client bases decisions upon is complete and accurate. This may mean telling the client a few things they don't really want to hear.

The following are some of the things you should expect your investment advisor to do:

- Evaluate investment options solely according to your investment objectives,

- Document recommendations and fully explain market risks,

- Provide full disclosure, including all fees and cost comparisons,

- Explain that past performance is an unreliable predictor of future performance,

- Keep the investment process an ongoing one,

- And, *be* a fiduciary.

If your consultant can't accept all that, perhaps they should consider another career. Unfortunately, many investment advisors were attracted to the business for the mountains of money they wanted to make, and for the opportunity to regularly experience the thrill of the sale. Then there are those of us who really do this because we want to play a vital role in people's lives, we want to take confusing topics and make them understandable, and yes, through that, our own financial and emotional lives will be terrific. I believe that, on average, you find more of the latter per capita running independent money management and consulting firms.

At my firm, we have always emphasized the difference between working with the owners of a firm and working with their employees. The owners of a small or medium size firm (we consider ourselves to be medium-sized) cannot afford to screw up for a client. We ARE the company, so there is no replacement for us. To our clients, we are not interchangeable with a hundred other advisors. We know them too well.

My two co-founders of Emerald Asset Advisors, Scot Hunter and Bruce Levy, have been together in business since 1984. Bruce often refers to it as a "marriage" and in fact it has lasted longer than many marriages, for sure. Scot doesn't often speak that metaphor, so I assume it's that testosterone thing. Yet, I see how they function, and it is like the business version of a marriage. It follows that the best client-advisor relationships are those in which they see each other as teammates, not opponents. There are no expectations of perfection or wizardry from either side, and there is an appreciation that both are trying to accomplish the same thing. I am happy to say that when my long time clients call, my initial reaction is just as when an old friend from college calls. Then, its down to business. Let's face it, there are enough forces conspiring against people on a daily basis. One of the most important people to have on your side is the person most responsible for directing your wealth. If that's not the case, it's another headache you don't need.

So, out of this "new world" of investing –the one we're on the brink of, there are some fundamental questions you should consider which will help you map your investing strategy. Let's look at another one of these questions a bit closer:

It's Time To Decide: Are You A Trader Or An Investor?

The financial services industry has done much to empower individual investors in recent years. Many experienced investors now take advantage of the increased, timely information at their disposal. Many others have taught themselves how to create and execute an approach that makes sense for them. This is all great stuff.

However, this revolution now puts potentially dangerous tools in the hands of many inexperienced investors. Discount brokerage firm TD Waterhouse has a commercial encouraging investors to use the tools offered by the firm. At one point, the stoic actor Sam Waterston says to the camera "You can do this!" I wish he'd say "Some of you can do this" instead.

It's not that people new to the markets can't profit from trading stocks. That would be foolish to say, since many have been successful. What is missing from many people's approach to the markets is their belief that they are **investors**. They are not investors, they are **traders**.

As Jerry Seinfeld would say, "Not that there's anything wrong with that". However, it is critical to an investor's long-term financial health that he or she recognizes the difference. It's easy to be a trader when markets are continually moving up, or when volatile Internet stocks make wild swings. However, even then it's not easy to profit from it.

Trading can become extremely more difficult when the environment changes. That is when long-term, experienced, out-of-the-box-thinking investors will sleep peacefully, while traders try to figure out why the techniques that worked before are now blowing up. The key is to understand the difference between trading and investing (or a combination), choose the approach that you are most comfortable with, and go with it—without second-guessing yourself. It is said that one definition of an investor is "a disappointed speculator". Don't be one of those.

Do You Think You Can Be Effective In Market Forecasting?

I wish I had a dollar for every market forecast I've ever seen. While predicting economic and market events has become something akin to a sporting event, sometimes a forecast can be useful. I advise you to consider the following anytime you read or hear a financial forecast:

1. **What is the motivation of the forecaster?** If a Small Cap stock fund manager tells you that Small Cap stocks are a screaming buy, is that as reliable as someone who's livelihood isn't directly impacted by Small Cap Stock performance? To take this a giant step forward, did you ever notice how a decided majority of guests on financial TV shows are optimistic, all the time? Now you know why.

2. **Is that person speaking in absolutes, or leaving open the possibility that they are wrong?** Don't let someone's high level of conviction influence you too much. For more on this, see number 1 above.

3. **What is the forecaster's experience?** In an era where any college kid, barber, or entertainer can get a web page and wax poetic about investing, you have to be careful.

Yes, making a lucky buy in a security which then experiences tremendous growth *does* occasionally happen (consider the experience of Ty Cobb and Coca-Cola, which we will discuss later in the book). The key, however, is *luck*. To use a more modern example, someone who bought shares of Microsoft in the mid-seventies would probably be very pleased with their investment—however, there were many other computer software companies at the time—some of which seemed even more promising than Microsoft—whose investors ended up losing everything. Luck more than wise selection was the contributing factor to success.

Predicting the future is a tricky business—one perhaps best left to the wizards and sorcerers of popular fiction and blockbuster films. Fortune telling may be useful for Harry Potter, but it is not going to help us here in the real world. Instead of wasting our time chasing the next Coke or Microsoft, we should focus on setting realistic and concrete goals, and creating a plan for realizing them.

CHAPTER 6 – WALL STREET'S BULL (SEPARATING THE INVESTMENT WORLD'S MYTHOLOGY FROM REALITY)

"Compensation Drives Behavior. Think about that the next time your broker asks you to look at something he's selling" – Matt MacEachern

Google This

In early 2006, just before releasing this book, I went to Google and typed in "Wall Street Scandal". Want to guess how many "hits" it generated? How about 11,400,000! But while the scandals make the headlines, those headlines are more about the bad apples who spoiled the bunch. I think that there are far greater concerns for investors in dealing with what investment firms and advisors offer. This chapter will cover some of those so that you can beware.

Taking The Shortcut

When I'm driving my family somewhere, there's nothing my kids enjoy more than hearing that we are "taking the shortcut" to reach our destination. Even if it's a 5-minute trip, they love it. In fact, if my wife and I simply tell them we're taking the shortcut (even when we are not), Jordann, Tyler and Morgan get a great sense of satisfaction. While shortcuts are great when you're taking your kids someplace, they can be disastrous in the investing world.

Wall Street has notoriously developed shortcuts in creating and managing portfolios. Products have been created for the sole purpose of being easy to sell. While an argument can be made that the investor has been benefited because there are more investment opportunities than ever before, the financial advisor community has been given tools to make them lazy. The problem is, how do you sort the good from the bad? Some clients fall for a good presentation, the more educated ones will realize there is no substance.

Brokerage firms, trust companies, and bank investment advisory firms also take shortcuts. But they are often not enjoyable for you, the client. Why are they taking shortcuts? Very simply, to increase their profit margin at your expense. They are not doing it with malicious intentions. On the contrary, they do it to make their businesses as efficient as possible. Its tough to keep thousands of brokers in hundreds of offices around the country in sync. And many brokerage firms, trust companies and bank advisors are part of publicly traded companies. If you are running one of those companies, you are there to do what is in the best interests of the shareholders—this is exactly what most CEOs say when they are interviewed about their businesses.

If the business increases profits substantially quarter after quarter, year after year, the stock price of that company you run will likely go up. This brings all kinds of good news for you, your board of directors and your shareholders. The stock price rises, shareholders make money, you earn a ton as your company stock options become more valuable, and the company gets more popular with investors. This is all fantastic news...FOR YOU AND THE SHAREHOLDERS.

Now, let's conclude that dream sequence and return to reality. You are no longer running a big brokerage firm. You are you again, and you've just met with a broker at that brokerage firm you were running in your daydream. You tell the broker what you want out of your money, and at some point a proposed portfolio is placed in front of you. It looks beautiful – colorful, slick, neatly bound, with lots of great information about the professional money managers and mix of investment styles the broker feels is the best fit for your needs. It looks like your broker worked with his team of internal experts for weeks on this. You feel like you are the broker's most important client. Life is good.

But wait, I hear the piercing sound of a car coming to a halt. Is this "personalized" presentation all it is cracked up to be? Or is it your version of a quickly prepared proposal based only on a few questions you answered in an investor survey during the meeting? Is this professional-looking advice really "mass-customized" advice – that is, have you been given a Big Mac dressed up to look like a Kobe beef steakburger? Sadly, the answer is often "YES". Now, like nearly everything I discuss in this book, there are exceptions to the rule. However, I have seen enough evidence of this practice for enough years to conclude that it is very common. In fact, as technology improves, it gets easier to create an impressive looking investment package that in reality has very little consideration for what makes you different from every other investor in the world. That is a BIG, BIG problem! Is the approach taken by the firm in this example for your benefit, or for the shareholders? I say it's the latter. Streamlining a national firm creates profit for them but does it create a platform from which you can live and retire in the lifestyle you aspire to? My response: NOT OFTEN ENOUGH!

You may like the sizzle that a slick presentation provides. You may even feel that you need it, to truly believe that you are wanted as a client. But you are hungry for personalized advice, and while it looks like you are receiving it, you are actually getting placed into a grand "model" portfolio that the firm, who doesn't know you (as opposed to the advisor, the one who knows you) put together so that thousands of people "just like you" could get streamlined advice.

Who Can You Trust To Get You To The Promised Land?

If the achievement of financial retirement is important to you, how do you find your way there? Two generations ago, this was a straightforward project. You put in your years at the company, saved a little, and retired with full benefits and that nice pension. A generation ago, you went to a stockbroker or maybe a trust company and they worked with you to decide how to invest your wealth. You bought stocks like AT&T (or "Telephone" as it was called back then) and General Motors (or "a successful, profitable American company" as it was called back then), and maybe some bonds.

We've all seen movies about time-travel. A person gets in a funky looking machine and blasts off to another era. If you were 50 years old in 1978, and you took a time machine that brought you to 2005, you would be in for a shock if you tried to figure out how people were investing their money today. Day-trading, wrap accounts, junk bonds, hedge funds…you would wonder what happened to the simple world of "I have money, I want to make more and try hard not to lose it, so that I can live the way I want to".

And to make matters worse, the people who are providing this information are everywhere. From your buddy to your bank, from your insurance company to the guy you met on line at Starbucks, everyone has something to say about how you should handle some of the most critical decisions of your life (the financial part, not whether to get a decaf mocha or a latte at Starbucks).

The situation I describe here is not unlike what today's investor often goes through in trying to determine how and with whom to invest their hard-earned wealth. This is not your fault. It has more to do with what Wall Street has become and the way it has changed the way it delivers its advice. A big part of the problem is that in many cases, "advice" is not delivered at all – it just looks that way.

Are You Being Advised, Or Sold To?

Dan Wheeler, a director with Dimensional Fund Advisors in Santa Monica, California, recently wrote an article which sums up this dilemma. He wrote that *"the financial services industry is designed to work against investors. Wall Street is not in the advice business, as most investors think and as most brokerage firms say they are. No, Wall Street is in the business of manufacturing and selling product. Its true goal is to create products that will sell and then use a sales force to push those products on investors. That's the game."* That's powerful stuff, yet in my experience, having worked at brokerage firms, trust companies and banks, and despite my generally-positive disposition, I'm inclined to agree with him. I have just seen, over and over again, how investors do not get what they really want from their advisors – a straightforward provider of advice and direction, who customizes their thinking to that of each individual client.

75

Instead, much of the financial advisory business has reduced itself to what I call a "factory" mentality: make it, sell it, go on to the next one. And to provide incentive to the advisor (who is more a salesperson or at best a facilitator, acting as a conduit through which you can buy investment "things"), the firm pays the advisor more. All but the most altruistic advisor (and there are some out there) will succumb to temptation and try to have the client invest in ways that put the advisor's needs ahead of the client's. If you're not sure whether to believe this, go to http://pdpi.nasdr.com/PDPI/ to look up your broker's disciplinary record. If your advisor is part of a Registered Investment Advisor (RIA) firm, you can look the firm up at this specific page in the SEC's website: http://www.adviserinfo.sec.gov/IAPD/Content/Search/iapd_OrgSearch.aspx.

You must ask yourself: in an industry where many are rated by their employers based primarily on the revenue they bring to the firm as "producers", and not how much better off their clients are for being with them, is there not a obvious *dissynchronicity* between the needs of the clients and the way those needs are being addressed?

The other issue in the financial services area that causes confusion for today's investor is the way the industry clings to the common wisdom of past eras, even when conditions have changed dramatically. Without getting into too much detail here, there was a study done about 25 years ago that determined that asset allocation was by far the most significant determinant of investment success. That is, if you have the right balance of stocks, bonds and cash in your portfolio, your probability of success is much greater. Many a financial product advertisement references this study in one form or another. This is, however, somewhat deceptive.

Simply put, that study does NOT apply to many of today's investors. To me, while asset allocation is important, it is not as important as having someone in your corner to whom you can talk about what you want out of life, and who has the experience and skills to craft for you a strategy that maximizes the probability that your money will get you there. Investors don't come to advisors because they want a stock or bond portfolio. They do so because they have accumulated money, life costs money and they want to make the most effective use of their money. The investments chosen are simply a means to an end, not the end itself. I read an article by an advisor who described this quite well. He said that his company exists "because the world is more complex—and we're all just one minute away from chaos. What we do is a risk management strategy for our lives". Investing is not really about what hot stock you just bought or the sleek hedge fund you snuck into while others missed out.

But too many advisors miss this as they mature in the business. Instead, they become part of the industry machine that says things like "here's a diversification plan for everyone" and other solutions we refer to as "mass-customized advice". Be wary of firms and advisors who take shortcuts with your money.

Fear of the unknown is why some clients stay with a broker or bank instead of going with an independent firm. But this is an irrational fear. If renaissance mariners had been unable to overcome their fear of the unknown, we would still believe the world is flat; and if a client cannot overcome their fear of stepping outside the traditional investment box, their returns may be just as flat.

As someone who is by nature a strategic thinker, a detail-seeker (you know, the kind of person who wants to know how the watch is made, not just what time it is), this concept was something I had to learn myself as I grew up in the business. This was the most important thing I learned in the industry during my twenties. No matter how much your firm says "do this for your clients", an advisor must resist the temptation to put anyone else's agenda ahead of their client's.

The best advice I can offer on the issue is this: do not allow yourself to get stuffed into a standard-shaped box. Find an advisor who will take a wide range of materials at their disposal and build a box just for you, with whatever shape you and they judge to be the best fit.

On Proprietary Products:

It is a common cry from independent advisors like me. "Proprietary investment products are the creation of the devil himself" or something like that. Plenty of Wall Street's trouble with investors and regulators stems from an advisor's use (or misuse) of products created by the firm offering the product. I've come to realize that there are two types of proprietary products. One I despise and the other I endorse so much that I've even created one.

The key difference between the two types of proprietary product is in how the advisor is paid.

One of the many recurring themes in this book derives from a quote I first heard uttered by my outstanding colleague Matt MacEachern, **"Compensation drives behavior"**. When a stockbroker is paid substantially more money by their firm if a client purchases a proprietary product, that's a problem with me. In that case, there is a burden of proof on the advisor to justify their decision. The same can be said for B-share mutual funds which pay the advisor handsomely upfront, but restrict the client's ability to reposition the assets without penalty for several years. Fortunately, enough heat has been put on the brokerage industry so that the use of B-shares has been greatly reduced.

I should also add that my thoughts in this area are limited to what investment advisors traditionally offer. Private real estate, mortgage investing, and some hedge fund approaches offer the opportunity for outsized gains if the managers are successful. If your advisor can access this type of extraordinary talent, more power to them. Just make sure that you don't simply fall in love with the track record of a manager. Fall in love with their investment process and credibility as operators before you trust them with your capital.

Now consider a different scenario. What if the producer of the proprietary product or strategy is not making any more money than if you bought another investment from them. That, to me, is a sign that they believe they have truly discovered a gap in the marketplace that needs to be filled. I say this from personal experience, since in 2006 I helped launch a private partnership in which I manage the Hybrid investment strategy I created in the 1990's, and have run for clients individually for years. In fact, we are spending an increasing amount of effort to design strategies that we think are a better fit in many portfolios than what Wall Street traditionally offers. Importantly, we have priced the investment in line with our other offerings.

John Lohr, a veteran securities attorney, one of Wall Street's leading thinkers since the 1970's and a man who was a great mentor to me in the writing of this book, has also published on this topic. Consider the following article, reprinted with permission.

"You're Known by the Company You Keep"

by John Lohr

The impact on clients has been lost amid the rubble of the fiduciary meltdown which occurred in the investment management community. Special deals, spotty disclosure (or the lack of even that), blatant disregard for rules and regulations and the complete dismissal of the trust imposed on them by their clients has resulted in these firms perpetrating civil fraud upon their clients, which so far has resulted in more than 20 principals arrested, 10 barred from the industry and estimated damages of more than $20 billion. A cursory search of the Internet reveals hundreds of thousands of references to "Brokerage Scandals" and "Wall Street Crime". Making money through deceptive and misleading practices may be quick and easy, and it may be possible to get away with it for a while, however it is no less unethical, immoral and downright criminal than stealing money from clients at gunpoint— and at least a mugger or carjacker has the honesty to make it obvious and use a gun when he steals.

In an attempt to recover face after the recent storm of negative publicity associated with this latest round of Wall Street scandals, investment management firms have had to cut their fees, make special disclosures, fire principals, throw out portfolio managers and dismiss employees (in some cases, the founders or principals). With various abuses of investment law and client trust perpetrated, condoned or even encouraged at the highest levels of these firms, it is ludicrous to assume that there has been no impact on the investment merit of the firms in question.

---

*Certainly no financial advisor **should** send any client assets to a firm which has proven by their actions they have no respect for the law. In some cases, however, investor fraud is not illegal, merely unethical—but does any advisor really want to play the game of seeing how close to the line one can get before an ethical breach becomes a criminal breach? Should a responsible advisor allow clients to invest with parties who are unethical? Since investment management consultants and most other financial advisors have at least some fiduciary responsibility toward their clients, the only ethical answer is a resounding "NO". Furthermore, clients whose advisors have not recommended replacing the firms in question should fire their advisors.*

Conventional sales wisdom in the financial advisory world has said that if clients are happy or at least satisfied, then the consultant is doing their job and shouldn't try to rock the boat. Financial advisors have historically been reticent to disrupt a client relationship for fear that it will give the client an incentive to change advisors.

There are more than 5,500 mutual funds in the country. About 500 of them have been charged with breaching their fiduciary responsibility to shareholders. Led by New York State Attorney General Elliott Spitzer and Paul Roye and Stephen Cutler of the Securities and Exchange Commission, regulators and government agencies have imposed fines, ordered fee reductions and jailed or permanently banned perpetrators from the industry.

The media, interested in selling a simple story with good guys in white hats (Spitzer and his Wall Street Untouchables) and bad guys in black hats (Martha Stewart and the like), has misled investors to believe that mutual funds have been the culprits, and have tended to downplay the real culprits—the individuals responsible—the investment advisors, portfolio managers, traders and principals who ignored the fundamental principles of fiduciary responsibility.

Public and media attention has been directed to late trading. This is the practice of allowing certain favored investors to take advantage of after-hours activities and trade on information not available to the rest of us. But late trading is more than that. It means that persons in a decision making position have allowed preferential trading privileges to certain "favored" investors. Why certain investors? Let's think about some possible reasons.

Could it be because certain investors placed large assets with the fund? Or perhaps, the investor is a significant institution, say a center of influence or referrals. The point is that allowing late trading is not a random act of kindness by the fund. It's illegal, it's fraud upon shareholders and it is a breach of fiduciary responsibility by the fund principals as well as a lapse in oversight by the fund boards of directors. Allowing a client to participate in late trading takes money out of the pockets of other investors. It is more than unethical; it is theft wearing a suit. I have read that the fund scandal will, in the end, not cost the average investor much money. But if your co-worker stole $20 from your drawer because he knew it was there, and didn't tell you until you asked him if he did it, would you be able to trust him as much as you used to? Furthermore, would you continue to keep money in that drawer?

Market timing has gotten attention because, again, "certain" firms have been permitted to trade in and out of funds quickly while the "Average Joe" investors are waiting for tomorrow's <u>USA Today</u> to see how they are doing. Clients pay the added expenses, lowering their already paltry returns. The problem with market timing is that while it is not specifically illegal, the firms which permitted the activity did not disclose the activity in their prospectus. The problem is epidemic: failure to adequately disclose special preferential arrangements of this nature is the most common violation of securities laws reported to the regulators. Reread that last sentence: failure to disclose is a crime. Some firms have actually said that they will not permit the activity, yet allowed it anyway. Asking the same question, why are only "certain" firms given preferential treatment, leads us to the same answer--quid pro quo.

Other abuses which have been committed by funds include front running portfolio managers who so fervently believe in their own research that they must trade ahead of the rest of us to test it out, the blatant disregard of regulatory sales practices and the failure to disclose revenue sharing deals to investors. The total cost to investors is incalculable. It is not a cadre of back office clerks or rogue traders who have committed these crimes against shareholders. It is fund presidents, senior executives, advisory firms' officers and chief portfolio managers who have been the guilty perpetrators. Media attention has focused on a few high profile individuals. Unfortunately, jailing Martha Stewart (whose paltry take in illicit gains is a drop in the bucket compared to the ocean of malfeasance and wrongdoing the industry is faced with) has little real effect. The entire financial industry needs a severe housecleaning, and this can only be provided from within.

However, the financial advisory community has generally adopted the analytical approach in addition to the traditional sales approach. The analytical approach says if the client has been satisfied with the results, AND the fund is meeting its investment objectives, AND if the performance has been consistent, don't rock the boat. From a higher-level analytical approach, if the science of investment management consulting tells us that the fund is okay for investors, then it's okay.

What is being ignored is a fundamental ethical question—Do you want to recommend or even allow your clients to be invested in firms which have blatantly thumbed their collective noses at their fiduciary responsibility to their shareholders? This is part of the "art" of investment consulting not found in analysts' textbooks. Trying to compromise the art by balancing it with the science is like trying to reconcile modern geography with the Flat Earth theory. Don't try. Trust the art.

Your fiduciary owes YOU a duty of loyalty. How do you know who your fiduciary is? A fiduciary is someone who is responsible for somebody else's money. Fiduciary responsibility is the ethical treatment of somebody else's money. The issue need not be made any more complicated than that.

Courts and regulators regularly apply a sophisticated theory called the "Duck Theory" when assessing fiduciary responsibility. If something looks like a duck, walks like a duck, acts like a duck and quacks like a duck, it's a duck.

Fans of the old comedy movie "Monty Python and the Search for the Holy Grail" will remember a scene that used this theory. In the movie, the Duck Theory is used by a mob of angry peasants to find a witch. Wall Street's witch-hunt may be in the late stages, but it doesn't mean that all the witches have been purged. My first reaction when I heard about the fines being paid by the brokerage firms was that while some of those who remain employed have probably been scared straight by this, others are certainly laughing at it and thinking about what gray-area shortcuts have not yet been discovered.

Mutual funds are trusts, or are held to behave like them. Using fund assets for personal interests rather than those of the shareholders is a breach of that trust, and it's either illegal or unethical.

Favoring one group of investors over another to the potential detriment of the other or for the benefit of the fund manager rather than all the shareholders is wrong and has no place in the investment management world.

Out of this period of scandal and controversy will emerge a new age of investment transparency. The industry will satisfy client needs with a more open, more shareholder-oriented investing world. Those who play by the rules will be winners and will benefit by remembering they're dealing with "Somebody Else's Money".

Models in the business

Look in any magazine at any mutual fund advertisement and you'll see model portfolios in action. By definition a mutual fund is a "Model" portfolio. Every investor in the fund gets the same mix of securities. The principal thing that distinguishes an actively managed private account from a mutual fund is the private account's ability (and requirement) that they be able to be customized. This is not to say mutual funds are bad; in fact, my feeling is just the opposite. They are a core part of our portfolios and those of many other top-quality investment advisory firms.

Now, I'll admit that model portfolios are necessary at some level of the portfolio design process. We even use some modeling in our practice, so that in particular areas, our best thinking can be reflected in each client's account. However, this is a long way from having the entire plan based on "the model". If the client's entire future well being is based on generalities and suppositions instead of the specific hurdles they will face in their lives, then most success that does follow is more the result of luck than good intentions and solid planning. And, as the expression goes, you are likely to end up with "the sizzle but not the steak".

To help you recall this most critical concept in the client-advisor teamwork process at a time when you need it, think of a fashion model (man or woman, take your choice). Generally, these women and men are on strict diets most of the time. If you saw a famous model in a restaurant, you'd expect to see them eating salad, not steak. Of course, when at that restaurant, many of us would eat salad AND steak (and appetizers, and dessert, and coffee, and…). So, try remembering this:

MODELS DON'T EAT STEAK.

YOU ARE NOT A MODEL.

YOU NEED STEAK.

Have you ever seen an ad that said something like: "Diversification Made Easy". I'm going to guess that it was not easy for you to accumulate the wealth you currently have. It took hard work, perhaps punishing hours and advice from people you know and trust along the way. Now that you've made the incredible effort to amass the funds to place with an advisor, does it make you feel good that your advisor slapped together your plan with a few clicks of their mouse, and wants to direct your money to a program they use because it's "easy". Whether advisors are simply passing on what their large firm tells them to say, or creating the appearance that your portfolio's design and ongoing care is a laborious effort, advisors have a lot of incentive to make their lives easier at your expense. Don't let this happen to you!

So, that's a challenge that exists for many investors today. How do you know you are truly getting personalized advice with your best interests in mind? When we first started our firm, I wanted to make it clear to prospective clients that we understand and sympathize with the due diligence process they must go through to decide who to place their trust in. Later in the book, I'll present a due diligence questionnaire that our clients have found helpful as they get to know us.

For some investors, particularly those starting out, the model system works. It gets them started and avoids procrastination. For more seasoned investors (let's say those with at least $250,000 in their portfolio and some investment experience), modeling some part of a portfolio also makes sense IF it allows them to get the best thinking of the firms investing their money. However, for these folks, it is important to avoid the trap of simply being short-cutted into a portfolio with no regard for who they are, what makes them tick, and what they really need out of the money.

The other shortcut that we see over and over again is assumption that the stock market in its traditional form is a reliable core investment for most investors. The discussion of secular bear markets is sprinkled throughout this book, but here's an image that will drive the point home: if you simply rely on traditional stock market investing as the key to your ability to retire, you are taking a big risk! The picture in the next section of this chapter will drive this point home.

A Shocking Fact

When you first learn about the stock market, you are liable to be taught that the long-term average annual return of stocks is about 10%. That figure is based on a widely-followed, documented history of the U.S. stock market (as measured by the S&P 500 stock index) by Ibbotson Associates, an esteemed research firm. Their data starts in 1926 and is updated each year. Ibbotson does terrific work, but recently I stumbled upon a stray fact that really challenges this conventional wisdom.

Morningstar also reports the history of the S&P 500 stock index, but their data only goes back to 1928. So, what do you think the historical annual total return of the U.S. stock market is if you take out those two measly little years, 1926 and 1927? If you guessed close to 10%, I wouldn't blame you. But you would be incorrect. How about 7.22%! How can two years make so much of an impact on an 80 year study? When those two years were the ones that led up to the Crash of '29.

The stock market at that stage of the "Roaring Twenties" was not unlike that of the late 1990's. In fact, it took nearly two decades for the market to recover from the damage that occurred during the crash of that period. This is just one of many historical facts that has been brushed aside by the investment industry because it does not sell well to the public.

I'm here to tell you that not only is the 10% stock market average a myth, but more importantly, that it doesn't impact your ability to reach your individual wealth goals. Why not? Because if you focus on making money and not being tied to the allure of the market averages, you can escape the fate of those who started investing in 1929 instead of 1926. They say what a difference a day makes. The same goes for a year or two, especially when you are talking about investing for your retirement.

In South Florida, my home, many retirees and pre-retirees escape the summer heat by going to the mountains of Colorado or North Carolina. Some eventually buy second homes there, or even move there for good. Now, check out the picture below. It's a "mountain" chart of the S&P 500 from 1998-2005. Can you imagine if you decided in 1998 that you would retire in seven years, and based that assumption on your advisor's projection that you would make a 10% annual return over that time? We often forget that when you hit your peak earning and investment years and when you retire are all somewhat random points in time. The markets do not care about that timing. The last thing you want is to get suckered into some advisor's line about expected market performance based on historical averages that may never, ever come close to the actual experience you have in the future.

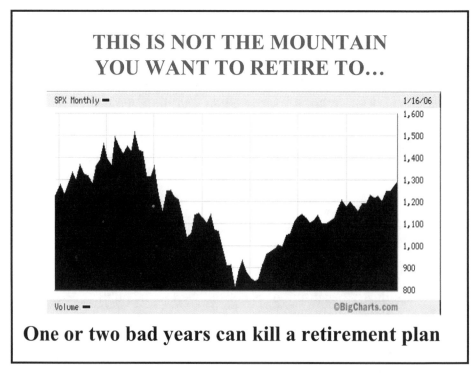

Fig. 4: A Mountain Not to Retire To--Source: BigCharts.com

Is It Time To Cut The "Wrap"?

For many years, mutual funds were on an island of their own. For anyone but the wealthiest of investors, the only way to gain access to professional money management was through these pooled vehicles. For decades, the world of private money management was closed to those building their fortune and even those who were simply well off. Investors resorted to funds they bought themselves, or they worked with stockbrokers.

The late 1980's and 1990's brought about the emergence of separate-accounts. For as little as $100,000 an investor could have their money managed by professional money management firms that typically worked only for institutions and the mega-wealthy. A new vehicle was created and Wall Street brokerage firms hopped in with both feet. Assets surged into these accounts and investors were willing to pay up to 3% for the privilege – a fact not lost on brokerage executives. They bundled the various fees owed to the manager, custodian, and themselves into a single fee – thus, "wrapping" it all together. The term "wrap-fee account" became a popular way to refer to these vehicles.

Before long, the industry was flooded with accounts – first millions, then billions of dollars fed into the managed account craze. Fees came down but only slightly in many cases. More damaging to clients, however, is what has occurred over the last few years: the reason people became attracted to wrap-accounts disappeared. What do we mean? Here are a few examples:

1. Investors wanted to have an account managed by someone who actually knew who they were. Now, most of the firms that manage these accounts are what we call "wrap-factories". They manage thousands of accounts, and everyone is a number. It has become indistinguishable from a mutual fund, so why bother? The client who sought something special now receives what some have called "mass-customized" advice.

2. These managers were supposed to provide superior performance. In select cases they have, but most are indistinguishable from their index-benchmarks, except that they seldom beat those benchmarks. Our feeling is that this is largely due to the fact that the firms that sponsor wrap programs (mostly brokerage firms and some independent providers) place more value on selecting firms that can manage thousands of small accounts than finding great money managers with something different to offer. The client is left with what we call the "usual suspects" – the same 20 or 30 wrap-factories that stand out only because they have the familiarity with the accounting systems required to manage large amounts of assets from different clients. If this gives you some sort of feeling of security, that's fine. But that security comes with a hefty price, and it's not necessary.

3. This is one of the reasons that Exchange-Traded Funds (ETFs) are becoming so popular—if you want index-like performance with simplicity, ETFs will deliver it. We prefer to use outside money managers to run accounts that give you a fighting chance to either deliver outsized returns in the long run and/or protect your portfolio when times are rough. Neither has been accomplished by the vast majority of "wrap-factories". If you are going to pay up for professional money managers to guide your portfolio, its best to find firms that truly do look at your account as different from the masses. Be a client, not a number, that's the way we approach it.

4. The wrap fee issue is one that evokes particularly high emotions from my partners and me. For years, we have talked to people who told us that their wrap account's total fee was 1%, and upon closer inspection by us turned out to be 2 or 3%. We're not saying that the fee should never be that high; we just wish that the brokers were more upfront about it. Compounding the problem is the fact that brokers have now become simply a place for managers to get "shelf space." For wrap managers today, distribution is the name of the game. Just like in insurance, the more your product is distributed, the more sales you will have. And they pay dearly for it. Managers complain to us that their share of the total fee has been cut dramatically over the years, even though the client's total fee is about the same. Who do you think gets the difference? That's right, the brokerage firm that forced the manager to work for less. We applaud companies that fight to reduce investors' costs...unless they take the cost reduction and pocket it themselves!

5. Finally, there is the proprietary product issue. Take a guess who the two largest wrap managers are? MLAM and SBAM. Who's that you say? Let me spell it out for you: Merrill Lynch Asset Management and Smith Barney Asset Management – the internal products run by the two largest providers of wrap accounts. Do you think there might be some internal incentives for brokers keeping the money under the firm's own umbrella?

Third-party managed accounts have been an important part of client diversification strategies at our firm and many others. But, as the deficiencies mentioned above became apparent over the last several years, we made adjustments to our offering. We try to avoid the "usual suspects" unless they are firms with a demonstrated record of superior long-term performance, a consistent investment process, and stability of personnel. We understand that clients today don't want index-like performance from these managers – they can get that from an index fund. We keep the fees manageable and we are open about them. Most importantly, we do not limit ourselves to volume-driven money managers. As an independent Registered Investment Advisor, we are free to hire any money manager who will work with us. What we require from them is that they will manage our clients' assets with as much customization as we request. That freedom of choice allows our clients to have a meaningful experience with separate-account advisors instead of buying a commoditized program. This is not the easiest way to run an investment business, but you don't want your advisor taking shortcuts with your money.

Rebalancing

I am often asked by prospective clients how we "rebalance" our portfolios. This is one of those questions which shows the positive aftermath of Wall Street's effort to better educate investors during the 1980's and 1990's. Just the fact that people ask about rebalancing, investment costs, trading turnover, and asset allocation is a fantastic improvement over the client-advisor discussions of twenty years ago. Yesterday's investor took a lot of things at face value, and today's investor knows better.

The investor of the 1980's has lived through the crash of '87, the recession of '90, the investment bubble of the turn of the century, and the decline since. They have seen scandals emerge from every corner of Wall Street. They have learned the hard way that they must ask certain questions of their advisors and the investments they make to reduce the chance that they will be misguided. Today's investor, as I see it, is far more on guard.

I try to make it clear during the first meeting with someone that I am not only sympathetic to their situation, but have thought of ways to allay their concerns and gain their confidence. Very often, I feel that the best relationships between client and advisor start in the first ten minutes of discussion at the first meeting or phone call. The advisor makes it clear that their job is not to sell the client on some approach that may not apply to them, and the client is open about what they need from the advisor. Even if the client does not have a grip on what they want, if they are ready to have the advisor guide them with an open mind, they have already done their part.

Rebalancing is a term used to describe the periodic adjustment of the different parts of your portfolio, so that the percentages you owned in each asset type have been restored to the figures you targeted in the past. For instance, if 30% of your portfolio was in stocks, and your stock portfolio performed extremely well for awhile, stocks could be, say 40% of your portfolio due to the outperformance of stocks versus other asset types. If your advisor's intention was for you to be at 30%, a 40% position in stocks would represent a relatively aggressive posture for you. Your advisor would probably recommend that you sell enough stocks to bring you back to a 30% weighting.

I believe in rebalancing, but I strongly believe that it is overused by advisors. In fact, it is one of the main casualties of Wall Street's move toward commoditizing and sterilizing the investment process. This is to the detriment of many investors. Here's why.

I think that simply rebalancing because it's "time" to do so is ridiculous. But that's what is usually done. It's done because it fits the demands of the investment firms whose approach calls for every portfolio to look the same, and so rebalancing every three months makes that goal easier. But that's their goal, not yours! Do you get your hair cut when it is getting too long or on the third Tuesday of every month?

In other words, rebalancing should be done when positions have gone well out of their acceptable range, and even then should be handled with care. Especially for taxable accounts, you have to be careful you don't simply sell solid investments that are performing well and buy more weak investments. Don't put good money after bad, as they say. In addition, there's nothing wrong with letting a winner run. In fact, if you are charitably inclined, the biggest winners in your portfolio are prime candidates to be gifted to charity. This allows you to bypass capital gains tax and get a tax deduction for your contribution.

When you rebalance a taxable account according to some mechanical formula, the only thing you know for sure is that you will pay taxes. So, my rebalancing rules are more relaxed than most people's. Its part of the personalized, human element that I believe is gradually but surely slipping away from many advisory relationships. Insist on reversing that trend and you become part of the solution, not part of the problem.

In The Long Run, We Are All...About The Same

About 70 years ago (around the time of a tremendous bear market), the economist John Maynard Keynes stated that "in the long run, we are all dead". Many a Wall Street pundit has since used this phrase to make the point that short-term investment decisions are important, and that one should not merely buy and hold forever. Since both sides of this argument have merit, we will not take sides. We merely want to present a set of figures that we found very interesting:

Fig. 5: Comparison of Overall Performance By Sector

Wilshire Small Value	15.67	6/30/1978
Wilshire Midcap Value	15.32	6/30/1978
Wilshire Midcap 500	14.99	6/30/1978
Wilshire Small Cap 1750	14.02	6/30/1978
Wilshire Midcap Growth	13.86	6/30/1978
Wilshire Large Value	13.41	6/30/1978
Wilshire Large Cap 750	12.95	6/30/1978
Wilshire Large Growth	11.97	6/30/1978
Wilshire Small Growth	11.51	6/30/1978

Returns through 12/31/05. Source: Morningstar

So, regardless of which part of the U.S. stock market you invested in, your long-term return was about the same (within a range of less than 5%). Yes, I know that there's a four point difference between the best and worst segments of this list of indexes published by the Wilshire group of California. But if you consider them to be what they are—proxies for subdivisions of the stock market—and realize that this past information does not predict the future (i.e. there's no guarantee that small cap value will be the best performer going forward), it makes you wonder why so much time and energy is spent by the masses arguing about the merits of this style or that style. That's why I prefer to throw out the style boxes and simply find managers that are out to make money—the fewer the barriers, the better.

Quarterly Reporting

The investment consulting industry has perpetuated the practice of giving clients a performance report every quarter. Clients have been "trained" to look at short term results. This has not done investors any favors. Clients who want to know how the broad market indexes have performed and what major issues impact portfolio returns can get that information from reading the newspaper once in a while. Advisors must provide something beyond that.

The quarterly review meeting – what's wrong with it?

I used to follow the crowd when it came to client portfolio review meetings. The nearly universal approach in the business for years has been to send the client an extensive report of portfolio activity and holdings at the end of each calendar quarter. This is one of the many ways in which Wall Street tries to apply (incorrectly) to individual investors what they have done for institutional investors for decades.

There's only one problem. Most families are not institutions. They don't have the same concerns. For one thing, they pay taxes. As for that good old quarterly review meeting, here's what I concluded after doing it Wall Street's way for many years: most of you do not want to be dragged through a discussion of what parts of your portfolio are doing well, which ones are not, and what new securities you own. After all, here in the 21st century, answers like that are available online. And if you prefer to get this information at 4AM while sitting in your Lazy Boy recliner in your pajamas, you can! Just log onto your account to see it. Most advisors offer online access to investment holdings and transactions today. If they don't they are dinosaurs and I would be wary of what else about their care of your assets is still back in the 20th century.

The quarterly review meeting sends a message: watch your portfolio like a hawk and check frequently to see what changes you should make. I think a more sensible approach is to have this kind of detailed review once or twice a year. By no means am I saying that your advisor should ignore you the rest of the year. For instance, in addition to the one or two detailed reviews each year, our clients hear from their portfolio advisor and our support staff several more times each year. They receive commentaries from me on topics that we expect are of interest to them. They are invited to client social events such as ballgames or perhaps charity events. They may have as many as ten, twenty even thirty contacts from us in a year. And we are also available whenever they have questions, as often or seldom as they wish. In short, it does not take a formal, quarterly meeting for you to get all you wanted and more from your advisory relationship.

I find that investors are more concerned with what issues are impacting their ability to reach their particular goals. Simply summarizing returns or giving market and economic commentary is not sufficient, and it is very impersonal. It is also backward looking without being forward looking and I think that any review session should be both. As I have mentioned elsewhere in this book, past performance is fine to look at, but it's a mistake to blindly assume that the returns of the past will repeat themselves going forward. Yet this is what some investors base their entire evaluation of an investment on.

Also, telling you that your best performers were bank stocks and that software stocks cost you some money in the quarter ended June 30, and mailing the report to you in mid-August is a waste of paper.

When I write, it's about what events or trends my firm and I are watching and WHY we think it will impact your wealth over the short-term and long-term. And if we are going to talk about what happened in your portfolio in the June quarter, if we do not get it out to you within two weeks of the end of that quarter, the ink is already getting stale.

"Wholesale" Problems

During my years in the advisory business, I've come in contact with dozens of investment wholesalers. These are salespeople whose job is to travel an area of the country convincing people like me that I should invest my clients' assets in their company's mutual funds or managed accounts. As with sales reps in other industries, from a professional standpoint some of these folks are not worth the value of the fancy suits they travel in. Others truly understand what their role is. Similar to an excellent advisor, an excellent wholesaler realizes that their client (the advisor) does not want a hard sales pitch. If the wholesaler listens well, and if the fit is right between the advisor's investment philosophy and that espoused by the wholesaler's firm, good things will happen.

As you might guess, I'm not one to respond favorably to being sold to. If I grant a meeting to a wholesaler, it is probably because my team and I have already researched one of their funds, and invested clients in it. In other words, we tend to find them before they find us. I think this is a good thing for our clients to know because it speaks to our research approach. We know what we are looking for, and when we find it, the door opens wide. But we don't answer the door if the proverbial Big Bad Wolf is knocking.

As a result of this approach to working with wholesalers, I have learned a lot about the industry. In fact, some of my best fact-checkers for this book are wholesalers. They know that any information they can relay to my team and me about what is going on at other firms is appreciated. In the past few years, here are some of the best insights I've gathered from my friends in the investment wholesaling business:

Overlap

Many investment firms have built their success by essentially spinning off similar versions of one of their products. For instance, if their original growth stock fund becomes popular, they come out with another growth fund. Oh, they find some way to make it appear quite different from the original. But it usually isn't. Over time, the trained eye will find that a mutual fund family offers many funds that look, act and perform very similarly.

Why would a company do this? In my opinion, it's to create the impression that you can buy several of their funds in the name of diversification. After all, if you have all of your money in one of their funds, even though that fund may own 150 stocks, Wall Street may try to tell you that you are not diversified. After all, you only own one fund. So, to help you diversify and capitalize on your positive opinion of them (you must have a positive opinion since you have your money there), they offer you a different fund.

This sounds reasonable except for one thing: there are only so many ways to invest in growth stocks…or value stocks…or stocks at all, using traditional approaches. What this points out is that there is much homework to be done. In the money management business, we call that homework on securities, funds and managers, "Due Diligence". We, in the industry pay professional analysts good money to slice and dissect performance results and qualitative as well as quantitative factors about investment vehicles. A "do it yourself" investor would find it extremely difficult to replicate the depth of intelligence we gather.

Here's something that might surprise you. Using data from Morningstar as of 1/31/06, I made a detailed analysis of the twelve largest U.S. Large Cap Growth Stock Funds. I compared their holdings and correlation to each other over the past 10 years. I discovered that the funds all moved in sync with each other, and with their benchmark, the Russell 1000 Growth Index. That is, they are all highly correlated to each other and their benchmark index. If you are thinking that 10 years is a long time and that things can change, consider that the correlations over the past three and five years were similar or higher. If anything, I was giving the funds the benefit of the doubt by using the longer 10 year period. It is worth noting that four of the funds were from American Funds group and three were from Fidelity, which is the example of what I just mentioned above – the idea of a large fund company creating new packages for essentially the same investment.

In addition, I looked at the top 15 holdings of each fund as of their last report (mutual funds announce their full holdings typically twice a year). Guess how many of the 12 funds I surveyed owned Microsoft? Answer: 12. How many owned healthcare giant United Healthcare? Answer: 12. I think you get the idea.

All in all, of the top 15 holdings across all these funds, 10 stocks were owned by at least 10 of the 12 funds. 13 of the top 15 holdings were owned by at least eight of the 12 funds. Bottom line: the investor must ask, "How many times do I want to own the same stuff"? Another good question is, "If these funds all correlate so highly with the index, why shouldn't my advisor use an Exchange-Traded Index Fund (ETF) instead of all of these funds to get the same result"? Answer: they should! Similar work we've done in the past in other traditional asset classes has produced similar results.

Now, I'm not saying that all funds that target investment in traditional asset classes are lousy investments. I'm simply pointing out what I've gravitated to over the years when it comes to selecting investments for the equity portion of my clients' portfolios:

1. There are managers that have consistently provided "alpha", or returns above the market return.

2. Those managers are typically not found at the largest, best-known firms.

3. A portfolio of ETFs, spread across the traditional categories, gives you a great chance to replicate what a portfolio of big-name mutual funds can, but without the "waste product" that is overlapping holdings. Hiring a manager who runs a portfolio of ETFs (the ranks of which are growing quickly) could be an excellent solution for many investors.

The conclusion: diversification means owning different assets that have very different characteristics. Investing in several funds that are essentially clones of each other does not satisfy that definition.

Senior Loan Funds Are Not Money Market Surrogates

These funds buy loans made from banks to corporations. Many of these corporations go to banks for their short-term financing needs. They are often the same companies that issue high-yield or "junk" bonds for their longer-term needs. The bonds in the fund have interest rates that fluctuate. Higher inflation leads to higher rates on these funds. Yet the principal value of the fund often stays steady or even rises. This makes Senior Loan Funds a potentially good choice to battle inflation. Again, these funds are comprised of bonds that are not very high quality, so don't confuse them with the bond funds I've maligned in other parts of this book. I believe that for investing in high-quality bonds, the bonds should be bought directly, not through a fund. For investment in lower-quality bonds, the diversification of a fund or managed account is a more attractive alternative.

I happen to like this asset class, but only in a certain form. The Senior Loan Funds we use have daily liquidity—that is, if we want to sell them today, we can. We don't have to wait. I don't like my clients to wait to get their money if I can avoid it. And this is one of those areas of investing that change very quickly. As soon as the rate of corporate bond defaults (i.e. companies can't make their payments on debt) increases, these funds can run into trouble. In addition, many Senior Loan Funds use leverage (i.e. they take the money you invest, and borrow more money so they have more to invest). That can add to your income and total return, but it can also bring a double-whammy if interest rates rise along with a rise in bond defaults. We tend to use funds with no leverage, with the aim of earning a return slightly above a money market fund, with little fluctuation in the principal and daily liquidity. On the occasion where we do use the leveraged versions, we do so with the understanding, and with communication to our clients, of the risks involved.

Well, it seems that these funds are often sold to clients by brokers as a money market alternative and used as a significant part of the client's portfolio. Whoa! These are a very nice addition to a lot of portfolios, and they can both reduce overall volatility and increase income. But they are not to be confused with money market funds!

For one thing, money funds do not lose value except in rare, catastrophic situations. Their price per share is $1.00 and it stays that way (the interest rate changes all the time but the principal protection does not). And I'm quite sure that most investors would not look at a leveraged investment that is only salable every three months as their next best choice to a money market fund.

97

When I asked the wholesalers how this could be, they were as perplexed as I was. In one case reported to me, a broker executed a $5mm trade in one Senior Loan Fund. The broker had a chance to choose another similar fund that paid 2% more in income. Both funds had quarterly liquidity. According to the broker, his reason for choosing the lesser yielding fund did not have anything to do with management, research approach or anything like that. The broker went with the lower yielding fund since it paid them 0.25% a year more than the other fund. On a $5mm investment, that's $12,500 a year, or over $1,000 a month more in revenue to that broker's firm. How about that for providing "advice" to your client! Yes, I know that this is one isolated case. But you don't want to be on the other side of that transaction.

While it is true that the client should have some basic understanding of what they invest in, I believe it is the advisor's scope of responsibility to gauge whether the client truly understands. I do not allow clients to "yes" me. If they do not understand the basic and most important features of their portfolio, we'll keep talking until they do. Or, we'll avoid that type of investment for them. This is particularly true with hedge funds. They are very well suited for some people, but they are too complex and opaque to put in just anyone's portfolio. And just because a client has a high net worth, it does not make them an appropriate candidate for any investment.

Who Cares About Mutual Fund Distributions?

Unfortunately, Not Many Advisors

As you know if you have owned mutual funds before, the funds are required to pay out to shareholders each year their pro-rata share of the income and capital gains earned by the fund. These payments are usually made in November or December. If you bought the fund in a taxable account, you pay taxes on the income and gains. These distributions come with the territory for fund investors, and if you've owned the funds during the period in which those gains were made, its only fair that you get your gains and the subsequent tax hit distributed to you. However, financially speaking, there are few things worse than receiving a distribution and paying taxes on capital gains you did not enjoy as an investor. This can easily happen if your advisor is not paying attention. And let's face it, with all the twisted motivations potentially out there for advisors to act on, buying a fund for you just before a huge distribution is not something they are likely to think twice about.

So how do you stay clear of paying taxes on what amounts to other people's profits? Some mutual fund companies make it easy for you. They publish estimates of their distributions weeks before they pay them. Some fund firms tell us exactly when and in what amount they will pay, and whether they are paying at all. For instance, a fund that has not made a lot of money the past few years, or one that tends to hold its investments for many years at a time has not generated a lot of capital gains from selling. The manager may also have been adept at balancing realized gains with realized losses to keep the tax burden on the fund very low.

Fidelity is usually an upstanding citizen in this area. The company often has all of their projected payments on their website in late October, even though the funds don't pay until November or December. That's treating your shareholders well! I am not a big fan of Fidelity and rarely use their funds, but I have a great deal of respect for them on this issue.

In our Hybrid Investment Strategy, we use as many as 25 or 30 different funds across our various portfolios at one time. That means that when we reach the fourth quarter of the year, we have to be very aware of which funds could throw a large distribution at us. We do not want to buy these funds until after they have paid out. To help us make the best possible decisions and avoid being blindsided by the fund companies, each year we assign a staff person to call the companies that run each of the funds our clients own, as well as those we anticipate buying. They make their first round of calls in late October and track the estimated payments and payment dates on a computerized grid we created years ago.

But several fund companies don't play fair on this issue. They don't give estimates (even though they know what they are), or they play dumb, saying they expect to pay out in December and then do so in November. Why would they do this? Because a large projected distribution could cause shareholders to redeem their shares prior to the payment and cause others to hold off on purchases. The fund companies may think this is a good short-term business decision for them but I think the negative public relations in the eyes of advisors and their clients far outweighs that.

Because of the uncertainty caused by distribution season, as the last weeks of the year go by, our staff calls the mutual fund companies as often as needed to update estimate information and to confirm that distributions due to be paid have indeed been paid. That frees us up to start using the funds again. Also, if we have a fund that is about to pay a big distribution, and we were planning to sell it anyway, we may want to sell it before the distribution is paid.

I'd like to think that the process we go through each year is performed by every advisor who uses mutual funds in their practice. I even thought that one day I would create a company that would service advisors by tracking all the distributions for them, to save them a lot of time toward the end of the year. But I've learned over the years that while my team and I are obsessive about not buying funds shortly before large distributions, many in our industry do not share that obsession. In fact, the wholesalers tell me that companies get relatively few calls from advisors on estimates, while there's still time to do something about them. I'm not patting myself on the back for making the effort. I'm just surprised that it is the exception instead of the rule in the industry.

The implications for you if you invest in mutual funds are enormous. In a high distribution year, on a portfolio of $1mm in funds, buying just ahead of distributions could easily cost you $10,000-$15,000 in unnecessary taxes! Heck, that's more than you pay your advisor in a year for "managing" your assets! Bottom line: your advisor better make the effort to dance around excessive or untimely taxable distributions, or they are not doing their job.

Who Is Your Advisor "Producing" For—You, Or Their Firm?

I think the best money management firms have figured out the types of people they best relate to, both economically and psychologically. I call this having a "good fit". Obviously, if you have read this far, you know that I believe that for most investors, an independently owned money management firm provides the best fit and best chance for ultimate success. This is especially true for entrepreneurs.

At my firm and other independent advisors, we are independent wealth managers—you work closely with the owners of the firm, not with a commission-paid incentive-driven broker whose interests lay more with how much they can charge than with your personal financial success. If you doubt this, just do some research into how brokers are evaluated by their firms and the industry. It is based almost entirely on "production". That is, how much was generated in sales by the advisor. Everything relating to success in the industry is tied to production. The brokerage firms just don't seem that interested in delivering to you a highly-qualified, well-matched advisor unless that advisor has also racked up big sales numbers for the firm.

It annoys me to no end that the image these firms portray on their TV ads is one of personal attention to life goals and coddling the client. In reality, I believe that while there are many brokers who match this ideal, there are far more who don't. In recent years, one brokerage firm after another has made life difficult for those who don't meet the firm's revenue targets. These brokers have their income and incentives cut, and some are let go or effectively forced to leave before they go poor. If I were a client of a brokerage firm, this potential instability would bother me a lot. It seems as if brokers' production levels are so important in evaluating the advisor's talent, there's no room to notice if they are actually doing well by their clients!

I can understand why the brokerage firms act this way. It goes back to what I said earlier in this book—if their choice is to satisfy the client or the shareholder, the shareholder usually wins. In the marketplace, this manifests itself through a focus on broker production for the firm instead of the broker's production for the client (i.e. meeting client objectives).

When I asked a 30-year industry veteran from a major brokerage firm about this, I was told that in their opinion, this problem boils down to one thing above all others: lack of training of the brokers. From what I have heard, Merrill Lynch has a better program for training their rookies, but even they produce a lot of salespeople who burn out quickly in the business. The idea that these firms take in and spit out brokers on a regular basis is a tough thought, but consistent with the "shareholder defeats client" idea.

So, do I have any ideas about how this situation could better? Sure, I could talk the party line of independent advisors and say that the brokerage machine is eternally broken. But I won't.

As a former brokerage trainee, and a former member of a brokerage team (in which there were two advisors working together, plus an assistant), I think the brokerage business would benefit greatly in the client's eyes (and ultimately their own wallets) if they pursued some adjustments to their training approach. For instance, they could take a lesson from Donald Trump's "Apprentice" program by recruiting and evaluating trainees based on their ability to complement each other's skills and work as a team. If they sought to recruit two types of brokers – those who enjoy and are successful at selling and those who enjoy and are successful at advising, and during the months of training, try to pair them off, that would help. They could even throw the investment assistants (yes, in the brokerage industry they often call them "sales assistants") into the mix by recruiting them for training classes that run simultaneous to the broker training. The end goal would be to produce three-person teams that could go out and create client relationships, conduct ongoing analysis of investment alternatives, and support the operation, with everyone on the team helping and even liking each other.

Of course, this would still leave one big, gaping hole in the attractiveness of the firm to the client: the members of the team are all rookies. It's like asking someone if they prefer to be guided by a soldier who's recently out of basic training, or a 4-star general. Since I'm long gone from the brokerage business, I'll leave this topic alone and let the bright people who run these firms sort it out. For the sake of millions of baby boomers, I sure hope they do.

CHAPTER 7 – INVESTING IN THE 21st CENTURY

"Life favors those who are prepared" – Troy Vincent, NFL football player whose career spanned more than 15 years (league average is 3 years)

In Chapter 5, we reviewed some of the most important issues for investors today. In Chapter 6, we saw that Wall Street may help or hinder as you seek to address those issues. In this chapter, I'll start providing my opinion and beliefs on how to create a solution for yourself. Put another way, **we have identified some of Wall Street's "bull" and will now move on to how to "bear" it.**

One of the most important pieces of guidance I've ever received is that there are some things in life that we can control, and some that we can't. At least once a week, something happens to remind me that this is so critical to remember. If we focus less on what happens to us, and more on what we can do about it, we are much better off. In this chapter, I'll point out some of the most important concepts you should understand as a 21st Century investor. I'll then share my thoughts on what types of investments I believe give you the best shot at living the lifestyle you envision. Note that I'm not going to call out a stock or market sector. I'm simply going to summarize many years of a "process of elimination" analysis about what you should focus on and what you should ignore as an investor today. I say "today" for a very important reason: as we saw in Chapter 5, there are rules that some of us grew up with as investors in the 1980's and 1990's that are fading into obscurity. If you and your advisor don't recognize this, your portfolio's value may fade too.

The Big Picture

The money you invest in the stock market should be money you are not likely to use for several years. It is much more important to have the money you need when you need it. Today's paper-value is far less important. You need to understand the investment process, the various dynamics that are in play every day, and, most of all, you need to understand yourself—your motivations and fears about whatever amount of money you have. Bond investing, on the other hand, is not simply a "safe haven" for money you don't' feel like putting in the stock market.

Volatility

Simply put, volatility is the amount by which the price of an asset changes over some period of time. Everything in investing is cyclical and the cycles can be days, weeks, months, years or decades. Volatility is part of stock market investing, and will always be.

From 1963-1998, the U.S. stock market's average daily price movement was six-tenths of 1%. We studied the S&P 500's daily moves for the few years after 1998, and found that the average daily volatility was often more than double the historical average! Roughly speaking, that translates into a daily move of about 140 points on the Dow Jones Industrials. But if this is a fear generator, don't let the daily gyrations of the market disturb your dinner, sleep or long-term investment goals.

Another important thing to remember about volatility is that it tends to be more consistent than performance for most asset classes. That is, while the investment return generated over a period of time by, say Large Cap Growth stocks or International stocks will vary greatly, their level of volatility will stay more constant. Stocks as a group don't tend to stop moving around in price for periods of time. Over multi-year periods, stocks will nearly always be more volatile (variable) in their returns than bonds.

Volatility is something all successful long-term investors must endure to ultimately reach their goals. The key is to understand it, so you can deal with it rationally, and keep your cool.

Market Volatility In The Context Of The Real World

How often do you change your mind about a business decision? Some market participants do every day. This is not rational, but it happens. Do you want to spend an investment lifetime thinking that way? We spend much time during volatile periods explaining to our clients that they shouldn't.

The way I see it, most of the information we receive from the markets can be classified as falling into one of three time frames: Temporary, Cyclical, or Secular. Some examples follow.

Temporary - a stock falls 5% in one day because one Wall Street analyst slightly lowers earnings estimates for the upcoming quarter. Temporary events are just that—temporary.

Cyclical – semiconductor companies say demand looks weak for the next 12 months and they have an excess inventory of chips, and they are reducing production. The stocks sell off. Guess what? A year later, the inventories come down, the same companies realize that demand is getting stronger and announce they must ramp up chip production. Wall Street falls in love again (this happened several times in the 1990's. Just look at a 10-Year stock price chart on Intel).

Secular – baby boomers start retiring en masse, and the money they pull out of the stock market overwhelms the amount that younger investors can add. Stocks go from being the long-term investment of choice to a smaller focus of people's assets.

So what's my point? Temporary and Cyclical reactions are not reasons to make dramatic portfolio changes. Professional Money Managers use these events as opportunities to buy into stocks that have fallen for no good reason, or they merely ride them out. They know that their good research will win out in the long-run.

Secular events are more troublesome, even to long-term investors. However, they come along very rarely. The contrast between these three types of event is depicted on the chart on the following page, and is explained in further detail below.

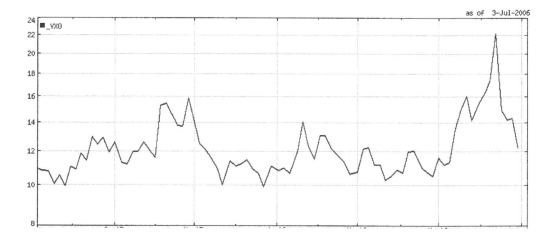

as of 3-Jul-2006

Fig. 6: Market Volatility Over Time

What does the market worry about most, and how would I classify these events?

1. **Fallen Valuations Of Certain Stocks – Cyclical**

   Every period of innovation in business history has followed the same pattern: Boom--Euphoria--Return to Reality--Excessive Decline--Recovery, start of the next Boom

2. **A Recession – Very Cyclical**

   Recessions occur in every decade, but don't often last that long.

3. **The Federal Reserve Not Raising (Or Lowering) Interest Rates "Enough" – Temporary**

   If the Fed doesn't raise or lower rates fast enough to prevent recession or inflation, you can be sure they will respond once we're in one. They may sometimes react late, but they always react.

4. **Continued Warnings Of Lower Earnings From Market Leaders – Temporary**

   How else do you explain that so often, a company announces a disappointment, the stock falls sharply, but joins the market on its next rally? Strong companies last much longer than most investors' memories.

5. **Rising Energy Costs – Cyclical Or Secular**

   If it turns out to be the latter, watch out and make sure you are prepared in your portfolio and your automobile.

6. **Increasing Default Rates On Low-Quality Corporate Debt – Cyclical**

More Tips For Volatile Markets:

1. **Beware Of The Crowd At The Extremes**

   As one example, panic selling can reach ridiculous levels in these circumstances.

2. **The Risk Is That The Market Becomes Cheap (Expensive) Before A Bear (Bull) Market Is Over.**

   There is no rule that says the market will bottom (top) at a fair price. Instead, it could occur far below (above) what is rational. This is the first rule my father ever taught me in investing, so I never forgot it.

3. **Beware Irrational Optimism And/Or Pessimism**

   If an investor's greatest allies are time and diversification, their biggest enemy is emotion.

SECULAR BEAR MARKETS – Ignore Them At Your Peril!

My son Tyler has the patience one would expect from a boy of his age – none (he was born in 1998). As with most kids, their time frames are not very similar to ours. In our family, we imitate Tyler's regular complaint that he utters in his typical, deliberate voice, "This...is...taking...a...long...time." He has applied the quote to everything from a quick trip to the supermarket to waiting for food at a restaurant to sitting at a traffic light (back seat driver!).

One day when Tyler is older and I want him to get some sleep, I'll teach him about something that REALLY takes a long time – secular trends in the investment markets.

As we discussed in previous chapters, a bear market is an extended period of time during which stock prices are roughly flat. That's right: not down, flat. Secular bull and bear markets have lasted between 8 and 20 years, and the average return across the length of a secular bear is slightly above to slightly below zero.

Wait a minute! Aren't secular bears huge, nasty declines? Yes…partly. Think of it this way: Suppose the S&P 500 index lost about 45% in 2 ½ years (as it did during 2000-2002). Using some basic math, that means it will take a 90% rise to return to the old highs. If that moves takes 10 years, we will have had a 12-year period with zero return. That's a secular bear market.

Bear market recoveries, however, are more often gradual than quick and exciting. If that recovery took 10 years to get back to the old highs, you'd average over 7% a year and finally get back to where you started 12 years before. Try explaining to your family that your retirement plan was based on an assumption that stocks always go up in the "long run" and that the plan you put in place with those index funds 12 years ago netted you about zip in return. I guess you'll need another phase on that retirement plan. With the rising concerns that employees of large corporations have about the future availability of their pension plans, avoiding the potential trap of failing to adjust to a secular bear market is, in my opinion, the greatest challenge faced by baby boomers, who will hit retirement age in large numbers over the next three decades.

Fig. 7: 102-Year Dow Jones Chart

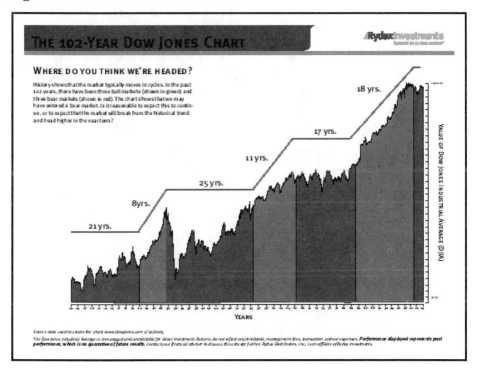

I gave a speech at an investment conference and stated that if the audience could only remember one thing from my presentation, it should be this chart. It shows how over the last century, the stock market (as represented by the Dow Jones Industrial Average) can be divided into "red zones" and "green zones". The green zones (visible here darker) are secular bull markets and nearly everyone who reads this book will remember the last one, as well as how it ended. The last secular bull market started in the early 1980's and ended in early 2000 (some will argue it was earlier, but I will not jump into that discussion here). The red periods, like the green ones, last many years. In fact, the shortest secular bull on the chart is eight years, and the shortest secular bear has been seventeen years. You may be thinking back to the table earlier in the book which contained similar information. I like this version of the story because colors and charts are naturally easier to understand and remember than tables The sections alternate red and green starting from the left .**IF YOU ARE IN AN UP-MARKET ZONE, GROWING YOUR WEALTH IS PRETTY EASY. NEARLY EVERONE DOES IT.**

2. **IF YOU ARE IN RED ZONE, YOU CAN GROW YOUR MONEY BUT YOU HAVE TO BE MUCH MORE FLEXIBLE IN YOUR APPROACH.**

3. **IF YOU THINK AND ACT LIKE YOU ARE IN A RED ZONE BUT ARE REALLY IN A GREEN ZONE, YOU CAN STILL EXPECT TO GROW YOUR MONEY (YOUR GROWTH PORTFOLIO MAY TRAIL THE RETURNS OF THE STOCK MARKET, BUT WHO CARES?!).**

4. **IF YOU THINK AND ACT LIKE YOU ARE IN A GREEN ZONE WHEN YOU ARE REALLY IN A RED ZONE, YOUR PORTFOLIO IS AN ACCIDENT WAITING TO HAPPEN!!!!**

OK, now I'll stop yelling. Secular bear markets call for very different investor behavior. In fact, I think that given the four statements above, it is essential to change the way we have been taught to think by the media, by brokerage firms, and even by many advisors.

Reprogramming Our Investment Thinking

Here are what I believe are the most important observations an investor and their advisor can make about what has changed in protecting and growing wealth.

To start with, there is the issue of what I call "de-worseification". I believe that the traditional idea of diversification is: overdone. I see so many portfolios that started with the idea of not having all the eggs in one basket, and apparently decided that starting a basket factory was a better idea. In other words, they took it too far, and now have what is no longer a portfolio but a "collection of securities". They and their advisors think they are doing what is necessary but they take it too far. Maybe it's the unending supply of investment strategies, but here's the rub— diversificaiton is about reducing volatility and risk through the addition of investment styles whose characteristics are different from the rest of the portfolio. Diversification is NOT simply adding more and more assets and styles with no strategy or direction. Adding more apples to your apples doesn't make fruit salad, it makes a bigger pile of apples! And at some point the apples go rotten, and there's nothing to save you. Similarly, there will be periods where the commonly used approach to diversification and asset allocation set families back for years.

Style Boxes: Out of Style?

Morningstar is one of my favorite companies. They are based in Chicago and for a couple of decades they have offered the premier research service for mutual fund data and analysis. Over the years they have added coverage of stocks, managed accounts, ETFs and other investment vehicles. I think that their stock research is among the best-presented work you'll find anywhere. Maybe its because their analysts tend to be liberal arts graduates who just like talking and writing about investing, as opposed to Finance MBA-types like me.

Morningstar is known for, among other things, the "Style Box". This grid contains nine boxes, and each box represents the type of investment (growth, value or core- mix of growth and value) and the size of the companies involved (large, medium or small cap). The style box spawned an entire segment of the investment industry. It literally took the concept of asset allocation and put it on the map. Morningstar even supplied the map. Style box investing was all the rage in the investment advisory profession during the 1990's. In fact, if you look at how mutual funds and managed accounts are created today, a lot of it goes back to the producer's desire to build a product to fit an area of the style box. It is common to see a company with a single mutual fund, which did not have a clear style bias, renamed, say the "Large Core Portfolio". The management company would then introduce a Large Cap Growth Portfolio and a Large Cap Value portfolio. Later on, they would build or acquire a small cap fund, and perhaps a mid-cap too. They'd keep going until they were confident that their sales force could now go out and market to advisors, armed with their own brand of box-filling products.

I think that this is very 1990's thinking, and it is potentially very dangerous to you as an investor. The reason is simple: style box investing does not reduce your risk as much as you think it does! Here is an example of why some funds transcend the style box approach.

What Style Box Does This Fund Fit Into?

The Permanent Portfolio (PRPFX).

The investment seeks to preserve and increase the purchasing power value of its shares over the long term. The fund maintains target percentages for investing in each of the following categories: 20% of assets in gold, 5% in silver, 10% in Swiss franc assets, 15% in stocks of U.S. and foreign real-estate and natural-resource companies, 15% in U.S. aggressive-growth stocks, and 35% in cash, Treasury bills, and notes.(Source:Yahoo).

Answer: None! It's A Hybrid.

Unwrapping The Box

A very crafty money management firm I know touts their firm's flexibility in being able to invest in any stock style whenever they want. At the same time, they run a fairly concentrated portfolio. They refer to their philosophy as "unwrapping the box," which is clearly aimed at refuting the style box mentality in today's post-bubble environment. I'm right there with them. Investing for the next generation, in my opinion, is more about maintaining the highest degree of flexibility you can, not clinging to a rigid, boxy style of portfolio construction. I don't see anything in the latter approach (style box) that cannot be accomplished by the former (flexible). I think that my industry is subtly starting to pick up on this.

As for Morningstar, I still love them. They have grown into much more than the authority on style boxes. When they announced their plans to merge with Ibbotson, another very reputable research firm, in late 2005, I realized that there's a real potential for a juggernaut in the business of serving advisors. Assuming that comes to pass, it will then be up to the advisors to make the best use of that combined research talent, and create their own personalized opinions and view of how to best take advantage of the resources at their disposal. For the sake of the client, it has to be more than just taking information at face value or plugging numbers into an investment proposal program and spitting out some canned analysis.

If advisors and their firms do not take a good look at the changing face of asset allocation and continue to live in the 90's, they risk going the way of the bulky, three pound mobile phones we used early in that decade. I think my little girl Morgan plays with an old one. And when she's done pretending to talk on it for a few seconds, she throws it on the floor and goes on to something else. My team and I don't want to be that mobile phone. You don't want your advisor to be one either.

Expense Ratios: Overrated

One of the mutual funds I have used for years has the distinction of being one of the few funds to beat the return of the S&P 500 Index in each of its first nine years of existence. At the same time, it did very well in down markets. In its first ten years, the fund averaged a return of over 18% a year. You would think it would be on every "top fund" search conducted by both professional and non-professional alike. But alas, the fund took years to get noticed. Why? Because for years its expense ratio (the internal costs of the fund for management, trading, administration, marketing, etc, expressed as a percentage of the fund's value) was nearly 3%. The cost scared people away.

I can understand this hesitation to look away from an expensive investment. But what's more important, finding the best or simply the cheapest? When it comes to hot dogs, mattresses, jewelry (OK, trying to impress the wife with that one) or investment strategies, take a look at what you are buying, and don't even look at the price tag until you have evaluated the "product". While the fund I described here is merely one example, I have seen enough others in my career to know there is a pattern.

Inflation: Is It Going To Become A Threat To Wealth Again?

Remember when inflation rates were over 15%? I don't. I was in grade school and, while I started my curiosity of the financial markets at a fairly young age, I was not infatuated with the study of markets just yet (still wanted to be a baseball player or a fireman or something). But it's not important whether you were old enough to remember the last period of hyperinflation in the U.S. What is important is that you are prepared in case such an environment were to occur again—and most likely it will. Why am I so confident about this? Because the economy, like human behavior and much of life in general, is cyclical.

What was gone forever somehow comes back. Bell-bottoms? Back. Coca-Cola in glass bottles? Back. Inflation so high it impacts your daily life and every financial decision you make? Back?! From the early 1980's through the beginning of the 21st Century, seeing your "cost of living" for most basic items increase by two, three or maybe four percent was typical. Maybe it will be for a long time. But history is against us on this one.

I am not trying to make a short term prediction here. This book is not about that. I'm just trying to plant a seed in your mind that your portfolio's life is VERY different in a high-inflation environment. Want a quick example? Let's say you and your advisor have great confidence in the plan you crafted, with an 8% projected return. You figure that this is all you'll need to get everything you want from your wealth. But what if inflation, which was 3% when you put the plan together, jumps to 8% and stays near that level for years? Your "nominal" return of 8% will be just enough to break even net of inflation. What will happen then? Ask someone who retired in the 1970's. It ain't pretty.

Fig. 8: A Visual Depiction Of Inflation

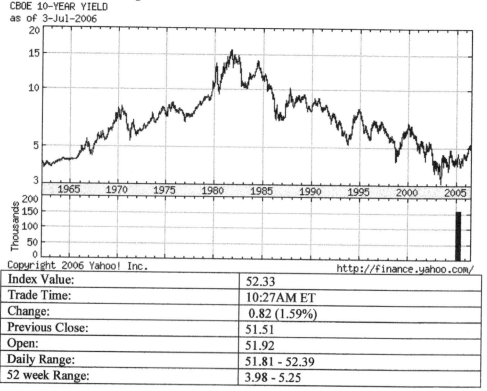

CBOE 10-YEAR YIELD
as of 3-Jul-2006

Copyright 2006 Yahoo! Inc.   http://finance.yahoo.com/

Index Value:	52.33
Trade Time:	10:27AM ET
Change:	0.82 (1.59%)
Previous Close:	51.51
Open:	51.92
Daily Range:	51.81 - 52.39
52 week Range:	3.98 - 5.25

Bond Investing: It's Not The Same Anymore

If you believe as I do that inflation is a real threat to your long-term wealth growth plans, it follows that bond investing will be a whole new ball game. A very different outlook is needed for the investor and especially for the advisor.

Why is this the case? A quick review of history and investment basics will explain.

For over a quarter-century now, interest rates have been falling. As discussed earlier in this book, high-quality bonds prices do not behave like stock prices. Stock prices are determined by everything from how profitable a company is, to what news events the company releases, to the desire of buyer and sellers (regardless of what the actual news is on the company). High-quality bonds are different. Their prices are determined largely by interest movements.

Now, interest rates can change due to a number of factors that are fundamentally-based (see the chapter on the Economy). But while a stock can go up or down regardless of the actual news (due to buying and selling forces of the market), bonds are more about mathematics. If interest rates go way down, bond prices are going to go up. Not maybe, not probably. They WILL go up.

This is what happened throughout most of the 1980's and 1990's with only temporary breaks such as in 1994 when the Fed raised interest rates seven times. If you were a bond manager in the last two decades, life was sweet. Your track record makes you look like a genius. In fact, it was actually the greatest bond bull market in modern history that made most bond managers appear heroic. If and when the party stops, it will hit many investors with a shock that will rival that experienced when the Tech stock bubble popped.

To clarify this, here's bond math made simple. See the chart below. While bonds may not fall as far as stocks in a rising interest rate scenario, it can still be a shocker. At least with stocks you kind of expect the volatility. But bonds? The investment version of "Lassie"? Old, reliable high-quality bonds? Oh, yes, they can put a hurt on your portfolio too.

Fig. 9: Sensitivity of Total Returns to Interest Rate Changes over a One-Year Holding Period

Maturity	Hypothetical Initial Yield	Change in Yield				
		-2%	-1%	0	+1%	+2%
2-year	2.75%	4.6%	3.7%	2.5%	1.8%	.8%
5-year	3.75%	11.4%	7.5%	3.8%	.1%	-3.3%
10-year	5.00%	20.6%	12.5%	5.0%	-1.9%	-8.2%
20-year	5.75%	32.7%	18.1%	5.8%	-4.9%	-13.9%

Note: Shows approximate total return (income plus price change) over a one-year holding period for the given change in yields for a non-callable issue, assuming the coupon rates shown. Source: Incapital LLC

The table above puts this in perspective. Look at that 10-year column. If rates on such a bond go up by 2% (from 5% to 7% in this example), your total return is negative 8.2%!

The income you took in was overwhelmed by the impact of rising interest rates. How much of a wizard does your bond manager look like now? Oh, maybe the manager was particularly savvy and traded in and out of bonds adeptly. OK, so maybe you lost 5% or 6% instead of 8.2%. Throw in your management fee and it gets worse.

I still think that the shock of seeing your high-quality bonds drop in value is a bigger emotional issue for most people than seeing stocks plunge. But there is a way out. The table below, courtesy of bondschool.com and Investment Advisor Magazine, points the direction.

Fig. 10: Bonds vs. Bond Funds

	Bonds	Bond Funds	
**Maturi y (Call) Date	Known	None -- 'Rolling'	
Minimum Investment	Varies from $1,000 to $5,000	Varies from $1,0 0 to $5,000	
Incremen s	Typically $1,0(0	Variable	
Redempti n	At Maturity (P r)	Any Time, at Cu ent NAV	
**Interes Rate Risk	Declines as Bonds Near Maturity	Constant	
Liquidity	Active Secon ary Market For High Quali y Bonds	Daily Liquidity	
Up-Front Fees	Commission r Issuance Fee Generally Buil Into Price	Some Have Commissions; Others No-Load	
Ongoing xpenses	Typically Non	Management Fe s and Other Operating Expe es Can Be A Drag on Perfo ance	
Default R sk	Depends on Cr dit Quality	Minimized by D ersification	
Portfolio ontrol	Customized Po tfolios	Professionally M naged	
Taxes	Tax Conseq ences are Typically Clea	Can Have Unexpected Capital Gains Di tributions	
Other Fa tors	Fully Invested	Fund Managers Must Keep A Portion of the Funds Ready for Reden ptions	
Types	Vary By Issu r, Maturity, Interest Rate, Redemption And Estate F atures, New Issues, Secon lary, Credit Quality, Step/C ll Structure	Open-End Mu al Funds, Closed-End Funds, Unit Investm nt Trust Exchange-Trade Funds (ETFs)	

117

To help you, I've put a pair of asterisks next to the two rows that most distinguish owning individual bonds from owning bond funds. Bottom line: individual bonds give you the predictability of getting your investment back at a predetermined date (maturity date). Bond funds don't. As a result, if you take the approach of buying bonds and holding them to maturity, you can't lose in nominal terms – essentially a high-quality bond is a contract for the issuer to pay you back on a certain date. Unless that high-quality company all of a sudden has a severe reversal of fortune, you can have confidence about how the story will end.

Bond funds, on the other hand, are perpetual. They don't have a contract to pay you back, so as the chart says, the risk of rising interest rates taking money away that may never come back is constant. That's why high-quality bond funds are as bad an investment in a rising interest rate environment as they were a good investment in the falling rate period of the 1980's and 1990's. Bond buyer beware! Based on the tremendous flows of cash into bond funds over the first half of this decade, I don't think the message is out there. And don't count on Wall Street to educate you on this. They are selling "the dream" and that includes making you believe that investments that performed well in the past will automatically perform well in the future. That is simply not always the case. In the case of high-quality bonds, the "new math" of this century could be very different from that of the late 20th century. Don't get caught in the past if that happens.

Hedge Funds: Growth Explosion => Implosion?

In a very short period of time, hedge funds went from a private beach to a public beach in a major metropolis. The influence they have on the markets is impossible to ignore. In fact, I have heard that as much as 70% of the daily stock market trading volume in 2005 was from hedge funds – can you say "under the influence"?!

Unfortunately, the rapid growth of hedge fund investing, like the rapid growth of anything, can lead to overheating. In the hedge world, this can be a spectacular sight (in a bad way). With leverage, high fees, unregulated investments and an overwhelming environment of greed and ego, the potential is there. This does not mean it will happen, and certainly there are some well-managed hedge funds that operate in a more secure and flexible environment. But it's kind of like living in Southern California. The big earthquake may not occur in our lifetime, but don't make the mistake of ignoring the threat of it.

Volatility: Learn How Use It To Our Advantage

Later in the book, I describe in detail some ways to make volatility our friend instead of our enemy. Its not exactly playing on the fears of others, but there is a strong element of that. Simply put, having a strategy that is always prepared to exploit dramatic shifts in the market gives you a major advantage.

Solid Long-Term Returns: Aggressive Investing <u>Not</u> Necessary?

I have seen over and over again that people automatically associate high returns with aggressive tactics. The "crash and burn" risk of investing on margin and focusing a lot of money in helter-skelter strategies often finishes second to a consistent, patient, lifestyle-oriented approach thinking. It's the tortoise-hare thing applied to your wealth.

Where Does This Lead Us?

The conclusions from all of this are clear:

1. Traditional asset allocation is not enough

2. Stocks alone are too volatile

3. Bond funds are no longer a reliable diversifier if the interest rate "tailwind" of more than 25 years ends

4. Hedge funds are at best a small part of the solution for most investors

This last point begs the question: "Rob, with so much money having moved into hedge funds in the last decade or so, why are you so damn opposed to using them"? The answer is that I'm not against hedge funds. What I'm against is the overuse of them by advisors for clients that either don't understand their implications or do not have sufficient wealth to deal with the "baggage" that hedge funds may come with. Also, there are hedge funds that have found ways to overcome the limitations of their peers. I view those funds as having the same potential to help a client as any traditional money manager.

Now, let's lay out the best and worst features of hedge funds. You can find these listed below. One very important distinction that needs to be made here is that I am referring to hedge funds and hedge-fund-of-funds that are focused more on consistency than seeking the maximum return they can get. The latter are the ones that typically have the biggest potential to blow up. There's probably a good reason to consider risk-controlled hedge funds to be a different asset class from return-maximizing, ultra-leveraged hedge funds, but I'll leave it to someone else to write a book on that.

Notable Pros And Cons Of Hedge Funds

<u>**PROS**</u>

- ❑ **Absolute Return Focus** – with our modified definition from above, the focus on making money instead of competing with some traditional stock index is desirable.

- ❑ **Flexible Investment Style** – with flexibility comes opportunity, as long as the money is in capable hands.

- ❑ **Top Manager Talent** – many capable hands have left other investment structures to run hedge funds. As long as they exploit their talent and don't let greed in the door, this is a good thing for hedge fund investors.

- ❑ **Well-diversified** – fund-of-funds typically diversify among as few as five or as many as 100 hedge funds. While the higher end of this range clearly qualifies as "de-worsification" or over-diversification, the principal of being smartly diversified is a key to hedged investing, or any other type of investing.

<u>**CONS**</u>

My colleague Matt MacEachern refers to the "TLC" of hedge fund investing – transparency, liquidity and cost. However, there is not much tender loving care going on when:

- ❑ **Transparency is limited**. If you and your advisor don't really know what type of activities are being performed deep in the bowels of your hedge fund, lost in the shuffle of a 60-manager fund of funds, there is the risk I call "what you don't know WILL hurt you.

- ❑ **Liquidity is limited**. If you took the advice of your broker and put a big chunk of your assets in a fund that can only be sold every six months, you had better not need that money unexpectedly.

❑ **The costs are high and layered.** We tell our clients that to figure out why hedge fund of funds have lost their appeal, we should start with this riddle:

Question: When Is A 10% Return Not A 10% Return?
Answer: When Management And Incentive Fees Shrink Your Returns!

Fig. 11: Hedge Funds—Gross Vs. Net

GROSS RETURN	20.0%	10.0%
Hedge fund management fee	1.0%	1.0%
Hedge fund incentive fee	3.8%	1.8%
Fund-of-funds mgt. fee	2.2%	2.2%
NET RETURN	13.0%	5.0%

Notes: Assumes hedge funds charge 1% management fee and 20% of profits after management fee. Fund-of-funds fee based on annual charge for DB Hedge Strategies Fund. Fees for other funds may be higher or lower. Source: MONEY Magazine, 2003

The chart above, while not based on any particular hedge fund of funds example, shows that in "the old days" (1990's until about 2001), if the hedge fund managers in a fund of funds made 20%, and the various layers of fees were deducted, a 13% return would result. I think that clients who saw a consistent return of around 13% a year were probably not asking a lot of questions about fees. 13% is a strong return, especially compared to bond rates at the time.

Now look at the far right column, which is where hedge-fund-of-fund returns may be going in the wake of a crowded marketplace and perhaps lower market volatility. If the underlying hedge fund managers only scrape out a gross return of 10%, after the pounds of flesh are taken out by the managers' fees, profit incentive fees, and the fund of funds' fees, the net return could be more like 5%. Again, when 20% nets you 13%, you don't ask a lot of questions. When 10% nets you 5%, and you are carrying all the potential baggage represented by the TLC of hedge fund investing, you WILL be asking questions. It stops being a prudent investment at that point.

Without a doubt, THE most overlooked aspect of hedge fund investing is taxes. Now, I'm not a tax advisor, but I do know that you can find out how a hedge fund or fund-of-funds is taxed by reading the documents that created it.

The following description of hedge fund taxation is taken from the website of LJH Global Investments, a hedge fund advisory firm:

> *A major investor concern in the alternative investment sector has been the potentially significant tax liability created by hedge fund investments. As limited partnerships, investments in hedge funds produce taxable income every fiscal year, regardless of whether the fund made any distributions. The trading strategies employed by the majority of hedge fund managers are generally short-term in nature and, thus, taxable at the (35%) short-term ordinary income tax rate regardless of how long the fund is held. As such, some investors have been leery to use alternative investment strategies as part of their long-term investment planning. Recent developments in the financial markets have, however, resulted in the creation of international insurance and swap contracts that could quell some of these concerns. These new contracts offer the maximum in tax efficiency, while enabling the investor to use hedge funds that engage in short-term trading strategies.*

LJH points out some ways that you can reduce the tax liability, but such strategies are typically only available to people with several million dollars invested in hedge funds. I look at it this way: if a hedge fund makes 10% after fees, and you are investing taxable money, you are looking at a 6.5% return after tax if you live in a low-tax state like Florida and you are taxed at the highest income bracket. If you live in a high tax state, perhaps you are netting under 6%.

How about one more example of this to really make the point? Remember our example from earlier in this chapter where a 10% gross return by the hedge fund manager turns into a 5% return after fees? I'm sorry to break it to you but that 5% "net" return has not accounted for your capital gains or income taxes on the fund-of-funds investment.

Let's keep it simple and say that your tax rate is 35%. That reduces your net return to a net after-tax return of 3.25%. You are reading this correctly—it's 3.25%. That's all that's left to our sample taxable investor in a hedge fund of funds after starting with a manager gross return of 10%. Heck, short-term municipal bonds often yield more than that. Granted, there's much more upside potential in a hedge fund-of-funds, but how much return potential do you need to justify the risk of ending up with 3.25%?

By the way, if you apply this same tax logic to the other example we saw before (20% gross return nets to 13%), your net after-tax return is about 8.5%. Not bad, but a long way from 20%, and not enough for most investors to justify the oft-mentioned "baggage" associated with this type of investment.

The last hedge fund conundrum has to do with what regulatory environment you are operating in. For investors who have used stocks, bonds, mutual funds and options, they are operating in the world of investments registered with and overseen by with the Securities Exchange Commission (SEC), one of the principal regulatory bodies of my industry. Where does your hedge fund-of-funds fit into this?

For some time, hedge funds and fund of funds did not have to register with the SEC. The SEC started requiring registration in February, 2006. While many hedge funds found loopholes to temporarily suspend their requirement to register, most are now doing so. However, even if the fund of funds entity and the hedge funds in it are registered, the investment made by those underlying funds can be in anything. That includes, well, just about everything.

In my opinion, this leaves room for many of the same abuses that people worried about when hedge funds were unregistered. This article from the website of Institutional Investor, originally published in the Wall Street Journal in 2005, expresses this thought via a description of a little concept known as "side pocket investments" within hedge funds.

More HFs Are Filling Their Side Pockets

Source: InstitutionalInvestor.com

Hedge funds' growing use of "side pocket" accounts may be creating a potential breeding ground for fraud, The Wall Street Journal *reports. For years – some trace it to the collapse of **Long Term Capital Management** in 1998 -- hedge funds have been placing a portion of investor money into these accounts for a variety of reasons. One advantage of putting poor performing funds in side pockets – which, in effect, operate like "a mini-private equity fund" within the hedge fund – is that hedge fund returns look better. At the same time investors have a tough time withdrawing their money because they are essentially locked-up in p.e. investments. Because these investments are exempt from periodic valuation, investors have no idea how well these so-called pocket investments are doing.*

> *According to the* WSJ, *hedge funds allocate between 10% and 30% of their holdings into side pockets, but the exposure of a client's funds to these side pockets could climb without the investor's knowledge unless the hedge fund agreement has a strict limit. The agreements themselves, however, are no real safeguard for investors. Hedge fund attorney* **David Nichols** *of* **Morgan Lewis & Bockius** *told the* WSJ, *that "partnership agreements are very broadly drafted on points of these kinds," and managers take advantage of their authority to bar withdrawals if they feel it's in the best interest of all investors.* **Kevin Campbell** *of* **Van Hedge Fund Advisers** *told the* WSJ *of an instance in which some clients of a hedge fund wanted to take out money, which would have forced the HF to cash in some holdings at a loss. To prevent this, the fund moved the holdings into a side pocket, which the clients couldn't touch. "It was done to save the investors from themselves," he says*

To Hedge Or Not To Hedge?

While I've covered this topic in detail, I'll summarize it very simply. Investors and their advisors must take note of the differences between today's investment environment and that of the 1980's and 1990's. When they do, they will find a need for alternative strategies to complement their traditional stock and bond styles. The temptation is to look for the best hedge-fund-of-funds to buy. The reality is that for most families, that is NOT the right decision. As this book goes on, what I believe to be the right decision will become clear.

Now that we've turned the corner into 21st Century wealth strategy, let's finish this chapter with a short look at a variety of additional concepts for you to be aware of as you forge through this decade and beyond.

The Golden Ticket For The Next Decade

Unlike young Charlie in the Willie Wonka movie, I don't believe investors will need a lucky break to succeed in the future. However, investment strategies for the 21st Century must be more flexible, more thoughtful, and less tied to the performance of market indexes. For years now, the trend in our planning approach has been away from the "usual suspects" in money management. For the most part these behemoth companies managing billions of dollars in plain vanilla investment styles are investment dinosaurs. In our opinion, the investment returns of the future will be created by managers whose mandates include hedging techniques using short positions and/or options, or those who don't base their decisions on how their portfolios are set up versus a market benchmark. A deep contrarian money manager who selectively buys companies they know as well as if they were the CEO employs one equity strategy for today and beyond. A manager who buys companies with solid balance sheets and shorts stocks of companies with weak fundamentals uses another solid strategy (note: shorting is an attempt to profit by borrowing stock, selling it and buying it back at a lower price). Buying and holding forever worked in the 1980's and 1990's. It ruined you in the late 1960's and throughout the '70s. Do you want to take the chance that you invest for many years just to come up with nothing? A passive buy and hold forever strategy does not employ the flexibility that today's global, nearly 24/7 markets will require.

The days of advisors telling clients things like "we are overweighted in healthcare, but underweighted in technology" are over. Asset allocation in its traditional form is extinct. Large cap vs. small cap vs. international has gone the way of the Tyrannosaurus Rex. Here's what we have learned: you the investor don't care about asset allocation! You have voted loud and clear to look at the results and the logic of the approach used to achieve those results. You don't want to hear that, "The market is down 20% and your portfolio is down only 17% so you should be happy". The old joke in our industry is that performance like that entices a pension fund to add more money to the account due to outperformance versus the relevant index. As an individual investor, you should look at it another way: it will take you that much longer just to get back to where your portfolio started.

So, don't fall into the trap that much of Wall Street still pushes on investors.

But let's face it, I don't think that investment advisors have ever worked harder to stay on top of what impacts the wealth you have entrusted to our guidance. We are continuously searching for ways to get you to your goals, regardless of whether the stock market makes it easy (like it did in the 1980's and 1990's). We are not magicians, but we have experience and perspective. And you have the patience and willingness to be educated, and let time and cycles be your ally. We don't know what that will net you in the next few days, weeks or months. But we are confident that when it's time to use the money you've entrusted to our care, you will have accomplished what you set out to do.

I firmly believe that my responsibilities as your advisor do NOT include rooting for the stock market to go up. I am an investment professional, not a cheerleader. I don't know when the bears will tire and the bulls will take over again, or vice-versa. I know it will happen, but there's no sense planning your portfolio around such events. With few exceptions, pure market timing is a loser's game.

What I think is far more critical is to assess for each of our clients how a variety of market conditions may impact your ability to eventually reach the goals you've expressed to us. If your stock portfolio was created in hopes that it would beat inflation and payoff in the distant future, then I want you to stay on track. Time is your friend. If your investment goals are more imminent (i.e. cash flow in retirement, etc.), I will have increasingly angled your portfolio toward a less volatile approach as the bear market progressed.

Either way, it's difficult to see your monthly statement yo-yo up and down each month. Let's face I—you worked hard to earn this money, it's annoying to give it back—ever. We understand this, but we also emphasize that this is the nature of stock market investing. As a study showed, it's usually feast or famine; there's no such thing as a "steady" 10% return. You get there by muddling through the bear markets, keeping your overall portfolio volatility below that of the market, and resisting the temptation to make timing decisions, so that you're there when the bull charges. As I've said before, even long secular bear markets create pockets of "bullish" opportunity which last months or even years. However, if you thought that your investment horizon was longer than it actually is, and/or your tolerance for price declines is lower than you once thought, that's a cause for action – the sooner the better.

It can be difficult to establish realistic expectations regarding time horizons. To better understand how the process *should* operate, let's set the way back machine for a time not so far back at all…

Lessons from the Bear Market of 2000-2002

Until March, 2000, many investors did not know what a bear market was. They had never invested in one. In fact as of 1999, American households were heavily exposed to the stock market, according to a Federal Reserve report. In 1999, Americans held $13.3 trillion in shares, nearly 32% of household wealth, ten percentage points higher than in 1995.

Why did stocks fall? Investors came to believe that:

1. Tech stocks were not cyclical.

2. Companies with no revenues were worth $20 billion.

3. Long-Term stock returns should be 20-25%.

4. These returns came with little risk.

The technology sector, which made up about 10% of the market at one point last decade, reached 35%. The bubble was primed to burst. Investors and their advisors did not want to believe that the good times would end. But they did.

Of course, for a lot of people, thinking about how much money you will leave to the next generation is not a priority. You are more concerned with your own long-term financial survival at this point. If you have already amassed enough wealth to ensure a comfortable retirement, or you are making a tremendous amount of income and saving it, you might be able to afford to be a conservative investor until you retire. But if you are not in that situation, you face a BIG decision. A decision so large and so important, if you don't make the right decisions, it could have serious implications for the rest of your life. I don't think I'm being melodramatic. It is fairly well known that many problems with family and marital relationships stem from issues about money. Feelings of inadequacy, regret, etc. also can be traced back to a person's financial situation or decision-making. In short, the strategy and philosophy that you choose to invest by is more than just a task or an ongoing project. For many people, it is among the most significant decisions they will ever make.

Now, let's take this thought one giant leap forward.

Retirement Planning: An Insightful View

Jim Otar is one of most intriguing thinkers I've encountered in the area of retirement goal planning. Jim, who runs a small advisory operation in the Toronto, Canada, area has won awards for his writing on the subject of retirement, and has developed a very insightful approach for charting one's path to reaching their goals. He claims to go beyond the accepted industry standard and I agree with his claim. With his permission, I present a portion of his work, taken directly from his website. In an area like this, I'd rather you hear directly from one who's expertise exceeds mine. As they say, "do what you do best and outsource the rest".

By the way, if you are an advisor reading this book and don't know who Jim Otar is, don't be surprised. His straightforward, humble approach to this critical area has made him a popular speaker at academic conferences, but it is not the kind of thing that appeals to the sound-bite segment of the financial media. I think you'll enjoy it though.

In particular, notice how Jim's explanation takes into account what most retirement analyses do not. Namely, that market conditions from the time you start preparing for retirement through the time you are done retiring (i.e. your death) are not predictable or average. They can also not simply be projected to be "random". There have been a wide range of market environments over the past century and he considers all of them a possibility. Put another way, if the period of your life in which you are saving the most money for retirement happens to coincide with a horrible secular bear market, that is a world of difference (and pain) from saving during a strong financial market period. So with that as a background, here is what Jim Otar says.

Over the next ten years, over 80 million North Americans are hoping to retire.

We have successfully landed robots on Mars and observed their amazing findings. We have successfully discovered cures for diseases. We have found solutions to numerous problems.

Yet our financial planning community still does not have the tools to answer realistically some of the most basic questions:

Do I have enough money to retire?

How long will my money last?

When can I retire?

How much do I need to save for my retirement?

No More Guessing!

The most popular tool now is the standard retirement calculator. We **guess** *average future growth rates and inflation. We plug in these guesses together with some basic personal information into a retirement calculator. We push the "calculate" button and get a projection of our retirement finances.*

Did you know that in 80% to 90% of the time, these standard retirement plans will fail?

Take for example, a retiree who has one million dollars in his investment portfolio at the beginning of his retirement. He takes out $60,000 annually, indexed to inflation. Assume his portfolio grows 8% and inflation is 3.5% per year. [...] Now, calculate the portfolio value if this person were to start his retirement in any of the one-hundred years during the last century using actual market data and inflation. Assume a conservative asset mix - 60% fixed income and 40% equity. Each black line shows the portfolio value over time for retiring in a particular year since 1900. Most portfolios expired well before [...] the projection of the standard retirement calculator.

No More Gambling!

I am not talking about taking your life savings to a casino in Las Vegas or Monte Carlo. What I am talking about is a mathematical model called Monte Carlo simulation. Some people use this model to forecast their retirement planning. While in theory it is based on probability of events, it does have several pitfalls:

The outcome of a Monte Carlo simulation is based on adding a degree of randomness to an average portfolio growth. However, markets are neither random nor average. They are made up of secular trends that can last as long as 20 years. The randomness of the markets are piggybacked onto these secular trends. Assuming an average growth and adding randomness to it does not provide a good model for the market behavior over the long term.

In reality, several factors influence the shape of the distribution curve, such as: time spent in retirement, asset allocation strategy, asset mix, withdrawal rate, management costs, to name a few. Any randomness generated based on the incorrect distribution curve will result in significant variations from the reality of the markets.

> *When the Monte Carlo model is applied to retirement planning, these two factors introduce serious flaws. These simulations generally fail to forecast the effects of multi-year secular markets. [...] I developed my model when I was writing my book "High Expectations and False Dreams - One Hundred Years of Market History Applied to Retirement Planning". My philosophy was very simple: Why guess? Why gamble? Why not use actual, unadulterated historic market data?*
>
> *The Otar Retirement Calculator is based on actual market data. [...] In many cases you will find that the assumptions you used in your existing retirement plans are far too optimistic. In many situations, the effective compound annual growth of the bottom decile (90% survival) is no more than 3% or 4%. Yet every day, I see retirement plans based on 8% or 10% growth rates.*

Conclusion

I cannot possibly exhaust the types of securities, factors, definitions and market forces in today's investing world because the number changes every day, but what I have given you here is a good start—a primer, if you will to be better educated as you plough through the myriad media reports and misconstructions of what is happening in the financial workplace. Next we will examine how all these forces impact the investor and the reactions they may cause.

CHAPTER 8: INVESTOR PSYCHOLOGY

"Avoiding trouble is more important than finding that next big winner" –
Michael Kahn

We discussed certain common misjudgments of investors in Chapter 4, but clients who are bombarded with loads of conflicting information by the way of dueling industry experts often become frozen into inaction, stiffened by the "Tip du jour". We continually hear excuses for doing nothing, or worse, something that is clearly a knee jerk reaction to media pundits' rantings. Don't get me wrong, sometimes nothing is better than something, but don't be part of the herd mentality paying homage to the conventional wisdom (CW) of today (Which often contradicts the conventional wisdom of yesterday). CW like the following:

"Stocks can only go down from here."

"I might lose all my money."

"Get me out of the market at any price, and as fast as you can."

"I know about market history, but it's different this time."

The more we hear things like this when markets are declining, the greater the likelihood that the decline is nearing an end. That doesn't mean that in some cases, subtle portfolio adjustments should not be made. For many reasons, when the US market is declining, global stock markets may be exhibiting "different" behavior. Investors throwing in the towel, dumping entire portfolios, or radically changing their investment objectives are capitulating and it often means very good news for the long-term investor.

What Should You Do Now?

(Or "Don't Be Revisin' Your Time Horizon")

It sounds so simple, but the cardinal rule of long-term, managed money investing is ***"Don't react to market events"***. There are only two reasons to change a well-defined managed money investment strategy: either 1) your circumstances change in a way that affects your long-term goals, or 2) something changes at your money management firm(s) that creates a mismatch with your strategy.

To emphasize this point, consider the following series of headlines taken from a mainstream financial website (CBSmarketwatch.com) over just a few weeks' time:

Stocks fall sharply on Google warning, weak data.

U.S. stocks gain on cheap crude, strong earning.

U.S. stocks close mixed after hesitant price action.

Dow closes at highest since June '01 after tame CPI.

U.S. stocks close lower as Treasury yields rise.

Dow closes at highest in five years.

U.S. stocks end down on higher oil, rate outlook fears.

U.S. stocks end lower; impact of inflation in view.

U.S. stocks end higher, helped by strong earnings.

U.S. stocks close up on cheaper oil.

U.S. stocks end higher; solid earnings ease rate fears.

U.S. stocks end lower; earnings warning weighs.

U.S. stocks end mixed; Middle East tensions weigh.

Investors gloomy about week ahead.

You are excused if, at this point, your head is spinning like Linda Blair in *The Exorcist*. The media may change its mind every day about what is important, but that doesn't mean that you have to – and you shouldn't. It's no way to live.

Don't judge your investment success over short periods of time. When most traditional money managers buy a security for you, it is usually because they believe the stock is selling at what they believe to be an attractive long-term (3-5 year) entry point. Trying to pick on such a manager for how they've done during a 1,3 or even 12 month period is not fair when their decisions transcend that time frame.

Many managers often look like goats when the market drops suddenly (and it does sometimes). Those same people often look like heroes later. In fact, they are neither. They are professional investors with advanced knowledge and advanced resources to successfully grow your wealth during the course of your lifetime. Remember that when the "High

Drama" of a day's activity in the stock market tries to throw you off course from the reason you are a stock market investor.

How To React To A Down Market

Or, Do I Just Get Out Of The Market And Wait?

This is a popular question in down markets. If we were magicians, we could have all bailed out just before a market decline. In reality, I can't even get a few simple card tricks to work in front of my kids—forget about performing real-life miracles.

What we <u>have</u> done is come up with ways to earn what we call "relative return". We are firm believers that if you want to grow your money well above the effects of inflation and taxes, you must take on some volatility. Our aim is to structure for you a portfolio that captures most of the market's upside, but noticeably less of the downside. Each of our clients has a unique portfolio structure, but generally, we are achieving that goal during this bear market.

It has become tougher to earn "absolute return"—that is, actually making money—without resorting to fixed income investments. But here's the key question for the investors who are selling: did they enter the stock market with the expectation of making money every month, every quarter, every year?

A more appropriate approach, in our opinion, is to treat equity investing like your primary residence: you buy it as a long-term commitment (say, 5-30 years, which is about the range of most stock investors' time horizons). You make upgrades from time to time (build a pool and a deck, paint it, replace the carpeting). You bought a solid piece of real estate, so you don't drive yourself crazy watching its value change every day or month. And let's face it, home prices are constantly changing (based on sales of similar homes, etc.). But if you see your neighbors selling for less and less each month, do you put your house up for sale? Stocks are re-valued all day long, so the temptation to "play" the market is there. But don't do it.

As we have written several times before, the question you should be grappling with as you plan and evaluate your investment strategies is not, "Do I sell stocks?", but "What is my true investment time horizon—when will I use this specific money". The cash, bonds and lower-volatility "Hybrid" investments are all liquidity sources you will use before touching your equities. We set it up that way so that you can ride out the "pain" as you pursue your long-term "gain".

133

If this does not sound like you, then your allocation to stocks may need to be reviewed. In fact, you may need to consider if you should be in equities at all. Remember, if you make bold changes to get out of stocks, you then have to make <u>two</u> good timing decisions, one to get out, another to get back in. Realistically, we don't know for years whether these timing moves were for the best. So we conclude that the guessing method is not one we favor.

Is There Anything Else I Can Do?

Yes! There are strategies for those who want to stay committed to their long-term objectives, but are willing to buy some protection against further losses. This is kind of like the "break in case of emergency" sign on the cabinet that holds the fire extinguisher. One example is buying "index put options".

The short description of this strategy starts by answering these questions:

1. How much of your equity portfolio should we protect from further losses?

2. How long do you want the protection for?

3. At what market level do you want the protection to kick in?

Based on the answers, we figure out what the protection will cost (we can also work backwards—decide how much we want to spend on protection, and see what other parameters will be at that price level). It is not an exact science, but it works out as follows: if the market falls below the level we choose (less your cost of the protection), you make money. The more the market falls, the more you make. This offsets some or all of the losses you incur as your stock portfolio falls. If the market goes up during your protection period, your out of pocket cost is limited to your up-front cost for the protection.

As we said, it's an extreme measure. Options investing, even for protective purposes, is something you should be well-educated on. To us, this is a much smoother and professional way of managing volatility than trying to jump in and out of the market.

Too Much Money Chasing Too Few (Good) Stocks

You've probably heard of "inflation", even if you don't know about it in much detail. When I was in business school, I was taught that inflation is simply a condition in the economy where too much money is chasing too few goods. That is, when there is a limited supply of "stuff" available compared to how much of it people want to buy, an imbalance exists.

What's the result? The price of the stuff goes up. This makes sense as long as you are a capitalist. If everyone wants what you have, you have the flexibility to charge more than if very few people wanted it. We've heard this over the years whenever gasoline prices go up. We hear that supplies are tight and that is what's leading to higher prices. The generous folks at OPEC then ride in on their white horses, release more oil for use, and the price drifts down.

When you think about it, this is the number one reason why stock prices move up or down. No matter how popular a stock seems to be based on what people are saying about it, if they don't put their money where their mouths are and actually place orders in the market to buy the stock, it can't go up. The stock market, bond market, commodities market and any other market is about how much buying pressure there is versus selling pressure.

My friends in the technical analysis (charting) world often talk about the market as if it were a drama in the movie theater. "The bulls have control, the bears could have taken them down this week but they didn't have enough muscle." That's the type of thing you'll hear from them. To a long-term investor, the supply and demand of the market in the short-term does not matter much. But I have found that the supply-demand concept holds true over longer periods of time too.

For example, why did the stock market start to fall in 2000, then accelerate in 2001 (prior to 9/11)? By some accounts, the market was overvalued back in 1997. Why did it take so long? The answer, in my opinion: demand for stocks finally declined to the point where supply was stronger. There were more sellers than buyers, more bears than bulls (in actions, not in words).

At the end of the day, that's what drives the price of anything—supply and demand. Heating oil, olive oil, castor oil, whatever. Understanding this basic idea will help you avoid the hype that Wall Street throws at us on a daily basis.

The reasons people decide to sell or buy is something that we can always debate. But the fact that they are selling and buying is the key, not why they are doing so. If you lost money in the stock market from 2000-2002 (and you probably did), do you really care why? Does it make you feel better knowing that Y2K was a major miscalculation on the part of the experts, and that the impending nightmare it was supposed to cause instead became a nonevent? No!

Charting Your Course

This is why I am a huge fan of charting or "technical analysis". Once considered voodoo by many in the industry, I strongly believe that there is definitely something to be said for watching human psychology and emotions play out on my computer screen. I have found that the charts show what fundamental analysis often doesn't: what price for a security is "high" and what is "low". This is based on tracking trends in prices and trading volume. This is not a statement against fundamental financial analysis. I believe the two go hand in hand. The charts show a picture of what is happening on the field on Sunday. The research you read or the news reports you hear are merely the equivalent of training camp.

However, when my clients ask me why news on rising inflation is greeted with rising stock prices one day and falling prices a few weeks later, I often find that a look at the chart tells the story. No event actually moves stock prices. It is market participants' REACTION to the news that does it. Furthermore, it is often the case that the buyers or sellers of a security, sector or the market overall get exhausted. Everyone who wants to buy has bought, and now the sellers are taking over. Or the reverse occurs. The charts tell this story the best because it is a habit of people to do the same things over and over again, including the mistakes they make. In fact, one entire philosophy of investing, the "contrarian" approach is in its simplest form, capitalizing on the mistakes of short-sighted investors. People panic, they sell securities of good companies along with bad ones, and contrarians wait for the sellers to get exhausted. Then they buy in.

Of course, buying and selling pressure as depicted on the charts is one way to explain all of this. The other is that the technical analysts are poking their voodoo dolls! Which one makes more sense to you?

Technical Analysis: What It Is (And What Isn't It?)

This next section is based on an interview I did back in 2004 with Michael Kahn, one of the finest technical analysts in the business. I have subscribed to his newsletter for some time and followed his writings as the technical analyst for Barron's magazine.

I get asked all the time about technical analysis and its place in the investment world. While it is a very useful tool, please be aware technical analysis is not the "Nirvana" of investing.

Technical analysis is simply the study of the markets using only data generated by the market itself and the actions of people in the market. In other words, company data like earnings and sales and economic data like housing reports are not used. There are no estimates and no revisions of data. While extremely useful in making forecasts of market action, the bottom line is to make the buy, sell or hold decision and nothing more. It will miss the absolute high and it will miss the absolute low but when applied properly, it will allow the user to capture the lion's share of any price move. More importantly, it will alert the user very quickly if the analysis was incorrect to minimize losses.

What is a technician actually analyzing and why is it important?

Technicians are analyzing the market like a psychologist analyzes a patient. They assess the market's health using indicators. They can profile market behavior based on past behaviors and use probabilities to determine what kind of future behavior can be expected. What does a technician analyze? The answer is market psychology and the behavior of crowds. Crowds, after all, make up the entity we call the market.

What makes technical analysis reliable (or not)?

It is reliable to the extent that it is based on experience and objectivity. What constitutes some technical conditions is subjective at times. However, when applied consistently, it will yield more winners than losers and then it is up to money management to lock in the profits. A significant part of technical analysis involves knowing when to acknowledge losers and locking in profits on winners.

Why don't more money managers use technical analysis?

The answer is culture and training. You can talk a great story with your knowledge of a company and technical analysis sometimes sounds like gibberish. Fault the speaker, not the analysis. Schools pound the message of valuations and fundamentals down student's throats and do not expose them to the "dark side." Little did they know that they were, in fact, the dark side and technical analysis was the beacon during the bear market. This is changing now as the Market Technicians Association has been working very hard to establish a foothold in academe. For-credit courses are not being taught in many business schools today.

What role should Technical Analysis play in portfolio management?

Technical analysis should be as important if not more important in portfolio management than any other kind of analysis. Personally, I do not know anything about reading a balance sheet and yet I make money trading. While I don't recommend it at all, I remember trading a stock based on its chart and I did not even know its name! Nice trade but that's a bit extreme. For a more reasonable approach you can do your fundamental research and do a final sanity check using the charts. Or, use fundamentals as a sanity check on the stocks you find using technical means. These two types of analysis need not be adversarial so use whatever works for you.

What is your long-term market outlook from a technical perspective?

This is easy to answer since I have been writing about it in Barron's and my own newsletters for months. We are going nowhere for the next decade. Buy and hold is not going to work during this period and in order to make any money, even as a long-term investor, you will need to actively manage your portfolio. There will be huge swings to play both long and short but you will have to keep tabs on what's going on at least once per month.

Is there anything else you would want high net worth investors to know about technical analysis?

Yes, technical analysis is not voodoo and it does not pretend to predict where the market will be at any point in time. It is only an investment decision making tool that can give you a framework for where it will be but it is a probabilities game, just like human behavior. "The market is likely to do X" but a good analyst does not leave it there. That is just one big waffle. A good analyst will describe why the market is likely to do X and then outline what has to happen to change his mind. It's all about buy, sell and hold and not proving how smart you are with fancy numbers and graphs. This stuff works in bull markets, bear markets and most importantly in sideways markets.

And Now, Meet My Maker

Everyone has people that have influenced them in their careers. I had one before I started mine. My father has been following the stock market in a non-professional capacity since the 1950's. I think that makes his experience sufficient to call him a professional market participant. Not only has he seen more market varieties than most of us currently working in the business, but he has made more mistakes than many aspiring investors will ever make – because he has survived them while many will not. He has managed to keep himself "retired" from his career in corporate America for over twenty years by managing his investment portfolio on a daily basis. When I was named to Robb Report/Worth Magazine's "Top 100 Wealth Managers" List in 2005, I felt that it was as much an affirmation of the way my parents brought me up as it was an honor for me. Since my father is the one who first taught me the importance of understanding human emotion in investing, and stoked my interest in technical analysis, I thought it would only be fitting for him to write the beginning of this chapter of the book. So first, here's what Carl Isbitts had to say about investment markets, human behavior and technical analysis. As the saying goes: those who ignore history are condemned to repeat it!

The Psychology Of Investing And The Role Of Technical Analysis

In the hunt for the best methodologies to achieve investment success, there has been an ongoing competition between "fundamental" analysis (financial information) and "technical analysis" (techniques using only price and volume). With mass-market accessibility of the Internet have come a plethora of technical analysis tools, many claiming to provide the most advanced capabilities. This would give the impression that these tools have recently burst on the scene. In fact, technical analysis is decades old.

John Magee has been considered to be the "father" of technical analysis. His book, "Technical Analysis of Stock Trends", written with a cohort, was first published in 1948, but is still in print today, having undergone several "upgrades". To understand his accomplishment, you have to place yourself in the environment of that era. The raw data of technical analysis consists of two items, price and volume. In 1948, this data resided on a paper tape called the "ticker". Typically, it resided in a broker's office and on the New York Stock Exchange.

Bear in mind, the American Exchange at that time was considered a repository of fledgling companies and a non-existent competitor to the NYSE. What is today called NASDAQ was an assortment of relative non-entities that were traded "over the counter". Trying to even get quotes was a labor. Mostly, they were on a daily document called the "Pink Sheets", printed on pink paper (which still exist today, albeit electronically). The investment world tended to concentrate on the "elites"—companies like RCA, Woolworth, etc. as well as some existing blue chips. Brokers knew about these companies, but when it came to the smaller ones, the investor was essentially on his own.

Magee attempted to bridge this gap, although his primary motivation was probably to bring a different perspective to the world of stocks. His principle was that a set of recurring patterns occurred across the universe of stocks, and that these patterns would assert themselves purely by price/volume analysis. Furthermore, this action could be charted, and the chart would be a meaningful barometer of future price movement. An investor essentially would not need to dissect the fundamentals of a company, because the chart would represent all of the factors that account for price movement—the expectations of profits, growth patterns, and the intangibles such as investor sentiment and risk or reward expectation. The charts were defined by bars that represented the high, low and closing prices for each day. If the user wanted, they could go through the laborious task of accumulating the figures to form a weekly chart. The daily newspaper was about the only source of this type of information. The desire for a more efficient method of obtaining the information later spawned some charting services. Every week, if you wished, you could get a series of charts that were up to date from the preceding Friday. Of course, it was usually Tuesday before you got the information, so you would have to pencil in the most recent data if you wanted to keep current.

The first premise was that all securities would evidence a definable trend, which could be determined by a straight line. If you tracked the price movement of Stock "A", and it was going up, it would continue to advance in a straight line. Of course, there would be periods of decline, but as long as the decline did not penetrate the advancing slope, it was in an "uptrend". You would also expect each decline to stop on the line and move above its preceding high price. The trend would be reversed when there was drop below the line. Many technicians still use this principle today as their primary measurement of market and stock direction.

Magee also divined specific patterns that would be very meaningful in determining the next direction for the security. Names such as ascending and descending triangles, symmetrical triangles, head and shoulders, rounding tops and bottoms, flags and pennants were the initial watchwords of technical analysis. It was also possible to make some predictions as to the magnitude of movement of a security after it identified its next direction. Also, Magee thought that securities exhibited a pattern of "support and resistance". Support was a prior price where a downslide would supposedly stop, and resistance would do that same to an advance. For a time, these techniques worked well, and to an extent still do so today. Despite the fact (or perhaps because of it), that there were a relatively small number of stocks with limited data availability, Magee's premises attracted some attention.

Bear in mind that all of the daily news was also confined to that same ticker tape, which had limited capacity, so that the tape could easily become crowded. An "active" day was probably a couple of million shares (as contrasted to nearly 1 billion today), and unless you were a floor trader, it was almost impossible to capitalize upon a news event, because by the time it reached you, it was history. If the level of activity exceeded the capacity of the tape, it would run "digits deleted". That is, only the last digit would be shown. It was presumed the investor would know what the first digit was. If this didn't solve the problem, the next step was "volume deleted"—no volume figures were shown. Even though tickers were later sped up and electronic tickers came into being, the "deleted" conditions continued to exist even into the 1980s.

Magee's approach spawned an entire industry of technical analysts and innovators. By the 1950s, "point and figure" charting entered on the scene. The theory behind this tool was similar to Magee's, except that it excluded volume. What it said was that everything that is known, or is about to be known in a stock could be measured solely by the price. Point and figure analysts claimed that not only the direction, but the magnitude of a price move could be predicted by point and figure. In fact, bar and point and figure charting worked pretty well, and still do today.

In actuality, someone preceded Magee on the technical analysis scene. This was R.N. Elliott, who in 1939 propounded the Elliott Wave Theory. This Theory identified all price movements as a series of five waves, upward and downward, each consisting of five subwaves. In addition, the magnitude of the movement could be determined by a precise series of retracement or "Fibonnacci" measurements. These were stated in percentage terms. In other words, all price movements could be predicted by the combination of these methods. In the early days, using such analysis was limited by the availability of data.

Some changes in the breadth and availability of technical analysis began in the 1990s. As computers progressed beyond the era of floppy disks, which were previously the only source of both data and programs, so did the breadth and magnitude of analytical tools. Dow Jones and others developed end-of-day price and volume figures, providing the day's action within the same day. This was followed by "real-time" data services. A geometric change occurred with the advent of the Internet. Now, data was commonly available real-time, and the number of measurement tools and techniques expanded dramatically. Triangles, trendlines and point-and-figure were augmented by what some providers claim are hundreds of diagnostic and measurement tools—but still using price and volume. Names such as "cup and handle" formations, "heuristics" (using complex formulas to predict future movement), directional indicators, relative strength, moving averages, stochastics, etc, are now commonplace in technical analysis; and, many have some merit. Many brokerages provide these tools as part of their regular service. Other vehicles have sprung up that are supposed to provide even the most novice investor with extraordinary profit-making tools. One uses lights as signals to determine when to get in or out. A green light is a "go", while a red light is a "stop". The investment world is now supposedly reduced to a couple of clicks on a computer.

All of this sounds wonderful, but is it so easy? The answer has to be no. In many respects, the current environment is considerably more difficult. One major reason is the availability of alternatives, and the ease with which action can be taken. In the 40s, 50s, etc. there was practically a unilateral market—the United States. Today, there are global markets, many of which are actively competing with the U.S. There has been a fundamental change in the manner in which markets are conducted. With today's capabilities, there is a worldwide securities market that operates 24 hours a day. Something that occurs in London or Japan overnight can affect domestic markets. The number of mutual funds has expanded from a relative handful to begin with, to over 5000, covering every conceivable manner of investment. Names such as hedge funds, closed-end and exchange-traded funds are commonplace. Trading methods have changed dramatically. The slow-paced trading of the 40s and 50s has been replaced by instant action. With active overnight markets in Europe and elsewhere, the stock you knew yesterday could be different today. With the advent of globalization, everyone is competing with everyone else. Foreigners own a huge portion of our national debt. Takeovers and consolidations are rampant, and even General Motors is considered as a shaky bet. Remember the quote "as GM goes, so goes the nation"? This is symbolic of the nature and magnitude of change that has taken place in the investment markets.

Additionally, there has been a considerable shift to a trading mentality. We now have pre-markets and after-markets. So-called third markets have expanded to the point where they are considered attractive acquisitions. NASDAQ is no longer the poor step-sister to the NYSE, but a powerful rival, and a home for many growth companies. Every DAY you can tune into CNBC for all of the information you need (supposedly).

The state of technical analysis today should more appropriately be called "tactical analysis". It still requires an investor to have a strategy, and to abide by it. While the tools are there and can be reasonably reliable, human intervention is still required.

Technical analysis can be a vital adjunct to an investment strategy, but it is not absolute. For instance, in a true downtrend, the first "support" level is usually broken. You cannot count on technical analysis to save you. A piece of negative news can invalidate an entire chart pattern. What do you do then? Frankly, this is a point where there is no replacement for experience and knowledge. Unless you have been through at least one complete cycle (up and down), you are handicapped in moments like this; and, they are occurring with increasing frequency.

143

The growing popularity of technical analysis caused the development of a new industry-market letter writers. They joined the growing chorus of individuals who had already embraced a fundamentals philosophy. Using bar charts, point and figure or a combination of the two, these individuals attempted to forecast long and short-term trends in the overall markets; and, in many instances made recommendations of individual securities. This, in turn, created another business—evaluating the evaluators. There are still services today that grade the degree of success (or failure) of market letter writers. While some have been relatively consistent, others have had good years and bad years. In one recent review, some of the best prognosticators in 2004 were among the worst in 2005. There is also the case on one particular writer who correctly forecast a downturn several years ago, and became an instant "guru". For a time he was a household name, appearing on all of the investment talk shows and offering his then current wisdom. He then forecast a greater downturn just before a major upturn, but his results were unfavorable and not well received. Subsequently, he correctly joined in a bull market consensus well into the advance. A few years ago, he again forecast a major downturn in the Dow Jones average in 6 to 10 months. His timing was off by about a year, and his target was about 2000 points too low. This is not meant to disparage such individuals. There is knowledge to be gained from them. The key point to understand is that following a mass-market strategy can have negative as well as positive results.

One factor that gets overlooked by many market analysts is the significance of periodicity in using technical analysis. The longer the period you are addressing, the more difficult prediction becomes. Daily and weekly charts are the most accurate vehicles for decision–making, even though there can be swings in both. One fact every investor has to understand is that all securities undergo cycles, even intra-day. The experienced chartist recognizes these factors, and chooses the periodicity that matches his investment strategy. Daily charts are beneficial to short-term traders. Daily and weekly charts work for intermediate-term traders. Monthly charts can outline a trend, but cannot accurately recognize trend changes because they are not sensitive enough. This is because such changes can be abrupt, especially at market tops. Putting aside all of the analytical factors, markets move from one of two basic emotional factors—greed and fear. Bull markets run until those who are greedy exhaust themselves. Bear markets terminate when those who are in a panic have dumped enough so that there is little left to sell. These turns can be recognized on shorter-term charts, but not monthly ones.

Sample size is another factor affecting proper technical analysis. The larger the universe that is being covered by the security, the less sensitive charting is likely to be. Mutual funds tend to have a mix of all stocks, all income securities or a combination of the two. They not only encompass stocks which can be moving in different directions, but income items which tend to respond to a different set of criteria. A mutual fund that has say, 100 stocks in its portfolio, offers a real challenge to chartists. The rules of traditional technical analysis seldom apply to these situations, especially since there is only one daily price (the closing) and no volume. Exchange traded funds and indexes tend to respond more effectively, especially in terns of support and resistance. This is probably because they are so widely followed they attract enough traders to produce measurable results.

One other factor virtually all market analysts talk about is the use of stop loss orders. They are supposed to safeguard your investment by minimizing losses. From experience, they work better in larger universes, such as indexes and large-cap stocks. These have lower volatility and higher volume, which makes them less vulnerable to "whipsaws"—selling out just in time to see the issue reverse itself to the upside. Stop loss orders are more difficult in more speculative stocks. Their volatility and, at times, lack of volume expose them to wider swings, which are magnified by trading in the pre-opening and pre-closing markets. It is also not unusual to see them whipsaw, since they often have wider spreads in their quotes. A smart market tactician will consider using electronic tools to place "mental" stops, so that he can make the decision when and if his price point has been reached.

The Internet age has produced a dazzling array of tools that, properly applied, can assist a technician in making effective decisions. Just as you would not buy a house without evaluating the nature of the market that you are going into, using technical analysis requires confirmation. A point and figure chart by itself may seem to make a cogent case for a particular stock, but the bar chart may show cracks in the picture. One or two sets of indicators may show a favorable outcome, while others show the opposite. The best decision is the one that involves evaluating all of these factors before risking any funds.

Chartists make money. They also lose money. A generally accepted principle is that if you make money on 60% of your trades, you are successful. This assumes that you will sell your losers and let your winners earn some very nice amounts of money. My experience indicates that it is impossible for any investment tool to assure which trades will fall into one or the other category. Even the best investors lose money at times. That is why technical tools followed blindly without a tactical approach will not achieve the desired result. Unless someone is prepared to take the time and have the dedication to become expert in technical analysis (and it can take years), don't try this at home!

Every investor needs to have a set of rules they will abide by, if only to minimize the natural emotions that surface when you are "in the game". Here is a sampling of suggested rules:

1. Never buy a security unless you believe the risk-reward ratio is at least 2:1 in your favor.

2. You never know how high a security price will go, or how low. Don't assume you can tell.

3. Stocks will almost always go down faster than they go up. If one of your holdings does something negative you didn't expect, be prepared to sell it.

4. Have a target sale price for every purchase. Be prepared to sell at or near your target. Be prepared to revise your target if conditions change.

5. Don't follow the crowd. They may lead you up, but they will also force you down.

6. In a bull market, even if you sell prematurely, another opportunity will arise elsewhere. Falling in love is for mating, not investments.

7. In a bear market, the odds are against you. Even the best looking situation can turn on you. That's why it is so important to have extreme flexibility in your investment process.

8. The greatest handicap to success in investing is <u>you</u> - your emotions and attitudes. Don't assume that what others think of you is based upon how successful you are. If you don't tell them, they won't know (and they probably don't care).

Thanks Dad, and thanks Mom, for everything.

CHAPTER 9: CORE INVESTING...AND BEYOND

"I am a great believer in luck. The harder I work the more of it I seem to have."
-Coleman Cox

There are certain factors about goal-oriented investing that all investors should consider. We look at some of the basic core principles, with a mind toward educating investors. Then we'll move beyond the basics and introduce a very different way of tackling the wealth issues most important to you. Let's start this chapter by laying out the three rules of investing (according to me).

The Three Rules Of Investing (A Recurring Theme, Remember?)

Benjamin Graham is one of the most revered investment visionaries of modern history. He is widely considered the father of "Value Investing". His disciples quote him often. While I am not a true-blue value investor, I do have a clear contrarian bent to my thought process. Graham is often quoted concerning his two rules of investing:

> **Number one: don't lose money.**

> **Number two: don't forget rule number one!**

I like to take that thinking a step further. Specifically:

1. **Preserve what you have (i.e. aim to produce a long-term return above that is above inflation and taxes).**

2. **Grow your portfolio as much as you can (and as consistently as you can).**

3. **Remember that when push comes to shove, rule #1 comes first.**

Show Me The Money

The money you need to live on comes from several sources, this is the time to realize that there's a logical order to this.

1. You keep cash on hand to fund your immediate and short-term needs

2. You have a bond portfolio to produce income.

3. These two sources may produce all you need. If not, the bond principal is stable, and there for you as a backup.

Years from now, if your required spending had diminished all assets you had in all the sources listed above, you'd be down to your stock portfolio. Here's the key: think about how long it would take for you to reach this point, based on the assets you have in bonds and cash. It is likely many years out. Then ask yourself, realistically: will my stock portfolio be noticeably higher at that point than it is today? While there are no guarantees, the odds are very much in your favor. The bottom line is that if you have time to grow your portfolio, give it that time, and resist the urge to veer off course.

Should your policy include stocks? Your reaction to volatile market activity will give you a strong clue. Fortunately, our use of **"Hybrid" investments** have allowed our clients to invest in strategies that are linked to the stock market, with a fraction of the volatility. For some, this has proven to be a nice substitute for low bond yields; for others, its just a way to keep emotions at a minimum, and prevent them from constantly changing their minds about what kind of investor they want to be.

Fig. 12: The Cycle Of Market Emotions

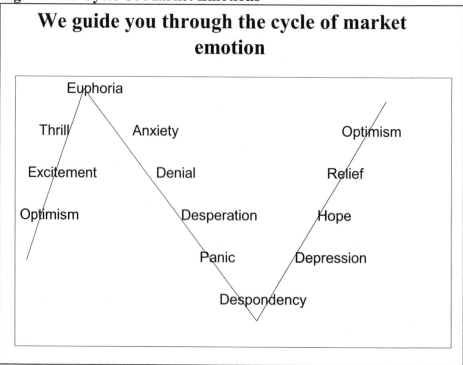

We guide you through the cycle of market emotion

Euphoria

Thrill   Anxiety   Optimism

Excitement   Denial   Relief

Optimism   Desperation   Hope

                Panic   Depression

                Despondency

This chart was originally created by Munder Capital back in the late 1990's. Over the years, my team and I have found it to be a very valuable, thought-provoking tool. I refer to this chart often when I try to assess the mood of the financial markets. As we covered in the last chapter, the psychological component of investing is not only critical, but may be as important as any other factor in setting portfolio strategy. Let's face it: collectively, all of us are "the market". For this reason, I'm always looking out for even the smallest piece of information that might help determine what significant, long-term changes may occur.

The turn of the century witnessed a strong emotional reaction in world stock markets. From the invincible feeling many felt in the late 1990's, to the stomach-turning drops of 2000-2002, investors have been through a lot.

The markets have and will always be volatile. This is the unfortunate but necessary reality. If avoidance of risk were the only concern for investors, there would be no investment industry—everyone would be putting their money into their mattresses or finding a decent rate on CDs at the corner bank. The implicit assumption of investing as a concept is that investors are willing to assume risk in exchange for potential reward.

It's a question most investors ask themselves at some point. Whether it is a retiree fighting to make the money last, or a young entrepreneur hoping to grow what they have accumulated, the stock market is looked at as an opportunity...but is it worth it? We'll give you three points of view, including ours.

This article was originally published by me and released to clients in 2003:

> *At a 2002 conference for investment professionals, two very accomplished speakers debated whether investments in stocks were still a core part of a retirement investment plan. The first was Jeremy Siegel, professor of finance at University of Pennsylvania's Wharton School of Business and author of a popular book called* Stocks for the Long Run. *As the title implies, he believes that stocks should play a central role in a portfolio. However, he says high valuations in the stock market will dampen returns in the future and we will unlikely witness the double-digit percentage returns produced through much of the past two decades.*

The second speaker, Zvi Bodie, professor of finance at Boston University and author of the book Worry Free Investing noted that there is no consensus among a broad group of investment scholars. In his opinion, investments like inflation-protected bonds and Series I savings bonds are a better solution to retirement planning than stocks. His bottom line: invest to beat inflation and be happy with that. He added that equities were not a good choice for people who are averse to risk, even over the long time horizon that applies to younger investors.

"Renting" the Stock Market

So how do you reconcile divergent opinions of two highly respected academics? We ask: "Should you use stocks to save for retirement, or should you use preservation-oriented portfolios? We respond with a confident "Yes." Stock investing takes many different forms. Our extensive use of a strategy we call "Hybrid" allows an investor to pursue some of the higher returns potentially offered by stocks, balanced with a lower expected volatility than a traditional stock portfolio. Whether it is an arbitrage strategy, where the money manager tries to make small gains consistently, or a long-short approach targeting positive returns in most or all market environments, or the employment of fixed income alternatives, Hybrid styles try to extract what is good about the stock market, while leaving the bad (volatility) behind.

We agree with the two professors: there is solid historical evidence for lower stock market returns in the next decade, compared to what this generation of investors is used to. But that is very different from saying there is not money to be made. We think there is.

Portfolio Design – It Depends On Who You Are

Investors are confused because they see stock prices rising and falling, and cannot distinguish between good companies to own and bad ones. They don't want to miss out on a winner, but are afraid of owning any losers. It's a conundrum, but one with a solution. Part of the solution is to figure out what you believe in as an investor. You may have professional money managers making the daily choices about what stocks to buy and may also have an advisor to determine what mix of styles gives you the best opportunity to achieve your broad investment goals. But more important than the approach of the managers and your investment advisor is that your professionals are doing what makes you comfortable. Very likely, it is not buying the investment with the highest potential return, because the flip side of that could be a big loss.

Part of your advisor's job is to figure out with you what investment approaches make sense. No one likes to see investment values drop. However, it is easier to sleep at night knowing that you believe in the methods used to manage your portfolio, and you have confidence in the people running them. We feel that we have built portfolios that reflect what our clients want out of life.

We are confident in our ability to navigate through tough markets for our clients. This confidence comes from knowing that we have narrowed down an exhaustive list of investment choices to a short list of what makes sense for each client. When we feel an upgrade can be made, we recommend a change, with the knowledge of what we are leaving behind, and what we are gaining from the change. We encourage you to do what we do: **figure out what you believe in, and be sure your portfolio reflects that.** We all know that it's hard work to earn our wealth. Many investors are realizing now that it's also very hard work to grow the wealth you save. While the late 1990's offered little pain and much gain, long-term investing is full of obstacles and tough decisions. The patient and educated survive; the emotional suffer.

Clients hire advisors to provide the education and the resources to guide them. In large part, our relatively conservative style has yielded better than average results for clients. However, since we are not magicians, sometimes we encounter difficulties that all long-term investors eventually face.

So, what do we do then? Well, we keep doing what we always do: research and determine what combination of investment strategies will, in our opinion, provide clients with the highest probability of reaching their investment objectives. A weak stock market combined with uncertain and even volatile interest rates has caused us to be very resourceful in the first half of this decade. The inability to be market predictors is the reason we have developed several main themes for our portfolio management art, as depicted in the chart on the following page.

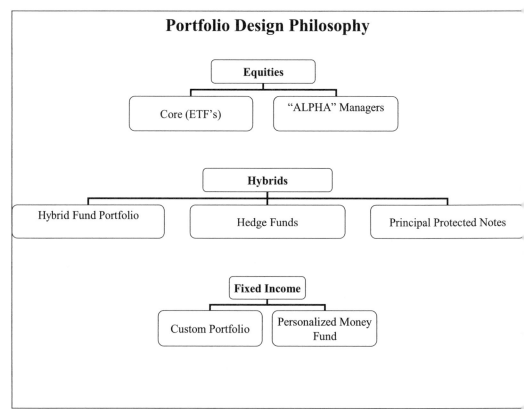

Fig. 13: My Portfolio Design Philosophy

Asset Allocation: My Way

So to me, a solid, long-term portfolio in my opinion looks something like this map, with explanation to follow. Call this the "punch line" of all the parts of this book related to asset allocation. <u>Now, here's an explanation of the different segments of the portfolio.</u>

EQUITIES

GOAL: Long-term growth of capital at a rate that exceeds the impact of inflation (by how much depends on the client's risk tolerance and wealth objectives).

Throughout this book I encourage you to focus on investing in a way that targets the pursuit of your desired lifestyle instead of trying to "game" the markets to make money with no plan in mind. You should have an investment strategy, a roadmap, instead of simply buying and selling "stuff". I also advise you to look at how you are getting to your own version of the Promised Land. This is where I think many investors and advisors settle. They settle for status quo, same old same old, and doing what the "experts to the masses" say works.

When it comes to the part of your portfolio that is invested in the stock market in a more traditional fashion, my thinking has changed over the years. It changed because the environment changed, and it changed because Wall Street's approach to equity investing for individuals changed dramatically.

For clients that we believe should have an allocation to stock market, we engage third-party Equity managers. For these clients I hire a limited number of highly specialized equity management firms. These managers range from passive Core managers with largely indexed portfolios, to active managers who run very concentrated portfolios (under 20 holdings) to managers with specialized styles that tend to exhibit low correlation to the broad stock market. Effectively, I divide the world of traditional, professionally managed equities into two very distinct camps: "Core Approaches" and "Alpha Approaches". After years of watching an infinite number of stock-picking styles, I've concluded that there are two approaches that give stock investors the greatest chance for satisfaction. Let's start with Core.

The Core Equity Approach

I have had many prospective clients tell me, with a sort of sarcastic pride, "Most money managers don't beat their market indexes". My answer to them is, "You're absolutely right". But then they are surprised that an advisor, whose job they perceive to be the promotion of active money management and sexy money management firms, not only agrees with them, but then proceeds to explain why over 90% of money management firms don't even make his research radar screen!

This does not mean that we just put our equity allocation into index funds and call it a day. Yes, that is the mantra of many advisors and it has served them well over the years. But I'm too wary of the potential for the stock market to rip away my clients' hard-earned wealth to simply bag the idea of actively managed equities. So, it would appear we are between a rock and a hard place.

Our solution for core equity investing is twofold:

1. Don't allocate too much to it.

2. Find a cost-effective way to do it.

Rarely will a client of mine have more than 30% of their overall portfolio in a style that seeks to perform roughly in line with the stock market. I just don't think that in the wake of the market bubble at the turn of the century, we should be counting on that style to carry us through the next decade or two. This is not the 1980's or the 1990's. Still, as I learned early in my career, always account for what would happen if your forecast turns out to be wrong. I often refer to this part of the portfolio as "manager insurance". It saves your portfolio during periods where your active management strategies deliver mediocre performance but the broad stock market flourishes.

So, after analyzing hundreds of money managers over the years, and having my heart broken time and again, I've learned to enjoy the benefits of Exchange-Traded Funds for core portfolio construction.

As we discussed above, Exchange Traded Funds (ETFs) are investments that track like index funds but can be traded like stocks. The best-known ETF is the Standard and Poor Depositary Receipt or SPDR (pronounced "Spider"), which tracks the S&P 500, however ETFs have been created which replicate virtually every major index. Some other well-known ETFs include Diamonds, which track the DOW, Triple Qs, which track the NASDAQ 100, Vipers, which track various Vanguard Index funds, and iShares, provided by Barclay's, which track a variety of domestic, international, and global indices.

ETFs provide an easy and inexpensive way to reduce risk and increase diversification in a portfolio. The risks are low, however, the return may not be high enough to justify investment. They are generally most appropriate as a balancing strategy in an otherwise complete and diversified portfolio (for example, 50% stocks, 40% bonds, 10% ETF).

Exchange-traded funds are bought and sold through brokers and traded on stock exchanges. Their prices change constantly throughout the trading day, unlike open-end funds whose prices are set only once, at the end of the day.

While similar to their index fund counterparts, there are some additional characteristics specific to ETFs that the client should be aware of, including:

- They consistently underperform the Index and their comparable index fund.

- They generally are not as quickly rebalanced when a change occurs.

- They are generally cheaper than traditional funds.

- They can be found on various exchanges: AMEX, CBOE, NYSE, and others.

- They can increase and decrease the number of shares outstanding.

- They can be traded.

- They can track an entire market segment.

Using ETFs:

Because ETFs are a good tool for portfolio diversification, they can be used in Core/Satellite Portfolio Construction. An ETF adds diversification cheaply if an Active Manager is the Core investment.

They also can be used to maintain equity exposure when changing managers, by shifting assets short term into ETFs until the manager change is effective. As an asset allocation component they can be used to rebalance, increase or decrease exposure in any area or sector.

Furthermore, I think that rather than try to just pick one or two indexes to include in your core portfolio, you are better off identifying a money management firm that runs a strategy that takes a long-term, patient approach and invests in a diversified basket of ETFs for you. We know of a few good ones whose research process is based on a solid foundation. Of course, these are independent firms. They also recognize that with the effort of doing individual stock research removed from their plate (since each ETF represents an entire segment of the market, not individual stocks), they do not have the right to charge you an arm and a leg. They also understand that their goal is to exceed the return of the broad stock market by a couple of points a year, and not trail it by much in its worst periods. They are not trying to create magic here. They are just trying to add a little value over the market's return through diversification and active management. Just the idea that they have cut out a lot of the headaches and risk of researching and owning individual stocks makes their process smoother than the "usual suspect" money managers one finds in wrap programs. At the end of 2005, there were very few firms running all-ETF portfolios with significant critical mass (assets under management), but I suspect that this number will rise quite a bit in the years to come.

I think of this segment of the portfolio as "manager insurance" in case the market does very well and your concentrated managers don't. Some advisors look at indexing through ETFs as a core strategy, and I agree that, for more aggressive investors, it can be. However, while many advisors will complement that indexing approach by finding the most risky asset classes they can think of, I prefer to put my "long-term high return" assets with Concentrated managers. I think that makes for a powerful combination, particularly for the baby boom generation.

At this point, you may be waiting for me to trash Wall Street firms for their approach to this part of one's portfolio. I will not disappoint you. I think the fact that brokerage firms offer managed ETF portfolios is a great sign. That they are charging too much for it is, well, par for the course. I have seen wrap fees as high as 2.5% for such accounts. That pretty much takes away most of the advantage these accounts had over simply putting your money in the ETF that tracks the Standard and Poors (S&P) 500 Index. This may be a simple investment approach on the surface – choose some index securities based on an asset allocation formula, and make changes once in a while. But there is more to it than that, and your advisor should understand this. Don't take the recommendation for an ETF wrap account at face value. Find out enough about the investment process used by the manager to choose the ETFs and what determines their decision to sell. Find out how much attention is paid to the impact of taxes. Again, this a good idea from the product creation team at the brokerage firm, but it can easily be negated by the need for the firm to generate fat profit margins. At least now you know there are other ways to pursue this part of your portfolio.

The Alpha Approach

The other part of my approach to equity investing involves the use of "alpha managers". Alpha, simply defined, is the ability of a money manager to produce a return beyond what the market provides on its own. I often say that in a stock market that earns zero return, alpha is the return that your manager provides. Most active managers have a history of producing negative or small positive alpha. Some defy the odds. You don't often find them in the brokerage wrap programs. You don't find these hidden gems in the investment department of your local trust company. In fact, you don't easily find them at all. And there aren't hundreds of them.

However, I do believe that a common theme among many of the most successful equity managers is this: they concentrate their holdings in a small number of stocks (typically 25 or less). These "concentrated managers" are typically not suited for the mass-customized world of Wall Street. And they don't really care, either. They are typically firms comprised of extraordinarily bright, experienced people who work well as a team. They do not split their attention in too many directions. And they approach portfolio management as a quest to invest in the best-managed businesses. The fact that shares of ownership in these businesses can be bought or sold on the open market (i.e. the stock market) from 9:30AM to 4:00PM most days is an added convenience, but its not especially important. These firms are all about finding entities they can own a piece of, hopefully for a long time. This way of investing used to be more popular than it is today. You might say that less is more in this case.

These money managers are more concerned with knowing the ins and outs of the businesses they own than hanging on every earnings announcement or Fed move. And if the idea of buying shares of stock for the purpose of owning a piece of the future success of a business reminds you of investing's good old days, there's a reason: it's a good strategy.

There is certainly more potential for volatility here, but the rest of your portfolio serves to counter that. I also think that one or two well-chosen concentrated portfolios will stand up well in the long run versus aggressive portfolio strategies and certainly against the "usual suspects" of the money management business as discussed earlier. As an added bonus, concentrated managers tend to exhibit low correlation to the broad stock market, which means that there can be times where stocks in general are struggling, but these firms still flourish.

By taking this approach, we focus the "risk" versus the market toward managers whose styles give them a high probability of outperforming over long periods of time. If you are going to pay a fee for managed equities, make sure you are paying for a realistic chance for superior returns. Mediocrity has no place here!

FIXED INCOME

GOAL: To address cash flow needs and/or complement a managed equity portfolio.

We run Individualized Bond Portfolios—buying individual bonds customized to the clients' cash flow, safety and liquidity requirements. As stated elsewhere in this book, I am NOT a fan of using bond funds or bond managers that heap on fees for managing in an asset class where there is little value to be added for most investors. I felt this way my entire career, but the feeling is even stronger now that interest rates have fallen for over 25 years.

We use high-quality securities to minimize credit risk, and concentrate on short-intermediate term maturities to minimize interest rate risk. We structure maturities so as to meet client cash flow requirements.

Many advisors now have capabilities beyond their own firm's bond trading desks. For instance, we have access to over 300 bond dealers, and we are able to buy bonds at very competitive prices. We are by no means alone in this, but you should steer clear of firms that are more "proprietary" and do not offer freedom of choice. High-quality bonds are a commodity, so don't fund your advisor's next BMW payment with your next bond purchase!

HYBRIDS

GOAL: To produce positive returns with a low level of volatility and low correlation to the stock and bond markets.

The bottom line here: capture most of the ups, avoid most of the downs, sleep well. Hybrids include a variety of strategies that seek to capture most of the stock market's upside, with a fraction of the downside. Some Hybrid investments are tilted toward higher potential growth (call them "stock substitutes") while others are tilted more toward preservation (call them "bond substitutes").

I won't steal my own thunder on the **Hybrid Investment Strategy** as it is the topic of the next chapter. However, there are other strategies I consider to be in the Hybrid asset class.

Hedge Funds

Despite my concerns about the hedge fund world expressed earlier in the book, there are exceptions – hedge funds that offer investors something that fits a piece of their profile.

Most investment firms today have agreements with a small number of outside hedge fund firms. However, the trend over the last couple of years has been to greatly reduce the assets managed by these firms for our clients. Instead, the strategy described in the next chapter has received a greater share of the asset mix.

Structured notes are like bonds, but with an interesting twist. The interest rates they pay are based on specific criteria, linked to the performance of an index or basket of securities. Banks issue them in the form of Certificates of Deposit or investment notes. For instance, you might find something like this:

"Equity-Linked Note" from bank ABC

Matures in five years

Coupon: 1% + 90% of the return of the S&P 500 Index

That is, you get 1% a year for sure. You also get 9/10ths of any upward movement in the stock index over the five-year period. What if the market goes down, you ask? Well, remember that this security is structured like a bond. That means that the issuer promises to pay you back par value at maturity. In the case of CDs, they even carry FDIC insurance. While there are many variables to consider with this type of investment, I'm finding more use for them as the years go on.

Defending Your Portfolio

Option strategies are used to hedge against the risk of losing a lot of money in a major stock market correction. Why not just sell your stocks if you smell trouble? Why shouldn't your advisor just "get you out of the market"? If the account is taxable, you will only assure yourself of one thing – paying taxes on any securities sold at a profit. By using put options, you spend a relatively small amount of money to hedge your stock portfolio. One of three things will happen, generally speaking:

1. The market goes up, your put options expire worthless (i.e. you lose the money you put up). However, your stock portfolio has probably gone up by quite a bit more than your options declined. You've made money and not had to sell any stocks. You kept your portfolio intact without engaging in wholesale dumping of assets. You've also avoided having to make two correct decisions (one is tough enough) - selling at the right time, and buying back in at the right time. This is a trader's game, and even most of them get it wrong, so don't try to beat the odds.

2. The market goes down, your put options make money. The gain on the options offsets some but not all of your portfolio's decline, but you have muted the size of the loss. If done prudently, this type of portfolio defense can be used several times over the years, in an attempt to allow your portfolio of expected long term winners to persevere through the market's ups and down, while providing you with the means to reduce the risk of a major shock to its value.

3. The market changes very little. In this case, you don't get the benefit of a gain in the portfolio, and the options expire with little or no value. This may result in a small gain or loss versus having not bought the options. But again, this has not done much damage to the portfolio.

There are many other factors that you should be aware of before using options, even if they are just for defensive purposes. A great online resource to find materials to educate yourself is www.islepress.com, a website operated by my co-author, Ian Lohr, and his father John.

CHAPTER 10: HYBRID INVESTING – AN ALTERNATIVE TO ALTERNATIVE INVESTMENTS

Introduction: Hybrid Investing In More Depth

So, with that history in the books (or at least in this one), its time to dig deeper into the hybrid strategy. Not to get to technical on you, but the so-called "modern portfolio theory" allows us to easily quantify whether hybrid investments are doing their job. Any hybrid portfolio should strive to produce consistent positive returns with low volatility and success with a low level of dependency on the market itself. Let us examine each one of these two components individually.

Consistent Positive Returns With Low Volatility.

The investment statistical crowd refers to this as having a low "Beta". For instance, the Beta of an S&P 500 index fund against the S&P 500 index is 1.00; the index fund is as volatile as the index. That makes sense.

Success With A Low Level Of Dependency On The Market Itself.

The fancy statistic for this is called "R-Squared" and it answers the question of how much of your portfolio's return was due to the movement of the market, and not the manager's particular skills. Recall a discussion earlier in this book about how people were so impressed by the returns of money managers in the bull market, only to find out that the same managers could be just as bad as a bear market. These investors learned the hard way that the market, not the manager's brains, were driving the returns in good and bad market environments. There's an old Wall Street saying that one should not "confuse genius with a bull market". I think you get the picture.

Unfortunately, there are billions of dollars invested in actively managed, professionally managed stock portfolios that have R-Squared of over 90. That means that less than one-tenth of the return produced by the manager has anything to do with the manager's skill; the market's movement is the real reason the performance is what it is. One of my favorite sayings is, "There are some things in life you can control and some you can't". I think that recognizing this is one of the grand keys to getting what you want out of life. I know this: if you are paying management fees expecting to get outstanding manager skill at your disposal and come to realize that their skill is not much of a factor, you CAN control that. You can stop paying for mediocre performance! Then your only decision is whether to pay less for market-driven performance (via an index or index-like strategy), or search for managers whose performance tends to be more a result of their own work, and not the whims of the market. This last point is what I have devoted a good portion of my career to researching and discovering for clients. It was this research that gradually led to the creation of the Hybrid Strategy.

We also try very hard to shrink the range of possible outcomes. That is, we don't want our Hybrid portfolios to have wild swings in their returns. While the stock market tends to gyrate between returns of 20-30% in either direction, we expect much smaller swings. This variation in returns among the best, worst and average periods for an investment defines the often-quoted term, "Standard Deviation". It means what it says: the standard (read "average") deviation ("variation or difference") of a typical period's return from the average return. While Standard Deviation is terribly overused by advisors to represent investment risk (I don't believe that its describing risk at all), it does serve a purpose. It allows us to compare the range of expected returns between Hybrid investments and traditional stock or bond investments.

So, where does the Hybrid Strategy rank on these measures? The returns were far less volatile the stock market, less than half of the returns had to do with the market's movement, and the returns from year to year were in a very tight range when compared to an all-stock portfolio. For a conservative strategy, that's good. In fact, the Standard Deviation for Hybrids is generally closer to the level of a high quality bond index than to the stock market. Bottom line: over the period that Hybrid investing has been formalized, it has done what it set out to do – deliver returns in a fashion that allows the investor to sleep better, knowing that the potential impact of market turmoil has been greatly reduced.

At this point, you are probably saying what people say when we present this strategy to groups of investors or investment advisors, "Enough about what Hybrids have done, tell us more about what they look like"! To end the suspense, here's a pie chart showing how we divide the Hybrid world into pieces. If you have worked with an advisor before, you are no stranger to pie charts, but you have not likely seen one like this unless you were investigating a hedge fund of funds investment. Again, every one of these styles is available in the form of a no-load mutual fund. It may not be in your broker's arsenal because their firm decided they can make more money (for themselves) by packaging a Hedge fund product for you. But I'm here to tell you that you don't need to resort to that.

Fig. 14: HYBRID MUTUAL FUND STYLES

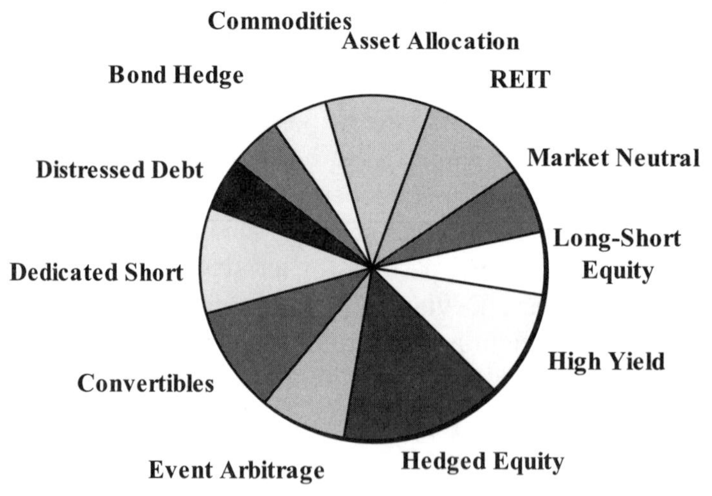

Description of Hybrid Styles Depicted in Figure 14:

o **Equity Market Neutral**

This investment strategy is designed to exploit equity market inefficiencies and usually involves being simultaneously long and short matched equity portfolios of the same size within a country. Market neutral portfolios are designed to be either beta or currency neutral, or both. Well-designed portfolios typically control for industry, sector, market capitalization, and other exposures.

164

o **Long/Short Equity and Hedged Equity**

This directional strategy involves equity-oriented investing on both the long and short sides of the market. The objective is not to be market neutral. Managers have the ability to shift from value to growth, from small to medium to large capitalization stocks, and from a net long position to a net short position. In the Hybrid Strategy, we separate this category into long-short and "hedged equity". The difference is the degree to which they short. A long-short fund typically shorts more than a hedged equity fund.

o **Dedicated Short**

The strategy is to maintain net short as opposed to pure short exposure. Short bias managers take short positions in mostly equities and derivatives.

o **Bond Hedge**

This strategy consists of Funds that short bonds. That is, as interest rates rise, bond prices fall and these funds appreciate in value.

o **High Yield Bonds**

Often called junk bonds, this subset refers to investing in low-graded fixed-income securities of companies that show significant upside potential. Managers generally buy and hold high yield debt.

o **Distressed Debt**

Fund managers invest in the debt, equity or trade claims of companies in financial distress and generally bankruptcy. The securities of companies in need of legal action or restructuring to revive financial stability typically trade at substantial discounts to par value and thereby attract investments when managers perceive a turn-around will materialize.

o **Convertibles**

Funds that invest in bonds and preferred stock issues that are convertible into the stock of the same issuer if the stock reaches certain price level. The convertible therefore has stock and bond features. It is expected to increase in price as the issuer's stock rises, while the bond structure of the convertible may limit its losses when the stock's price falls.

- o **REITs**

Funds that invest in publicly-traded Real Estate Investment Trusts, which are real estate companies that trade on the stock exchanges.

- o **Merger Arbitrage**

Specialists invest simultaneously in long and short positions in both companies involved in a merger or acquisition. Risk arbitrageurs are typically long the stock of the company being acquired and short the stock of the acquirer. The principal risk is deal risk, should the deal fail to close.

- o **Asset Allocation**

In these funds (which are also referred to as "global macro" styles), managers carry long and short positions in any of the world's major capital or derivative markets. These positions reflect their views on overall market direction as influenced by major economic trends and/or events. The portfolios of these funds can include stocks, bonds, currencies, and commodities in the form of cash or derivatives instruments.

- o **Commodities**

Funds that use derivatives or stocks to gain exposure to the performance of a basket of commodities such as energy, metals and grains.

When To Say Bye To Your Buy

As with any portfolio management situation, one of the critical elements of success is having a sell discipline. In fact, not having a good one was the single biggest cause of investor losses in the 2000-2002 stock decline. So, how do we decide when to exit a position in a Hybrid account? There are a few guidelines I follow:

1. The **Price objective is achieved** – when we buy any investment for a client, we feel an obligation to know at what point we will "bail out" on both the upside and downside. This may be based on a combination of the nature of the investment and the client's individual risk tolerance. Either way, if we decide that, say a 10% loss in an individual investment is the maximum pain we are willing to allow, we have to stick to it.

2. **Economic/market changes** – as with any investment in a traditional style such as large cap stocks or muni bonds, changes in the market or economic environment can prompt us to make adjustments in a Hybrid portfolio. However, it is important to understand that these adjustments are a response to long-term changes, not today's latest economic headline. Nothing should be more frustrating to you as an investor than to think that someone is flipping around your hard-earned wealth based on the latest inflation report, jobs report, or economic growth estimate. But if, for instance, interest rates gradually rise for over a year, for the first time in over two decades, that might be something to react to and reposition the portfolio.

   For instance, we along with the rest of our industry were looking for ways to enhance clients' yields when money market rates dropped below 1% in 2004. Two years later, money rates were pushing 4% so the need to get creative in boosting yields on cash was greatly reduced. But also had implications for the high yield bond market. While rates on the safest bonds rose quite a bit, rates on lower quality, "high yield" bonds did not rise as fast. This created what we call a narrowing of bond "spreads". Translated to English, when money markets were at 1% and high yield bonds were at 7%, the latter looked good. When money markets hit close to 4% and high yields were only at 8%, high yield looked less attractive than before. What does all this mean? We watch closely to see if our exposure to high yield bonds in the Hybrid portfolios should be reduced.

3. **Manager changes at a fund** – if a manager leaves, we have to ask ourselves what impact this will have on the ability of a fund to perform in the manner we have been accustomed to. If the manager was part of a strong team, their departure is no big deal. If the whole team leaves it IS a big deal. If the fund is run in a manner that is more mechanical than intuitive on the part of the managers, that would argue for more patience in making a decision to sell the fund. Bottom line: in the majority of cases, the people who created the track record of the fund are more important than the fund company. If they leave, the record of the fund effectively leaves with them.

4. **The fund firm becomes too institutionalized** – this is something that in my opinion has received insufficient attention in my industry. Different money management firms handle success very

differently. There are companies that can grow from managing $250 million to $50 billion in less than a decade, yet maintain the level of experience the client receives. In other cases, cracks in the armor appear as assets grow. As an advisor researching these firms, my team and I have to look for signs that things are not run as they were when the firm was a mere mortal, before it became a superhuman, bureaucratic goliath with national ad campaigns, a well-known spokesperson, etc.

5. **Our investment thesis is wrong…yes, it happens** ☹ - I could write a second book about all of the times I've been wrong about how an investment theme or idea eventually played out. But by acting quickly to limit losses in most of these situations, those mistakes had a low impact on the portfolio's return and no impact on the client's ability to achieve their desired lifestyle. Yes, it bears repeating once again – investing is about getting what you want out of life. Its not a competition with yourself or your friends about how much you can accumulate, and its not about finding what worked in the past for other people and simply mimicking it. If you believe this, then it follows that large losses are the easiest way to screw up an otherwise profitable experience. Admitting your expectations were not accurate, and doing something about it, is the best thing you can do for your portfolio. You advisor should know this too.

Other possible reasons to make a sale include a change in the fund's objective or process, consistently lagging performance for unexplained reasons, tax-related concerns, or in cases where a superior investment has been identified.

I mentioned that we run several portfolios using the Hybrid Strategy and some that don't. Together with my portfolio management team I share the responsibility of maintaining and changing the models. I review each internally managed portfolio on a regular basis, with a focus on consistency with the model and any client-specific requirements. The model portfolios are also reviewed by the team simultaneously so that there can be a clear distinction made between how each is invested. I strive to avoid the problem of having the models mimic each other, preserving the inherent independence of the various sub-strategies.

The concrete, quantitative objective of the Hybrid Strategy is to produce a consistent stream of absolute returns with low market correlation over a minimum rolling 3-year time period. I begin with the idea that the assets clients place under my care are not to simply accumulate, but to fund their future and/or current lifestyle. Many people do not want to see tremendous fluctuation in the possibility that they will achieve their desired lifestyle. It follows, then, that their portfolio should be designed to keep fluctuation in value low, while still maintaining the potential to grow at a competitive rate.

I believe that for most people, investment success is about getting what they want out of their money, not about beating a market index. Thus, most investors can benefit from allocating a portion of their funds to low volatility, absolute return strategies.

Another basic tenet that has formulated my thinking about the use of Hybrids is that traditional asset allocation has many flaws. Too many asset classes tend to look like each other over time. For instance, according to Andex Associates, Inc. in the 20 year period that ended 12/31/04, the annualized returns of Large Cap Stocks, Small Cap Stocks, and Non-US Stocks were within less than two percentage points of each other. Other periods of market history have often shown similar results. Since we don't know in advance whether Small Cap Value, International Growth or something else will perform the best in the next decade, we must ask, "Why bother trying"? When I realized that there were few good answers to this question, I expanded my work on Hybrid investing.

My conclusion: diversifying stocks with other stocks does not always add value to the investment process. Therefore, many investors need to look beyond traditional stock investment styles to fill their growth portfolio.

Fig 15: Stocks plus stocks equals...stocks

	Portfolio 1	Portfolio 2	Portfolio 3
Asset Mix	100% S&P 500	75% S&P 500, 25% Russell 2500	50% S&P 500, 25% Russell 2500, 25% MSCI World ex-US
Annualized 10-Year Return (as of 12/31/05)	9.06%	9.80%	9.14%
Best 3-Year Annualized Return	29.65%	26.35%	23.33%
Worst 3-Year Annualized Return	-16.08%	-14.25%	-15.01%
Beta	1.00	0.98	0.92
R-Squared	100	96	92

Source: Morningstar

On the other hand, I view investing in High-Quality Bonds very differently from much of the advisory industry. To me, bonds issued by the U.S. Government, its agencies and high-quality U.S. corporations and municipalities are NOT a vehicle to use in pursuit of total return. They are best used for preservation of capital and predictable cash flow only. We buy these bonds for their "fixed return" (the rate of interest they pay). Whether the bond price goes up or down after we buy it is not something we are very concerned about, since we know that we are getting our investment back when the bond matures. This approach favors individual bonds over high-quality bond funds. For our individual clients, therefore, we buy individual bonds, not bond funds.

However, bonds other than those we classify as high-quality may have a place in Hybrid portfolios and are often used in our Hybrid strategies. Examples include Convertible and High-Yield ("Junk") bond funds. While I would not recommend a client put all of their assets into speculative fixed income, I view these asset classes as being non-stocks and non-bonds; more of a combination of both. Thus, they fit the Hybrid definition as I apply it.

Fig. 16(a): Traditional

□ Equity

■ Fixed Income

□ Cash

□ Hybrids

Fig. 16(b): Hybridized

□ Equity

■ Fixed Income

□ Cash

□ Hybrids

170

Fig. 16: Traditional vs. Core Hybrids Strategies
Source: Lohr

So, in my opinion, stocks, bonds and cash do not provide adequate diversification in today's market environment. A more flexible approach that includes Hybrid styles is required. Note that very often, Hybrid investing is not a substitute for stock and bond investments. It is a complement to them. In other cases, some of my clients have told me that they are most comfortable in a portfolio that is primarily Hybrid-oriented.

I view Hybrids as the "Core" asset class in our clients' portfolios. Stocks and bonds are secondary, or "Satellite" parts of the overall plan. This is the opposite of how most advisors view the world. This tends to make my strategy very complementary with theirs, though it can also function as a substitute for "traditional" portfolio construction. This difference is expressed graphically above, in Fig. 16. Here, the graphic on the top shows the usual way of doing business, and the graphic below demonstrates my innovative and successful approach.

For one reason I feel strongly about this new approach in today's environment please refer back to the chart information we reviewed briefly in Chapter 3, showing over 200 years of "secular" or long-term trends in the stock market. We can see that secular bull and bear markets each have lasted between 8 and 20 years. A long secular bull market (and the greatest in terms of magnitude) ended in the year 2000. This is now common knowledge. However, the fact that we are only five years into the new secular bear market has us wary that sub-par stock market returns could continue for some time. At the same time, market interest rates have been falling for 25 years. The possibility that this secular trend is reversing is an equal if not greater consideration in portfolio strategy today. This is why Hybrid strategies make so much sense to us. They have proven the ability to persevere through difficult environments for stocks, bonds or both. Put another way, **"there's always a bull market somewhere"**. That somewhere could be in convertible securities, arbitrage strategies or even in shorting a major market (for instance, buying funds that short stocks will allow us to benefit from a falling stock market—i.e. a bull market for shorting). **This shows clearly that the investor's best friend now and always is FLEXIBILITY in the investment process.**

In developing and refining the Hybrid models, I use a combination of fundamental analysis (both top-down and bottom-up), quantitative analysis and technical analysis. Examples of each in the process include:

1. **Top-down:** determination of the allocation to each Hybrid sub-sector.

2. **Bottom-up:** selection of funds that are attractive Hybrid investments.

3. **Quantitative:** factors such as dividend rate, turnover, expense ratio and imbedded unrealized capital gains in a fund are all considered in the evaluation of a fund for the models.

4. **Technical:** once the other screening methods have been completed, charting analysis has been a very useful tool for us to determine the best entry and exit points for a fund, as well as to analyze general market conditions.

The Hybrid Strategy is a discretionary model. While my colleagues and I maintain The Emerald Hybrid Strategy, which we designed as an educational tool to help investors understand the concept of this asset class, we feel that there is much value to be added through an active process. We have not managed the Hybrid models as passive index funds.

As an independent firm, we are able to access a wide range of resources for research and analysis purposes. Also, as I stated at the beginning of this book, I read nearly every trade publication in our industry. In addition, our frequent appearance in the print media has attracted much attention from the hedge fund and mutual fund industries. Firms of all shapes and sizes send information to us about their products. This helps us stay quite current on what is being offered in the less liquid/higher cost/less transparent segment of our peer group, and helps us continually refine the Hybrid strategies.

Hybrid investment evaluation is a cumulative process taking into account stock market valuation ratios (p/e, p/b, yield, etc.), Bond interest rates (from short-term rates through 30-year maturities), Broad and narrow economic indicators (broad such as CPI/PPI, Productivity, Trade and Budget deficits, etc. Narrow such as expected adjustments in ARM mortgages over the next year, for example).

Because our Hybrid Strategy spans such a wide variety of markets, my colleagues and I closely track indicators that have particular relevance to one or more sub-styles within the Hybrid world. For example, Merger and Acquisition activity impacts arbitrage strategies. Corporate default rates impact High Yield bonds, short interest impacts the upside and downside potential of the stock market, and a long list of factors influence commodity prices.

Technical indicators have probably had the biggest influence in our process of finalizing our decisions to buy or sell individual funds. At all times, I try to keep a "Real World" Perspective as to what is going on and the impact on our clients' portfolios. To this end, I often liken the approach we take to what an NFL football team's schedule is like. Each week during the season, the team prepares for its opponent. This is similar to the research process any market participant uses to determine what portfolio actions to take. For the football team, the week's preparations are important, but winning and losing only occurs on Sunday—game day. To the portfolio strategist (us), technical analysis gives us a very good idea of what is likely to happen going forward, or least what the probability of success is. The charts are "Sunday". Because regardless of what pundits say on television, and brokerage firms say in their published commentary, the only thing that ultimately determines whether money is made or lost is the changes in security prices in the markets. This is why we back up every fundamental decision with technical analysis.

While technical analysis has a psychological component to it, we also pay close attention to traditional sentiment indicators. In particular, we have observed that many well-known indicators are counterintuitive. A common example is the variety of investor and market advisor sentiment indicators that consistently show participants to be most bullish right before declines and most bearish at the bottom. A very wise person once said that the markets wring out the maximum amount of pain. As we have seen this proven time and again, we try to look ahead to what is likely to happen next, and not get too caught up in what just happened.

Technical analysis is often our most reliable indicator as to our probability of success, but fundamental and quantitative analysis may tell us that a move we are about to make "looks" right. However, I may find that in looking at the chart, the fund we want to buy is overbought, oversold or somewhere in the middle. I may still decide to buy something that is not at an ideal purchase price, but the allocation will likely be lower than if I felt the current price was more attractive. It is a constant tradeoff between allocating to reduce volatility and market correlation, and trying to buy what individual funds look most attractive at any point in time.

The various non-technical indicators used in analyzing Hybrids also result in differing levels of confidence to us. For instance, if GDP is very strong for a quarter, that quarter is not looked at as a trend. As long-term investors, we put more emphasis on trends that have been established and confirmed, not events that could ultimately be determined to be "outliers" or temporary noise in the long run.

As our process is more than simply producing a quantitative conclusion and acting on it, our indicators and weightings are always subject to change based on new information. Weightings, as with our sell process in general, may change based on factors related to overall market fluctuation, changes of personnel and management at a fund, when we determine that our investment thesis is wrong, or that an idea that we saw high potential for has run its course, or under other circumstances, according to the client's best interests.

Because I focus on Absolute Return, my goal is to make money for my clients regardless of market conditions. Therefore, we are largely environment-neutral. However, from an absolute return standpoint, the portfolios I construct tend to make their highest returns on the "coat tails" of a surging stock market. From a relative return standpoint, the more the stock market declines, the more Hybrid portfolios tend to outperform the broad stock market benchmarks.

While past performance is not an ironclad indicator of future returns, many experts believe that consistent returns of 6-10% per annum over any three-year term are a reasonable expectation for the Hybrid strategy. These figures may be adjusted down or up for a more conservative or aggressive version of the strategy, respectively. However, as I have explained to my clients, targeting a percentage return can backfire if inflation rises. For instance, aiming for 6-10% will do our clients no good if ten-year bond rates go to 13%. Our answer to this, as with many investor concerns, is to strive for maximum portfolio FLEXIBILITY. For example, if inflation skyrockets, having the ability to allocate assets to short the bond market or take a position on the direction of the U.S. dollar, but do so through an SEC-registered mutual fund, is a major advantage of the Hybrid approach over traditional strategies.

For the purposes of comparing the performance of the Hybrid Strategy to other investments over a long-term period, we have constructed the Emerald Hybrid Strategy, a hypothetical portfolio which traces the performance of many of the current Hybrid funds we use backwards in time, to approximate the performance of the Hybrid strategy over years and decades. Based on analysis of these data, several comparisons between the various Emerald Hybrid strategies and a full range of traditional investments can be made.

As mentioned before, the Emerald Hybrid Strategy has experienced a long-term standard deviation of about 4%. While this could certainly change in the future, it is reasonable to expect our Hybrid portfolios to achieve a standard deviation that is no more than that of the S&P 500. Our Turnover historically has been between 25% and 75% per year. That is, we replace between ¼ and ¾ of the portfolio each year. This is influenced by the amount of tax-related transacting we perform during the year, to minimize the capital gains burden on our investors to the extent that it is reasonably possible. We believe the Dow Jones Moderately-Conservative Index (whose goal is to track a portfolio with 40% as much risk as the stock market) is a strong fit as a benchmark. However, we do monitor the Hybrid Strategy versus the S&P 500 (over a complete market cycle), and benchmarks that reflect the performance of traditional "Balanced" funds (such as the Dow Jones and Morningstar Moderate Allocation Indexes). The accumulated data indicates that Hybrid models have been very competitive with the benchmarks over several time periods.

Many of the best performing funds in our portfolios are those whose styles allow for the most flexibility. In other words, if you identify outstanding fund managers AND give them the flexibility to go and make money in a risk-conscious way, they can add tremendous value (Wall Street sometimes calls this "alpha") over traditional investment styles which are more restricted within the "style boxes". This is something we have seen over and over again in our observation of the Hybrid asset class over the years. We understand that part of the process of creating an absolute return strategy involves owning something that will be down in value during the year. Why is this expected? Well, if a portfolio contains strategies that have low correlation to each other as well as the stock market, the chance of all of them going up or all of them going down in the same year is not likely. But by owning a diversified and non-correlated group of assets, we get the smoother returns we are aiming for without having to trade in and out of funds aggressively as in a pure timing strategy.

We also turn this situation to an advantage for our clients by converting these losing positions to tax-losses. Bottom line: the portfolio's short positions insulate it from market volatility. When those short positions lose money, the realization of those losses allows us to offset realized gains from sales and fund distributions that occurred during the year. I view this as another important part of the FLEXIBILITY of the process we use.

175

The Emerald Hybrid Strategy has over 20 years of hypothetical performance, in which an allocation of fifteen mutual funds representing the Hybrid style is analyzed. We have a live track record on actual separate accounts we have run which dates back to March 31, 2003. While the knee-jerk reaction to that last statement might be, "Rob, that's a short track record for the Hybrid Strategy", remember that Hybrid investing as we define it has not been around for very long. While some of the funds we use have been around since the 1970's and 1980's, it was not until 1997 that the door opened wide for this approach to be developed. What happened in 1997? The short-short rule was repealed. For a brief, straightforward summary of the tax law change that led to all the good things we're talking about, here is a section of an overview of the Taxpayer Relief Act of 1997, from none other than Paine Webber (which is now part of UBS). If you want to see this on the web, go to http://www.seaserpent.com/portfolio/web/taxrel97/prov.htm is the link.

---

30 Percent Limitation ("Short-Short" Rule)

The 30 percent limitation on the sale or disposition of securities held for less than three months by regulated investment companies is repealed, effective for tax years beginning after August 5, 1997. The repeal of the short-short rule will allow mutual funds to engage in sophisticated trading techniques involving hedging transactions, selling short and potentially investing in derivatives.

The Hybrid model I originally created years ago has evolved significantly over time, and continues to evolve today. The limited pool of funds we had to choose from in 1998 has grown to over 80 funds and counting. We used to run a single model, and now run several, each providing a separate twist on the Hybrid theme. We have identified numerous additional investable Hybrid styles and funds as time has gone by, and have added them to our research process. We need to be able to adapt to changes in the market, if that means overriding the model then so be it. FLEXIBILITY is key!

And up at the top of the next page is a little whimsical reminder of that, which we borrowed from the slideshow we use to educate investors and investment advisors about the Hybrid Strategy. No, that is not a picture of me from the past (although it could have passed as caricature).

Fig. 17: Hybrid Investing is all about flexibility

Volatilty: How To Make It Your Friend Instead Of Your Enemy

Every investing strategy has its own basic assumptions relating to risk and return. In analyzing risk, I attempt to take a realistic approach. I attempt to make a clear distinction between risk and volatility. We reviewed the idea of combating volatility earlier in the book, and now we'll apply it to Hybrid investing.

If you ask most people what their greatest financial fear is, "needing money to pay for something and not having it" is probably it. That is what we call "risk". It is permanent erosion of capital, as opposed to the wax and wane of the markets. This is something that is personal to each client. In the case of running a customized portfolio for a client, this can be discussed in detail with the client. I closely scrutinize the client profile that I develop with my colleagues for each new account, to make sure it is consistent with what we can reasonably expect to deliver.

Many experts define volatility to be the amount by which a portfolio or security will fluctuate, particularly over periods of time less than two years. This is what most clients likely mean when they talk about risk in their portfolio.

I think risk control starts with a close look at the client's individual circumstances. While I may be simply the strategist and not the client's one-on-one advisor, it is very important to me that the client's investment disposition and expectations are aligned with the style I invest in. That is not only for the client's protection, but also for my own, and that of other involved firms. As professionals, we have a responsibility to ensure that we follow the proper procedures, to dot all of our "I"s and cross all of our "T"s, so to speak.

Within the Hybrid Strategy, the most important risk-control method is the nature of the strategy itself. A central tenet to Hybrid investing is that the combination of funds owned will have several natural offsets to each other. There is some stock shorting in the portfolio that neutralizes risk versus an all-stock portfolio. The use of styles such as arbitrage and market-neutral greatly reduces the impact of stock market movements. The ability to short the bond market or currencies via mutual funds allows us to offset some of the client's exposure to interest-rate sensitive segments of the portfolio.

To summarize, Hybrid investing is a risk-control vehicle to begin with. My job is to make as high a return as is prudently possible, given the natural constraints of the style.

In addition to the numerous aspects of the risk control system noted above, I have established other guidelines, along with my colleagues, to reduce volatility. For example, we do not typically take a position of more than 20% in one fund (at cost) or 25% at market value. We will not invest more than 35% of the fund (at cost) in any one sub-style of Hybrid (REITs, Arbitrage, etc.) except for short equity, which we allow up to 50%. This is for protective, not speculative purposes. We want to reserve the right to shield our clients from a down stock market of historic proportions. We also closely monitor our weightings in each Hybrid sub-style in relation to our weighting in the Emerald Hybrid Index. Extreme discrepancies in portfolio weightings versus the Index (over 10%) may occur for limited periods, but will be watched closely if they are in place.

As you can tell from the description above, the key to this risk-control methodology is also the key to the overall approach: FLEXIBILITY. We do not put hard constraints on ourselves because the motivation for using a Hybrid approach is to minimize the negative aspects of traditional investing. However, despite the flexibility, there is a discipline that we follow to keep portfolio fluctuations as low as possible without significantly impacting growth potential.

When creating or changing a Hybrid portfolio, it is necessary to consider the possibility of a worst-case scenario. We run back-tests of our models to see what their worst case has been then make a discretionary judgment as to what could make it worse. For instance, the vast majority of strategists in the business today did not manage money during the last sustained period of rising interest rates (which ended 25 years ago). We also analyze past trades to see why they worked or didn't work in this model. We look at what the technical analysis was telling us as well as the fundamental analysis. What we look for is to make sure our thought process is consistent (though this does not mean we were always correct in our analysis). We have been preparing for the possibility that the rules of investing as this generation knows them will change if the secular decline in rates has finally reversed itself. Past history may not reflect what will happen in the future but it certainly can be one factor in our modeling process – so we use it. We also analyze past trades to see why they worked or didn't work in this model. We look at what the technical analysis was telling us as well as the fundamental analysis. What we look for is to make sure our thought process is consistent (though this does not mean we were always correct in our analysis).

We do not use optimization models but we do run our models through a back-test system as described above. When we do this, we are looking particularly for data such as best/worst performance in a period, alpha, beta and R-squared. That is, our volatility control measures and the portfolio's potential to deliver returns not highly-correlated to the stock market.

Managing portfolios in this "alternative" fashion is something we, have been doing since before it was fashionable. In fact, we still don't see that the advisory business has been nearly as active in the Hybrid asset class as they should be. We believe we are ahead of our industry because we have become very familiar with who the Hybrid managers are, which ones have a process that promotes success, and where to look next for opportunity. In addition the balancing act we refer to within the portfolio (allocating to a number of strategies that are influenced very differently by the same market events) is something that can only come with experience, in our opinion. As the creators of a very comprehensive Hybrid portfolio strategy, we feel that we are in as good a position as any advisor in the industry to direct portfolios of this nature.

So, Hybrid portfolios are in the business of reducing pain while still allowing for great progress. The natural balancing of many different and uncorrelated investment styles within the same portfolio provides a strong solution for those investors who are concerned about their financial future hanging on where the stock market and interest rates go next. **I feel we provide an all-weather portfolio which can be appropriate for many investor needs. Because of our relatively long experience, we believe we will be on the cutting edge as this investment strategy continues to evolve and gain ground.**

CHAPTER 11: MAJOR LEAGUE SOLUTIONS

"It ain't over 'til it's over" Casey Stengel

In T-ball as in life...

When you walk into my office, one of the first things you notice is the wall full of baseball-themed items. Baseball is my favorite sport. Not simply because I enjoy the game, and because taking my kids to several games a year allows me to hand down my love of the game to them. One of the things I enjoy most about baseball is the nuances of the game. There is clearly a right way to play the sport to be successful, and I enjoy seeing plays executed correctly, even if it is the other team doing it.

I do not consider myself to be just a casual fan. I go to games in the rain and heat (there is plenty of both in South Florida). I've taken my kids to playoff games, giveaway days and doubleheaders. But I've also taken them to games when our team, the Marlins, were terrible. I've even taken them to the annual game in which dogs are invited to attend, in exchange for a small donation to the Humane Society. The team used to call this "Dog Day Afternoon", and when it switched it to an evening event, it became "Bark at the Park". And who can blame them for that. In South Florida, in the summer heat, the vendors were not the only ones with hot dogs to take care of!

As my kids reached elementary school age, Dana and I joined the legions of parents who encouraged their kids to play team sports. In the case of my son Tyler, it was an easy task. He likes baseball almost as much as I do. From the time he was four, he was playing ball on a team and I have coached his team. I can't help but notice a great number of similarities between people's approach to their investment portfolios and the way baseball games are played. This is true even at the T-ball level, with four and five year olds, not major leaguers, running around.

Here's a prime example of this. In T-ball, the children put a soft, rubberized baseball on a stand which looks like a three-foot high golf tee. They line their bat up with the ball and then hit it. At that point, the ball is in play just as in a regular baseball game. That's when the fun starts.

Typically, the team in the field swarms around the ball. Regardless of which fielding position they were playing before the hit, it becomes a mad scramble for this piece of gold that jumped (or dribbled) off the hitter's bat. Rarely are outs made, and when they are, its often because the hitter or one of the runners forgot to run to the next base (or the coach was not paying attention). It's a thrill for the parents, the kids learn to have fun and get along as a team, and during the course of the season, they learn a bit about the game. The analogy I see in investing is the way that the kids all run to the ball. Even in the remote possibility that they all get to it quickly, what will happen next? There's no one to cover the base to throw it to, so no outs will be made. In other words, they are playing for the moment, with no regard for the consequences of their actions, or any forethought as to what will happen next.

They should act this way. They are little kids, not accomplished baseball players. They are not thinking about getting the lead runner out to keep a force play in order, or backing up a throw in case it gets past the player in front of them. It will be years before any of this will matter, and by then many of them will not be playing organized baseball anymore.

Now, think about investors. Like T-ball kids, they also tend to move in packs. They often succumb to doing what all the other "kids" are doing as they perceive safety in numbers. They are certainly not thinking more than one step ahead. Their attention can easily be taken "off the ball" by insignificant, extraneous items. When we interview prospective clients, we often ask them what their reaction would be if they received their monthly statement and their portfolio was down 10%. In addition to different levels of concern they might express, one of the choices we give them is to ask if it is time to increase their investment in what went down. Many people laugh at this suggestion, and really do think it is in there as a joke. But we don't joke about things like this.

I am not saying that one should automatically buy more of a security that has fallen in price. There is great debate among investment professionals. Some will say, "Never buy something that you already have a loss on", and others counter with, "If you liked the stock at $40 a share, you should like it even more at $35 a share". My answer is not as black and white. This type of question must be answered in the context of the overall portfolio and objective of the particular client. Or, if the decision is being made by the manager of a pooled investment such as a mutual fund, it should depend on what is most consistent with the objective and approach of the fund. In any case, simply dismissing all investments as "good or bad" ones ignores the context which is such a vital part of all investment decision-making. We emphasize over and over to our clients that a portfolio should be judged in its entirety, not by pulling out the parts that worked best or failed the greatest. That's what asset allocation is. And even though I practice a different version of it than most advisors, the validity of this mental approach to portfolio management is no different.

There are so many other baseball analogies to the management of wealth. It has even been suggested to me that it would make an interesting book. Well, I'll work on that one and get back to you! For now, simply remember this when you are tempted to make an investment decision based on what the crowd is doing: do you want to think like a major leaguer, or like a T-ball player?

Long Term Investing: Patience, Skill And The New York Yankees

Investing is much more like a professional baseball season than a professional football season. In football, there are only 16 games so they are all critical. In baseball, the pros play 162 times, leaving much room to succeed through the ups and downs of a season. In fact, the 1998 New York Yankees lost their first four games, then recovered to post the best season in nearly 50 years! The team didn't panic and change its strategy one week into the season. They played through the tough times and in the "long-run" of the season, came out on top. Investors can learn a lot from this.

"Long Term Investing" has many interpretations these days. Ask a day-trader, and you may hear, "I'm a long term investor; I buy a stock on Monday and don't sell out until just before the weekend". Others hire a money manager and say, "I'll see how it goes for a year. If you don't beat the S&P 500, I'll find someone else".

Both of these attitudes have nothing to do with long-term investing. They have more to do with impatience and lack of investment education. So what is long term investing in the stock market? I say it starts when you readily agree to the following statements:

1. I don't need to use the money for at least 5 years.

2. I understand that the only thing that matters is that when it is time to use the money, it has grown to an amount I am comfortable with.

3. I realize that in any one year, a money manager can falter because of things beyond their control (e.g. Value managers in 1999, when fast-moving tech stocks ruled the market).

4. I make changes to my portfolio based on what I expect to occur in the next several years, not weeks or months.

5. If I take an aggressive approach (like having 75% of my portfolio in tech stocks), I am prepared to ride out several large, temporary declines on the way to achieving my objectives.

6. I look at my portfolio's value no more than once a month (or if I look more frequently, I don't get emotional about it – its just a quick update as part of my daily or weekly routine).

Still not convinced that everyone shouldn't just trade their way to riches? A study published in the Journal of Portfolio Management found that the more investors trade, the more they reduce their expected returns. In fact, the authors concluded from studying the activity of 10,000 brokerage accounts that traders who have early success become overconfident, begin to trade more actively, act on their "misguided convictions" and reduce their returns (As reported in "The Courage of Misguided Convictions," by Brad M. Barber and Terrance Odean, published in *The Journal of Portfolio Management*, November / December, 1999). Next time you feel the urge to join them, remember the 1998 Yankees!

Fig. 19: The 1998 New York Yankees

1998 New York Yankees
Won-Lost Record: 114-48
Finished 1st in AL Eastern Division

Game	Date	Team	Opponent	Result	Score	W-L
1	1998-04-01	NYY	@Anaheim	Lost	1-4	0-1
2	1998-	NYY	@Anaheim	Lost	2-10	0-2

	04-02					
3	1998-04-04	NYY	@Oakland	Lost	3-7	0-3

Source: Baseball-Reference.com

Cobb-A-Cola

Ty Cobb, perhaps the most talented baseball player of all time, made very little money playing ball. He played in the early 1900's when baseball was not a way to get rich. However, the Georgia-born Cobb started buying shares of an Atlanta-based company by the name of Coca Cola at a young age, and it helped him become a very successful businessman. He is also regarded as one of the nastiest, most disgraceful people to play the game, but that's not the point here. But as an aside, if you want to see the good and bad of a fascinating life, rent the move "Cobb" starring Tommy Lee Jones. I know many people who said they could not appreciate the movie because they were so repulsed by how Cobb was portrayed, but I really enjoyed it. See for yourself.

The following is from the National Baseball Hall of Fame's official website, and tells the story of how the man known as the "Georgia Peach" came to make millions.

A shrewd businessman, Cobb bought his first stock in the Atlanta-based soft drink company in 1918 at the suggestion of friend Robert Woodruff, the son of the president of Coca-Cola and later himself the leader of the company for more than six decades. Cobb took out a loan against his future baseball earnings to buy his first 1,000 shares and continued to invest in Coca-Cola throughout his lifetime. Quickly, Cobb and Woodruff developed a close relationship, harbored by their common Georgian heritage — Woodruff a native of Atlanta. Like Cobb, Woodruff was a sportsman and an intense competitor, and he would often invite Cobb to go quail hunting on his 30,000 acre hunting plantation in Ichauway, Georgia.

Cobb's Coca-Cola investments paid off handsomely, helping to make him one of the first athletes to become independently wealthy. In sharp contrast to other athletes who squandered their money and retired broke, Cobb built an enormous fortune over the course of his playing career and beyond. Confident in Coca-Cola, Cobb encouraged his friends and family to invest in the "Pause that Refreshes," as well. Future Hall of Fame second baseman Charlie Gehringer, who debuted as a rookie with Detroit under Cobb's leadership in 1924, recalled that Cobb would give the younger players financial advice. "He told us about Coca-Cola and egged us on to buy the stock, but we weren't making enough money to buy shares," Gehringer recalled years later.

One of baseball's highest paid players, Cobb continued to put money into the company, later purchasing three Coca-Cola bottling plants, in Santa Maria, California, Twin Falls, Idaho and Bend, Oregon. Eventually he would own more than 20,000 shares of Coca-Cola stock, making him one of the major stockholders in the company and earning him a place on the board of directors. As the company grew, Cobb's fortune swelled. At the time of his death in 1961, Cobb's estimated worth was between $10 and $12 million, "a large volume of it generated by Coca-Cola stock," according to Coca-Cola spokesman Phil Mooney. Due, in large part, to these investments, Cobb was able to establish the Cobb Educational Foundation of Atlanta, which paid college tuition for thousands of young people, and to build the Cobb Memorial Hospital of Royston, Georgia, just a few miles from his home town.

I am not endorsing the idea of a one-stock portfolio, and I'm not suggesting you conduct yourself the way Cobb did on the field (allegedly the dirtiest player of his era). But I have come to the conclusion that to be successful in a stock portfolio over a long period of time, you are better off having your manager own 10-20 stocks at a time instead of 50-100. Academic research tends to back this up. Several studies have shown that in traditional stock investing (i.e. just owning stocks, and without using hedging techniques), the advantages of diversification are minimal beyond a twenty stock portfolio. Adding more stocks does not reduce volatility very much, and it dampens the positive impact of your biggest winners. So, why bother? Ask the trillions of dollars residing in overly-diversified stock portfolios, and the people that bought or recommended them. I readily admit that I was part of that group for some time, but I feel my clients and I are much better off for my having seen the light. In fact, I have come up with a term for portfolios that have effectively diversified away any chance to do anything but track the broad stock market—"De-worsification". But with the average mutual fund owning over 100 stocks and the average separate account likely holding about 50, what's an investor to do? The answer, in my opinion, is the same answer as how to avoid a car accident, solve a tough math problem or avoid pissing off your spouse because you didn't listen to a word they said (Dana knows this one well from dealing with me since 1990).

Concentrated managers approach equity investing in much the same way as private equity investors do. They take a very close look at management's intentions and plans to execute their business strategy, and make sure it is consistent with what is in the best interests of shareholders. Many leaders of concentrated portfolio management firms have been very willing to pursue "activist" investment strategies, whereby they put pressure on management to do the right thing on behalf of the shareholders, the owners of the business, if they think that this might not be happening. This is also common in the private equity arena. I find that when I present the idea of concentrated equity management to professionals in the private equity world, they "get it" immediately. It's something they can relate to. The same goes for people who have been in a situation where one or two stocks comprise the majority of their net worth (often because they ran a public company or were bought by one and received stock). And while there is often greater volatility with a concentrated portfolio, in the right hands this is NOT the same thing as having more risk. To remind you, my definition of risk is permanent loss of capital, or needing money and you don't have it. Superior concentrated managers have such a strong "batting average" in their stock selection that this risk is probably a lot less than with a traditional, over-diversified equity manager. Look no further than one of the most famous concentrated investors in the U.S, Warren Buffet, who said "wide diversification is only required when investors do not understand what they are doing". There's nothing else to say on this subject except I'll drink (a Coca-Cola) to that.

"Capturing" Profits – Separating Statistics From Reality

So if we want think like major leaguers, breaking down a manager's record between good and bad market environments is a critical part of the analysis. To perform this work, we study databases that separate a manager's benchmark index into calendar quarters in which the index rose or fell. Next, we separate the manager's performance in those good and bad quarters for the market. The result is a "Capture Ratio".

I first described this in an article I wrote to my clients not long before the stock market started to fall apart in 2000, reproduced in part below. At that time, many of the best traditional stock managers were doing extremely well in both up markets and down markets. In fact, many managers who, on the surface, appeared to have aggressive strategies, actually were doing better in the tough quarters than more conservative firms. This is NOT normal and as time went on, people saw why.

During the height of the bull market from 1995-1999, technology stocks performed very well in good markets. That's no surprise. What was shocking was how well tech did in the down markets. If you read between the lines, and think back to that time (if you were an investor then), you realize that tech stocks were so highly regarded back then, people were hesitant to sell them as vigorously as other sectors of the market. As a result, they lost a lot less than the market during the few down quarters that actually occurred during that period.

What's the takeaway on this? That the Capture Ratios used by many aggressive money managers were not a good indicator of how these firms would do in a prolonged down market since they hadn't seen one in over a decade! I cautioned clients about this back then, and boy did those observations and warnings ever help!

For example, the two hypothetical managers depicted on the chart below have identical 10-year performance; however, their performance was achieved very differently over this period.

Manager	Annualized 10-Year Return	Up Capture Ratio	Down Capture Ratio	# Up Quarters	# Down Quarters
Manager A	11%	130%	120%	30	10
Manager B	11%	85%	50%	35	5

Fig. 20: Comparison Of Hypothetical Managers

Manager A has "captured" 130% of the market's move in calendar quarters in which the market was positive. In other words, for every 10% gain in the market, they have made 13%. Similarly, they have lost 12% for every 10% in the market's down quarters.

Manager B didn't do as well in up quarters, performing slightly under the market (85% Up Capture, or 8.5% for every 10% upward move in the market). However, they preserved capital much better than Manager A in down markets. Manager B also had only 5 down quarters in 10 years, while A had twice as many.

Which Is Better?

It depends on who you are as an investor. Both types can be effective, and they can even co-exist in your portfolio. However, the ride you take toward long-term success will be very different. More aggressive investors will want more of their portfolio to be invested in managers like A. However, if the next 10 years are not as strong as the past 10, managers like B may fare better than A, since their style is expected to hold its ground better in tough markets. This will cause more conservative investors to flock toward managers like B for the majority of their assets.

The bottom line is that this is a big part of the advisor's job. Capture Ratio information and other types of detailed data on money managers is expensive to access and difficult to interpret. This is the type of insight that only a well-trained advisor (notice I did not say salesman at a major national investment firm) can readily interpret and act on with you.

CHAPTER 12: WHAT DO YOU LOOK FOR IN AN ADVISOR?

"Honesty is such a lonely word. Everyone is so untrue. Honesty is hardly ever heard, but mostly what I need from you." – Billy Joel (who, as far as I know, was NOT thinking of his investment advisor when he wrote it)

If I have a mantra, then I think it's summed up in this line, taken from a Worth Magazine article from 2004: "If you go into a bank, and they give you a Chinese menu, that gives a client a lot of choice, but not what baby boomers are coming in to buy…they are worried about life problems, and they want someone who can relate to them."

When some people enter into investing, what they really want out of it is income without work. They want to see that they are making money every day. They are looking for instant financial gratification. They really don't have any long-term goals. This is a dangerous approach—it shows a gambler's mentality, not an investor's.

I want to take the time to get to know my client, and understand the objectives, the emotions and the motivations of their driving forces. Only then, I believe, can one do justice to clients as their financial advisor. I don't take an "Ivory Tower approach", but rather look on our investing horizon as a partnership. I want the client to think it is perhaps wiser to look towards the future enjoyment of their money rather than the immediate dollar value. It isn't as if the numbers on the statements or on the quarterly reports are increasing *in and of themselves*. Money is, after all, worth only what one can get out of it. A wise investor is willing to put aside immediacy in exchange for the ultimate realization of specific and carefully planned goals—to achieve financial independence, to retire early, to pay for college and medical school, or whatever.

My job is to help my clients become wiser investors, even if that simply means they develop only a broad understanding of what we are trying to accomplish – often that's all it takes for the relationship to work. In this way, I really view myself as an educator, albeit one with a passion for the business of financial advising. One of the key points I think an investor should understand is that investing is a means to an end, not an end in and of itself. Again, if the client and advisor are working as a team, the client's main job is to communicate what kind of lifestyle they want to get out of their wealth. The advisor's job is to figure out how to deliver that dream with the highest probability of success.

Do not allow yourself to get stuffed into a standard-shaped box. Find an advisor who will take a wide range of materials at their disposal and build a box just for you, with whatever shape you and they judge to be the best fit.

How Should You Interview An Advisor?

I think that when meeting an advisor for the first time, many investors don't know what to ask. As a result, if they are in the wrong hands at the beginning of the discussion, their potential disappointment will be at the back end of the relationship – when it costs them money, as their portfolio did something they did not expect it to do. I created this "due diligence questionnaire" in 1998, and we provide it to prospective clients at our first meeting. I think it helps them to focus on the new discussion and minimizes the chance that an important issue will not be covered.

Questions You Should Ask An Investment Firm Before You Become A Client (Or, "Why Should I Hire You To Manage My Money?")/

1. What is your firm's experience in the investment management industry?

2. What is the experience of the advisor(s) who will be working with me?

3. What is your approach to managing assets?

    a. What determines how a portfolio is structured?

    b. What use is made of Asset Allocation Strategies?

    c. If current income is an objective, how is it pursued?

    d. How are taxes controlled in your management process?

    e. How personalized is the portfolio construction?

    f. How are risk and volatility controlled?

191

4. What information and technology is used to create, analyze and monitor portfolios?

5. How is my current portfolio converted into one you create for me?

6. What input do I have into the conversion and ongoing management process?

7. Who holds my assets? How do I know my money is safe?

8. How and when do you communicate with me after I am a client?

9. How many client relationships do you manage?

10. Who are your competitors? How are you similar/different?

11. If you use money managers for my portfolio, what type of access do you and I have to them?

12. How do I know your advice is objective? (i.e. that you put my goals ahead of your firm's)

13. What does it cost to invest with your firm? Which assets are subject to fees/commissions, and which aren't?

Similarly, We As Financial Advisors Should Ask YOU, The Client Questions Like These:

1. What is the ultimate purpose for these funds?

2. If your portfolio were down 10%, how uncomfortable would you be?

3. What is your time horizon? By the way, if you can't invest for 3 or more years, you probably should just put it in a checking account at the bank.

4. Who do you look to for investment information?

5. How much do you think you need to achieve your goals?

6. How often do you feel you need to communicate with your advisor?

7. Do you have any issues with giving a professional discretion to manage your portfolio?

8. Are you O.K. with not getting confirmations on transactions?

9. What are your current investments?

Investing is a two way street. If you're using a driver, make sure they know the way. If you're driving yourself, buy a GPS!

Best Practices Of Investment Advisors – My Opinion

Here are some additional thoughts about how I think investment advisors can best serve their clients. As you might expect, these are also features of my firm's approach, process and philosophy.

We operate our investment advisory business in the manner we believe investors are really looking for. At our firm, portfolios are team-managed, though one primary advisor is assigned to each client relationship. I think that this gives us the best chance to deliver a high level of personal attention.

I think an advisor is best thought of as their client's "Investment Quarterback", but they should be equally comfortable as "Role Players" within the overall portfolio. A diverse array of backgrounds among partners and staff allows the best firms to find that "good fit" with many different types of client backgrounds and requirements

I strongly believe that independent firms have an excellent vantage point to review someone's existing portfolio. My team and I have collectively analyzed thousands over our careers, and we have a solid understanding of how to separate what is consistent with the client's interests versus what is more likely to benefit the advisor and their firm. In the months leading up to the stock market's peak in 2000, we saw countless portfolios managed elsewhere that were not nearly on the same page as the client's stated goals. When you think about it, how can you reasonably expect to have the perspective that a professional has when you have analyzed one portfolio (yours) in your lifetime, if they have seen thousands? It's like assuming you know more about a strange-looking lump on your arm than a doctor does.

When someone requests an initial meeting with us, we suggest that they send their existing portfolio statements to us to review prior to our getting together (at no charge, of course). We do this for several reasons. First, it allows us to comment on the portfolio with no biases – we don't know much about what the client is trying to do. Based on our review, we can enter the first in-person meeting knowing what your portfolio is trying to do. If, in our discussion, it turns out the client's objectives are not consistent with the portfolio, there's obviously a deeper discussion needed. I think that's a healthier way to approach the start of a relationship than just talking about the future.

I think that any advisor should feel that, just as the client is interviewing them to see if there is a good fit, so too should the advisor be evaluating the prospective client. That's why the question list shown earlier in this chapter has two parts. And if you are the investor, you should want that! If you work with someone who eagerly takes on all comers, guess what? You are working with a salesman. The best advisors have been around long enough to know what works, and how to spot a relationship that will not work for one side or the other. In fact, we have had a few situations over the years where we actually decided to release a client from their agreement with us because we no longer wanted to work with them. I don't know how common this is in the business, but my guess is it doesn't happen often.

Let's face it: life is too short to keep room for business relationships that for one reason or another are not functional. Our position has always been that if we can help you, let's go for it. If you don't understand the value we add, there's no need to prolong the mutual agony. Hopefully its refreshing to you to hear someone in my industry talk like this.

Mr. And Ms. Client, You're Fired…No, Really, You're Fired

Don't get the idea that we look for reasons to play Donald Trump with clients ("You're fired!"). We go to great lengths to try to educate our clients about why decisions are being made, what we believe is a real problem that will impact their wealth, and what is short-term noise to disregard. We help them understand the variety of traditional as well as funky investment styles we employ to get the job done. But sometimes, the connection just does not happen, in spite of the best efforts of all involved. Here are some examples that we present in hopes you will learn something from our experiences, just as we have.

Two Psychological War Stories

I'd like to think that my team and I do a good enough job for our clients that they do not feel the need to go elsewhere. Fortunately, our client retention rate is extremely high. I tend to hear the same from other independent advisors. I think that our working in an environment free of the usual conflicts of interest that shackle most brokers and trust companies is a big reason for that.

Typically when clients do leave it is because they decide they want to invest on their own without an advisor (we've had some do that and return a year or two later), or they find someone who has a seemingly magical formula that they believe will make them a lot of money. Two client departure stories in particular are, in my opinion, so bizarre that I felt they should be shared in this book-briefly, and without any references to names. I just want to show what can happen when people get certain inaccurate ideas in their head. Before you decide that any story about an advisor losing a client is some version of "sour grapes", read these.

The first case was the family who refused to meet with us to discuss their portfolio, then decided to leave because they felt we were not meeting their investment objectives. Over the course of more than a year and a half, we tried via phone, letter and email to convince these folks that we should get together and communicate about their wealth and our management of it. We use regular meetings to review hard numbers such as performance and holdings, and this family did not feel that much was accomplished by doing that. However, the most important part of the review meeting with any advisor is the opportunity to update them on changes in your life that could impact how your money is invested. Experienced advisors are particularly skilled at identifying portfolio-impacting news from a client. Often, a discussion that you may think is just shooting the breeze and "relationship-building" on the part of the advisor is actually an attempt to make sure that new, key information will not be ignored. Now, I know that in some areas of Wall Street, the review meeting is just an excuse to get in front of you to sell you something. That's not what I'm talking about here. This is a straightforward way of making sure we don't later regret that we were not in close enough touch with the life and lifestyle circumstances that a portfolio is based on.

The other part of this client-exit story that was so tough for us to understand is that at the time, this family's assets were managed by us on a "non-discretionary" basis. That is, we could not make any changes to their portfolio without their prior approval. That, combined with a lack of response to our multiple communications to them resulted in a "catch-22" situation. We wanted to get together to see if changes needed to be made, the client would not meet with us, and we could not act without them.

This is one of the events that caused my partners and me to move our business toward a discretionary service where the client authorizes us at the beginning of the relationship to buy and sell securities within their portfolio on their behalf. When we use outside money management firms for part of the portfolio, they also have discretion, but we can't replace a manager without client consent (though the client has the option to give us discretion to do that too). As the years have gone on, I have noticed a trend away from the client watching our every move as if they were managing the portfolio themselves. The majority of our clients are too busy to take on a second career (managing their money). They want bottom-line reporting, updates on a regular basis (but not constantly), and ready-access to their advisory team. The days of talking to your stockbroker three times a week about your stocks and entertain "pitches" of new ideas have faded, and are nearly gone. In my opinion, that's to everyone's benefit. If you trust your advisor's ability to deliver for you, the best way to allow them to do that is to let them run your portfolio's day-to-day operations-your Chief Investment Officer. You sit back and be the "chairperson" of the company you call "my portfolio".

The second client exit story worthy of inclusion in this book is one that boiled down to the advisor and client not speaking the same language. I don't mean this literally. I speak enough Spanish to get by and I can count to 10 in Japanese, but that's about it. This client's primary language, like mine, is English. But sometimes, for reasons I honestly cannot explain, my words of advice and education don't get absorbed by the client, and their objections don't make sense to me. It is like we speak different languages.

The issue that caused the client to leave had to do with their portfolio's overall performance. Their account had a large percentage of assets in one stock, which they had bought a very long time ago for about $10 a share. Since the stock was held in a taxable account, any sales of stock would be subject to large capital gains taxes. From the inception of the relationship, the client and I identified this as a significant hurdle to diversifying their assets. My solution for most (but not all) of their shares was to place an "option-collar" around the stock price. This would limit the loss and gain the client could experience from the stock over the next couple of years.

For instance, for a stock selling for $50 a share at that time, market conditions might lock in a range over the following two years of $45-$60, with no out of pocket cost (I'll spare the details here as they are not pertinent to the story). They were planning to retire in about two years so in my mind, protecting the downside risk of the stock plummeting was the number one objective. Once they retired, the stock could be sold off if needed, hopefully at a higher price than today, but with the comfort of knowing that they had established a "worst-case" scenario for the downside. Not doing this would open the client up to the possibility of the stock falling, let's say to $30 or worse. Without option protection on the stock, the client would have lost 40% on their largest holding. In hindsight, they would have been better off selling the stock when it was at $50, which at a 15% long-term capital gains rate would have generated $6 a share in capital gains tax, netting them $44. Of course, if the stock were at $30 and they sold it they'd still have to pay the tax on the gain they had since they bought it years ago, netting about $27 a share after tax. Hopefully you can see the difference in having the protection.

This option transaction saved the client a lot of money. However, as time went on, their life situation changed and they needed some of the money tied up in this stock to fund a large purchase of something. I explained to them that while selling some of the stock was necessary, given the facts they gave to me, they would incur some capital gains taxes as a result. The stock subject to the option collar was unaffected by this. They understood and agreed, and a portion of their stock was sold.

Then came the strange part. During the following year, the client told me that they were moving their assets to a trust company. I asked why and was told that they did not like the fact that they had to pay so much in taxes on the sale of their stock the previous year. I reminded them that with highly appreciated stock, selling causes taxes. I then asked them how the trust company was going to handle the remaining stock position. When they told me that the plan was to sell the stock immediately to invest in other stocks, I was floored! For some reason, paying some taxes in their account with me was less attractive than paying more in tax through another institution. Like I said, sometimes we speak different languages.

The bottom line: make sure that you are on the same page with your advisor. When even a slight deviation in thinking occurs, address it.

The lesson from the war stories and that to be learned from investor psychology is to not be over-reactive, be patient, and as we have said repeatedly here, "Have a plan, and stick to it".

What Else Should You Look For In A Financial Advisor?

We've talked a lot here about what to watch out for, and less about what to seek in an advisor. If you've read this far, then what I'm saying must hit home with you from personal experience or at least curiosity. So let's conclude by pointing out some of the other essential qualities you should seek in a true advisor.

Believe it or not, an advisor who does not wax poetic about how you've performed in a short period of time (say, two years or less) is OK. Let me repeat: It is OK if your advisor is not a short-term performance hawk. Think about it: if your portfolio were to grow by 2% in a year in which your friends all made 12% in the stock market, does that mean that your advisor is a dunce? The reverse is true as well. A great start to your portfolio's performance with an advisor is not a signal that you have unearthed some kind of genius, and now must throw all of your money into what they are doing for you. Here's the point: Your advisor's job is to meet your specific objectives over the time period you need to meet them. And "making money this year" is not an objective; that's a game you play. Choose an advisor who discourages you from playing this game, or who is willing to vigorously talk you out of playing when you tell them you want to. I'd even encourage you to test the advisors you interview. Ask them how much they think they can make for you in the next six months. How they answer it will tell you much about whether they are an advisor or a "player" (i.e. someone who plays with your money instead of investing it). You have worked too hard to earn your wealth to put it in the hands of the latter.

Unfortunately, there are many players in the field of wealth management.

You want one that is unconflicted. There are typically two ways that financial professionals are compensated for their services: either by fee or on commission. In some cases, a broker working on commission may feel encouraged to trade at an unreasonable rate, simply because he is being paid per trade. Think of it like the "paycheck running out before the end of the month syndrome". Commissions are archaic—Why should you pay your trusted financial advisor on piecework? Furthermore, the commissioned salesperson has little incentive to perform independent due diligence or provide service and analysis for existing accounts, because these duties do not increase his or her personal revenue stream. This is a mistake in focus—the money does not belong to the broker—it's "Somebody else's money". The money belongs to the client.

While the broker should certainly be paid a reasonable fee for their services, if anyone is going to get rich off of the investments involved, it should be the client. An industry friend of mine years ago wrote a great little article about sitting on the same side of the table as clients. He called it, "Where are the customer's yachts"? For an advisor who does fee-based business, the incentive is turned around—he has good reason to ensure that his client's assets grow, since he is being paid a percentage of those assets. He can trade once a year or three times an hour, and it has no direct effect on his revenue stream. The only he makes more money is if his clients make more money.

The explosive growth of the managed money market in the past few decades has changed the way accounts are handled. Nowadays, everything is designed for efficiency. Less time spent on personalization, which is how it was years ago. The bull market of the 1980s and 1990s fostered greed, which made the idea of specifically matching a portfolio to a specific investor's needs too time consuming. Avoid any vestiges of that mentality.

Some investment professionals, even entire firms, appear willing to do or say anything to get a client to sign up without being too scrupulous about whether or not what they were selling had anything to do with what services they actually provide. This is like a politician lying to get into office. Once they have the votes, they are all too eager to forget why those votes were given. This may produce momentary and immediate results, but the long-term prospects of any politician trying to base a career on promising to be all things for all people are not very stable. Likewise, a broker or office that is willing to bend over backward to get assets in the door may not be able to deliver on their promises. Paradoxically, the more effort that is put into the sale, the less effort is put into providing quality service and delivering consistent return for clients. This breeds public mistrust, and gives a bad name to everyone in the industry.

Look for an advisor that understands that a lot of their work is a commodity. They should recognize that what is far more important to you is to focus on where you want to get to in life and how your money is a means to that end. How you get there is far less important than getting there. There are very few "magic bullets" on Wall Street – strategies that are available to only a select group of individuals. At the same time, financial firms seem to have fallen in love with the concept of "mass-customization", where they present something that looks far more unique than it is.

Here's an example. 15 years ago the industry fell in love with "wrap accounts" in which a professional money management firm with, say a $10mm account minimum would manage your account for a mere $100,000 investment. The panache and exclusivity was a turn-on to many investors. Over time, many of them came to realize that to a large extent, what they really had was a portfolio run more by computers than people, and that the people who were involved had no idea who the client was and didn't really care. Investor access to hedge funds is heading in the exact same direction as we speak. Having an advisor that understands both the opportunities and limitations of the environment they work in is extremely valuable to you. At the same time, just because some of the investment choices are similar does not mean that the advice has to be one-size-fits-all. Milk should be homogenized, wealth advice should not be. Again, if you can find an advisor who gets this, it probably means that their relationship with you will be deeper and more meaningful than the figures that appear on your statement each month.

Selecting a wealth advisor is no easy task. But then again, most things in life that are worthwhile are not achieved easily. You know that from your own experience. By the time we hit our late 30's, we have developed our own "core competencies", a skill set that allows us to see through the industry we work in, as if we had X-Ray vision. Think about how much you know about the field or fields you are most familiar with. Where do you have X-Ray vision? Then, seek out someone who has the vision to take what you have created for yourself and your family, adopt your passion for what's best for you, and work with you to navigate the financial hurdles life will inevitably throw at you. I wish you the best in your efforts.

Making It Work

So, how do you make the client-advisor marriage work? From my vantage point, here's what I see:

An advisor should be looking for clients that "get" what they do and see what makes them different – the best relationships are when we find that "good fit". At our place, we strive to create a "Multi-Family Office" environment. Clients feel at home at our office and get to know the partners and staff well.

Advisors should develop a tradition of investing back into the business to provide the latest technology and research capabilities. This is important in an age where technology advances continuously by leaps and bounds.

Advisors must respect the privacy and security of your personal information. Confidentiality is the golden rule of our business!

Advisors should use a reputable asset custodian, and use more than one if the situation calls for it.

I started each chapter of this book with a favorite quote of mine. I"ll end this chapter with another one.

"I came to realize that a life lived to help others is the only one that matters." *Ben Stein*

CHAPTER 13: PUTTING IT ALL TOGETHER

"If it were easy, everyone would be doing it" – Scot Hunter

So now that you've survived the unabridged version of "Wall Street's Bull and How to Bear It", here's a summary of what we've covered:

Core Beliefs To Commit To, For Advisors And Their Clients

1. A client's portfolio should be a personalized reflection of what that client wants to get out of life, not an off-the-shelf package. Model approaches *within* this portfolio are fine.

2. It is not necessary to invest aggressively to produce solid long-term returns.

3. Taxes and inflation are the enemies of the high net worth investor, who must enlist professional help (i.e. an Advisor) to plan to minimize the negative long-term impact on their wealth.

4. Understanding market psychology helps avoid the most common investor pitfalls (see Chapter 4 for more information about avoiding them).

5. The best investment advisor is an independent portfolio manager, not a salesman (e.g. broker) from a large corporation – brokerage firms have a choice between the needs of their clients and the needs of their shareholders. The shareholders usually win – YOU should win.

6. No single investment style holds the key to long-term success. A diversified group of styles holds better prospects.

7. Clients and advisors MUST act as teammates and not opponents in order for the plan to succeed – it's a two-way relationship, both sides must cooperate, not compete.

8. The ultimate role of the advisor is to maximize the likelihood that every client's portfolio will achieve the goals they previously established.

9. A team approach to managing wealth works best; no stars, no egos, just hard-working team players.

I believe a client comes to an advisor to meet certain goals. They are not looking to buy a stock or bond portfolio. They are looking to develop a concise investment strategy, which will meet those goals. The strategies we use are a means to that end. Our clients' investment success is about getting what they want out of their money, not about beating a market index or other performance target. It's goal oriented investing—a disciplined, results- focused approach, and each client is different. We take the matter of being a fiduciary of our clients' assets very seriously.

There are some basics we discussed in this book that could be appropriate for nearly everybody. Most investors can benefit from allocating a portion of their funds to low volatility approaches, and many can benefit from absolute return strategies.

I believe that too many asset classes tend to look like each other over time: diversifying stocks solely with other stocks may add minimal value. A stocks-only portfolio is by this proposition under-diversified. So stocks-only is not the optimal solution. Neither is simply adding bonds to the mix.

High-Quality Bonds are NOT a total return asset class – they are best used for preservation and predictable cash flow. This favors individual bonds over high-quality bond funds. So as with stocks, bonds alone cannot provide an adequate level of diversification.

In our opinion, a more flexible approach that includes hybrid styles is required.

Communications

When I took a course on "communications" in college, I though it was the most boring subject ever. In the classroom, it was, but in the practice of investment advisory, it's the pinnacle. I think that most advisors truly get a thrill out of helping a client through a life-impacting decision. My best days in the business are when someone tells me how much our team helped them with something. In addition, the advent of the Internet and email has made it so that "phone tag" does not stop us from making progress with our clients.

My team and I enjoy being educators just as we enjoy learning new things from others. Our natural curiosity has produced many great benefits for our clients and ourselves over the years. We want our clients to be as informed as possible, and we want to know as much as we can about their financial circumstances. We conduct regularly scheduled portfolio reviews with consolidated reporting. This allows us to focus on the entire portfolio. Let's face it, the only way you can make important decisions is by looking at the whole picture. Although this did not make our list of top investor misconceptions earlier in the book, it deserves honorable mention. When a client only gives the advisor part of the story, or shows the advisor part of their assets, they are inviting uncoordinated advice through the door. And once Mr. Uncoordinated comes in, it's tough to get him to leave. Actually, given my career as a wannabe athlete, I should stop the references to Mr. Uncoordinated right here...but I digress. The key is, if your advisor is truly your advisor, show your hand. Don't keep secrets that will inhibit the planning process. At the same time, if your advisor does not ask the questions necessary to draw out all the information they need to plan for you, that's their fault.

Because we have garnered some publicity, we have a number of published articles and commentaries. Many of those were the basis for this book. Also, as I have become recognized as one of the leading voices for Hybrid investing, we have built a "library" of sorts that contains many articles we've found about the subject. Some contain quotes from us, others don't.

In summary, the investment process I believe should be emphasized more in the advisors business is to identify the financial liabilities a client has to fund - their expected future income, charitable and estate intentions, etc., and make a reasonable estimate of the assets that will be used to tackle those liabilities. From this information, we figure out a comfort zone, delineating the best and worst return that client can stomach over a short-term 1-year and 3-year time frame, as well as longer 5-10 year time frame. Heck, the stock market has had several 5-year periods of flat returns. Are you more interested in avoiding that (the tortoise) or seeking a higher return (the hare) and the greater stress that comes with it? If you don't know, start with the former, NOT the latter, after all, the tortoise did beat the hare.

To Conclude:

If there is one thing I would want the reader to come away from book with, is an understanding of the concept of Wealth Management. This is clearly distinct from "investing", although this may be an essential component. Wealth management is all about funding the liabilities of your lifetime. These liabilities include retirement, paying for big events like marriage and education for children, being able to afford the lifestyle you desire, and being able to maximize the size of the estate you leave to your kids and to charities you support. After all, why do we invest at all? To have money to afford our future, and to sustain and enhance our current lifestyle. Its a lot like the decision process that defined benefit pension managers or foundation directors go through in their decision-making process. This process, called "immunization" looks at the total expenses that the assets of the plan or foundation will have to meet (such as X number of employees planning on retiring in 2010), and then balances these financial liabilities against safe investments with predictable rates of return (traditionally, government bonds; however I advocate Hybrid strategies as a more viable alternative in many cases. Income from these investments should be equal to the total cost of future liabilities. When you think of wealth management in this way, all of the common distractions investors experience get crowded out. Instead, you focus on what's important to you, now and in the future.

Good Luck,

Rob

APPENDIX A: DEALING WITH APPRECIATED STOCK

"The stock market never really changes that much. What happened before will happen again and again and again." - Jesse Livermore

Joseph Ricketts once said "It doesn't matter to me if my stock is 12 or 20- I'm not going to sell at 20. I didn't get rich by diversifying, I got rich by concentrating." Joseph Ricketts' Net Worth was estimated at $850 million by Forbes Magazine in 2001. But Mr. Ricketts' approach to investing does not suit everyone.

The following are what we call "high-class" problems. Have any of the following happened to you or someone you know?

1. You sold your business for shares of your acquirer's stock

2. You bought many shares of a company like General Electric or Microsoft back when it was a baby, and have now accumulated a fortune

3. You invested wisely over the years, and now have several big winners

In each of these scenarios, you now hold "appreciated stock". Unless it is contained in a tax-deferred entity such as an IRA or 401k plan, you may feel the need to choose between selling your stock and paying a chunk of taxes, or letting it ride, praying that nothing bad happens to the stock. So, do you sell or hold?

The risk of having a very large part of your portfolio in one stock is high. Ask anyone whose net worth consists of shares of General Motors. Once one of the world's most admired companies, GM has been mired in endless debt and an uphill struggle to repair its tarnished image. Naturally, this has taken a former "Blue Chip" stock and sapped the wealth from its shareholders.

While most companies will never go through an episode of this magnitude, this shows that any stock can falter. If you are at a point where most of your investment eggs are in one basket, it may be time to consider the alternatives.

There are as many as a dozen alternatives to the "Do Nothing" approach to your appreciated stock position. The strategy or strategies that best fit your situation depend on what combination of features are most important to you. To help figure this out, ask yourself these questions:

1. Do I want to diversify my portfolio, to spread my risk across other stocks and/or types of investments?

2. Do I want to hold my stock, but protect myself from a sharp, drastic decline, though there may be a cost to do so?

3. Do I want to create more income from my stock? Today, most companies pay very low dividend rates, but there are ways to increase your stock's annual cash flow.

4. Do I want to use some of my accumulated wealth to help support the work of community organizations I feel strongly about?

5. Is one of my primary goals to reduce or delay the taxes I will ultimately pay from diversifying my stock?

The various strategies introduced here involve a wide variety of techniques. Some may take advantage of the increasingly popular options market. Note, however, that while many investors use options to speculate on stocks, the options strategies discussed here are used exclusively to protect your stock holdings.

Many basic strategies are easily implemented through public transactions. The more advanced strategies often require the assistance of a major financial institution, which creates a customized, "private" strategy for you.

There is one common thread among all of these strategies: you must understand them fully before they are carried out. Your appreciated stock positions likely exist because of a combination of hard work, savvy investing and perhaps a bit of luck. To successfully convert it to something that allows you to realize your life goals, seek out the guidance of those who can educate you.

A friend of mine is a securities lawyer, and he makes his living, as he says "punishing the bad guys". He represents disgruntled clients against advisors. The most fascinating story he has told me concerns an elderly man who, by the mid-1990's, had accumulated $5mm in stock in EMC Corp., one of the tech-mania's darlings. His position grew to $120mm at it peak, but within a couple of years (2000-2001), it had fallen all the way back to $5mm without him selling a single share. Now, $5mm is still a nice amount of money, and a flat return over several years is better than losing money. But the attorney correctly focused on the fact that at no time was the client advised to do anything in response to the sharp rise in EMC's price. While the gain and loss did not change this man's life, it may have changed the fortunes of his heirs and the charities he may have supported.

Why do I bring this up? Because it is the type of story I have heard so many times – a single position appreciates to the point where it is a very high percentage of one's portfolio, and inaction eventually causes the investor to regurgitate the large gain. Sometimes, as with the case my attorney friend ultimately settled in favor of his client, it's because the advisor either did not know what alternatives were available to holding the entire position or they just didn't pay attention. Now, how any advisor cannot pay attention to a $120mm position (or even a $120,000 position for that matter) is beyond me, and beyond the comprehension of most people. There are other cases (many in fact) where the client's greed prevented them from taking action.

Phrases like "its doing so well, how can I sell it?" and "their earnings for the upcoming quarter are supposed to be great" seem to be a part of investor human nature. I'm here to tell you that that attitude will more likely than not cost you a lot of money in your life. So, since you are reading this book, I feel compelled to both share my experiences in counseling clients in this situation, and provide a basic outline for a better way to handle it.

Take It To The (Investment) Bank...Or Else!

I have worked well with many entrepreneurs over the years. This makes sense since I've approached the business as an entrepreneur for most of my career – the "birds of a feather" thing, if you will. I think that the same is true of many advisors, even it they work for large firms. For the most part, my dealings with self-employed and self-made clients have been wonderful. They understand the nature of a private business, and how firms like mine pursue growth. They are excellent businesspeople, whether they are still working or retired.

However, there is one aspect of some entrepreneurs' situations which I have seen to be quite troubling over the years. This is the case when a business owner is "held hostage" by investment banking relationships. For instance, consider the plight of the aspiring entrepreneur who has taken their business idea, incubated it, and is now ready to take it to the next level. They are raising money for a private placement of stock or perhaps a public offering. They are chasing the entrepreneurial dream, but unfortunately they feel like they are really at someone else's mercy—the investment banking firm that is raising money for them.

During my years in the brokerage business, I worked at firms that had significant investment banking groups. They would do an excellent job of raising capital and awareness for a growing company, but that came with a price. Investment bankers, for obvious reasons, wed their clients to them for as many services as possible, including wealth management. It's a very successful business model for these firms. Find private firms who need their expertise to push their companies into the big time, and build an allegiance to them for other services when the big money comes their way. This type of mutual back-scratching is very common in business. Our firm practices it to some degree as well.

However, what about the entrepreneurs whose independent thinking extends beyond what the investment bankers are comfortable with? What if you want to use your investment banking firm for what they are best at: raising money for your company and telling your story to investors? Can't the partnership end there? Sadly, I have heard many stories where it could not.

I have no problem with the banking firm controlling all aspects of the financial life of a client. I do have a problem with the implied penalties that concern the business owner if they decide that their personal business is their business. The most severe situation of the many I've witnessed in this area concerned a client of mine whose banking firm prevented him from moving some of his corporate stock to an investment that was permitted with company approval, but they denied him approval. Ironically, the company would have been much better off letting him move his stock to the investment vehicle he wished. The stock did not trade heavy volume and my client's move would have been a better alternative to selling the stock aggressively on the open market. But the banking firm wanted to express the dominance they were allowed under the law instead of making the best business decision. I was only an observer in this, but the time and mess it caused for the parties involved was unfortunate, and frustrating to watch.

I have also seen many cases where a client was "strongly recommended" to place some of their investment portfolio with their investment banking firm's brokerage division, as an unofficial part of their relationship. In other words, "Do it our way if you want to get the best results for your company". I thought that the Chinese Wall that existed between bankers and brokers at the same firm could not be breached, but obviously someone built an elevator that moves Wall Streeters easily over the Wall to the other side. I guess that's why you've never heard the expression "Chinese Wall Street".

Easily the most frustrating aspect of the tie-in to one's investment banking firm is a saga I have seen so many times that I feel I can almost predict when it will occur again. I have worked with many clients over the years that when I met them, had most or even all of their investment assets in one stock. Typically, it was the stock of the company they built. It is common for a successful entrepreneur to look at selling stock in their own company as sacrilege. But I think that in many cases, maintaining this type of portfolio strategy it is imprudent, greedy or outright dumb.

If this sounds like I'm full of sour grapes…you bet I am! Why? Because I have seen over $100mm of asset value owned by my clients vanish into thin air because they ignored one of the central tenets of prudent investing: diversification. My best guess as to why this occurs over and over again is that successful people believe they have made so few mistakes in their careers, they have no fear. It's like my son Tyler when he plays a game of PlayStation football against me. I play it close to the vest, trying to execute a game plan, and punting when it's fourth down and long. Not Tyler. Like most young boys, he has no fear, especially when competing in a video game. Fourth down and 20 at his own 32 yard line? "Dad, I'm going for it." Even when he lines up to punt, half the time he fakes it and runs with the ball anyway. The point is, he is not thinking about the downside risk of what he's doing. And why should he? It's a game.

But having millions of dollars in one stock, so that it is the majority asset in your portfolio is not a game. Some entrepreneurs will argue that selling stock is a sign of weakness. I'd counter that not diversifying any is a sign that you are not putting enough emphasis on the responsibility you have to your family – this generation and beyond. And Wall Street has created a whole sub-industry for helping concentrated holders of stock to get diversified. I know that for some corporate insiders this is not so easy. I'm aiming my comments at those who have the flexibility to diversify and don't.

APPENDIX B: SOME REFLECTIONS FROM 9-11-2001

September 11, 2001

"9-11" was the worst day many of us have been a part of. Not only did it cause such a horrible loss of life, but like Pearl Harbor, the Cuban Missile Crisis, and the Cold War, it reminded us of how vulnerable we are as human beings. Did any of us in the general population really have any way to prevent ourselves from being victims that day? No way. If you happened to be in the wrong place at that wrong time, your fate was sealed.

Everyone has their own connection to the events of that day. For me, it was a chilling time because I was in the World Trade Center in 1993 when terrorists blew up a car in the basement. Fortunately for those of us in the building that day, the terrorists' plan was not executed well and we survived. Though for a few hours, up on the 94th floor of tower two, I wasn't sure what would happen. Naturally this pales in comparison to what those in New York, Washington and Pennsylvania experienced on 9-11. And for those of us who lived through that day as merely fortunate spectators, our sense of security in our daily lives will never be the same.

As an investment advisor during that time, there was really no protocol for what to do. The financial markets were closed for several days, and many people were focused on the aftermath, not what to do with their money when the markets reopened. But understandably, there were plenty of people who were very concerned about how to react to such unique and sudden circumstances. My team and I spent the days after 9-11 calling clients and following the news, trying to make some sense of it along with everyone else. It became obvious to me then that in that situation as with any other, the needs of our clients varied greatly. Never was there a time that I can remember having to react to such a diverse group of concerns. For some of our clients, we were part of the mass therapy that ensued for months after that day. For others, it was back to business very quickly. At the same time, I was trying to make sure that all of my friends (including some former co-workers in the World Trade Center) were alive and OK.

I debated whether to include anything about 9-11 in this book. But since it is such a memorable time in my career, I decided that presenting a commentary I issued to clients three days after 9-11 might help keep things in perspective. Striving to attain or maintain a desired lifestyle is important, but not as important as reminding ourselves how lucky we are just to be here every day.

INVESTING IN THE NEW WORLD

Originally published on September 14, 2001

To our clients, we say "Thank You".

In a week that has been one of the most emotional and difficult in all of our lives, Allan and I have learned a lot from all of you, and shared your feelings. We put aside all other business activities, and spent the last four days staying in touch with our clients.

We have seen your emotions move from shock, to sorrow and now to anger. Yet during that time, I sense that we have never been so close as citizens and neighbors. We hope that continues.

This week, we did enter a New World. Most of us will never look at the basics of life the same way again. While financial concerns have been a low priority to most of us this week, they will start to increase in priority as time passes. With that in mind, I can tell you with a high degree of confidence that **even in the New World, the Old World rules of investing have not changed.**

We have spent this week discussing first life, then livelihood. None of us knows what will happen when the U.S. stock market opens on Monday, but I do know that it will be one day in a lifetime of investing for your goals. I have felt no sense of panic from you, and I didn't expect to.

Based on what Lockwood Financial (our Broker-Dealer) told us yesterday, **your calm reactions mimic those of independent investment advisors and their clients across the country**. Lockwood supervises about 30,000 investment accounts. As of yesterday, there have been only two requests for complete liquidation.

We present below a compendium of what we feel are the most useful writings of the past few days, to help you understand what long-term investors are thinking *now (the first one really says it best, the others are also helpful)*. We believe they are all worth a quick read. Your feedback and questions are always appreciated.

212

COMPENDIUM OF CURRENT INVESTMENT THINKING

September 14, 2001

From MJ Whitman Advisors

This new world and the shock of recent events may cause some market participants to react in ways that will seem irrational. There was a great analyst, Sigmund Freud, whose greatness revolved around his belief that no one was really off-the-wall and demented completely. Rather, Freud's approach was to dig deeply for the reasons why a person acted the way he or she did. Freud sought rational explanations for what appeared to be irrational behavior. If Freud had written the Robert J. Shiller volume, Irrational Exuberance, it would have been titled, Rational Overexuberance. We, too, ought to try to understand why other investor-speculators do what they do.

In the weeks just ahead, many market participants may panic or be near panic, given what may be the aftermath of September 11th. For many of these market participants, panic, or near panic, may be appropriate, rational, behavior, provided these people are influenced by one, or more, of the following:

1. They are on margin, or otherwise heavily indebted;

2. They know little, or nothing, about the companies, or the securities, in which they are invested;

3. They believe their livelihood depends on the near-term performance of stock market prices;

4. They own junior securities, especially common stocks, of companies that are debt laden;

5. They need to raise cash over the relatively near term via the sale of securities;

6. They are strictly outlook conscious, rather than price conscious, in the selection of securities to buy, own or sell;

7. They believe that the macro outlook for the economy and for markets is more important than corporate details.

Keep an Even Keel

From Morningstar.com

by Pat Dorsey | 09-14-01 | 06:00 AM |

Early Thursday morning, I participated in an interview about what individual investors should do once the markets reopen. It made me angrier than I've been in a long time.

While waiting to begin the interview, I listened to an extensive piece on some company that does background security checks; the reporter suggested the firm could be "a good play" as both the government and private firms keep closer tabs on who is who. Then, once I was on the air, I was asked whether security-services firms like Wackenhut would be good buys once the markets reopened.

Moral issues aside for the moment (I'm not sure how appropriate it was to discuss "good plays" just 48 hours after the disaster), this is just plain silly. The strong likelihood that security-services firms will see increased demand over the next several months is not exactly a secret, so it's reasonable to expect that this information will be priced into the stocks when they first open for trading. In general, markets are pretty darn good at reflecting available public information very quickly, especially when investors have had a few days to think things over.

Back to the interview. After security firms, the interviewer wanted to know whether oil firms would be a good place to put some money, since crude oil spiked right after the disaster, and there's an increased risk that oil supplies could get disrupted some time in the future. All very logical, but all very public as well, and all very likely to be reflected in the share prices of oil stocks whenever they reopen for trading.

Finally, I was asked where investors seeking safety should hide--cash, gold, or other commodities. I almost blew my stack. For one thing, there's no point in "hiding" now, since the attacks have already occurred. More important, there's simply nothing to hide from. Although the attacks will undoubtedly do some short-term damage to the U.S. economy, they should have little material affect on where this country's economy (and stock market) will be three to five years from now.

Moreover, "hiding"--if that's even the appropriate word--doesn't help you accomplish your personal goals. If you're 40 years old and thinking about retiring in 20 years, that's what your investment plan should be based upon, and I can flat guarantee you that a portfolio of gold, cash, and oil stocks won't get you there. If you have a regular investment program set up, there's no reason to stop it.

So instead of spending your energy trying to game the crisis, spend it donating blood or giving comfort to someone who lost a loved one in the disaster. In the grand scheme of things, the financial impact of the disaster isn't that great--certainly not relative to the enormity of the personal and emotional impact.

How the Fed keeps cash flowing

From CNBC.com

By Scott Gerlach

The Federal Reserve keeps reminding us it stands by, ready to provide liquidity. But what is liquidity, exactly? And how does it help the financial system?

Just as firefighters swarmed the rubble of the World Trade Center in a search-and-rescue operation this week, the Federal Reserve has quietly engaged in a rescue effort of its own aimed at saving the global financial system. Central bankers promised plenty of cash to keep businesses and markets rolling. And boy, have they delivered: a $38 billion liquidity injection on Wednesday and a potential record of $70 billion on Thursday. The amounts are staggering. But what do they mean?

The Fed is flooding banks with extra, temporary cash reserves that serve two purposes. Most immediately, they ensure that banks can handle any conceivable demand for withdrawals, preventing "bank runs" like those so destructive during the Depression and basically unheard of since then. And in addition, the extra reserves may spur more lending, a key financial stimulus.

"The banking system needs funds just in normal everyday operations," says Kim Rupert, an economist at the Standard & Poor's MMS advisory service in San Francisco. "Now that we're in pretty extraordinary circumstances, the Fed is being super-generous in adding reserves to the system."

These reserve boosts typically last a short time and cost hardly anything. In fact, the biggest operations this week were "overnight reverse repurchases". The Fed bought certain kinds of bonds from financial institutions with the understanding that it would sell them back the next day at a discount. The money that flows into the accounts of these securities firms becomes, temporarily, part of the pool of bank reserves.

Wall Street bond firms routinely facilitate the Fed's reserve actions. In fact, reserves are the Fed's primary means for influencing interest rates. Banks flush with reserves are more able to lend them. Once Fed chief Alan Greenspan and his colleagues decide on a rate target, the central bank adds reserves to lower rates and drains reserves to raise them. Some analysts see Thursday's $70-billion Fed operation as a de facto half-point rate cut.

Thursday, when the bond market finally started trading again, short-term interest rates fell sharply, while longer-term rates generally held steady. That's actually a very good sign. Banks can borrow cheaply and lend at higher rates -- a classic pattern for making banks more profitable and thus potentially stimulating the economy.

Besides overseeing the U.S. financial system, the Fed works hard to grease the global money wheels. One of its most innovative efforts came to light Thursday. It established a $50 billion "swap line" with the European Central Bank that will let overseas banks draw dollars through their own central banks in emergency situations. Market watchers credit the swap line with helping to underscore worldwide confidence in the greenback. No one needs to worry about getting caught without enough dollars.

APPENDIX C: INVESTMENT VEHICLES – THE BASICS

Equities

Equity is the ownership interest in a business venture and is usually represented by securities, which evidence that ownership, most commonly stock. There can be several classes of stock, each with its unique characteristics. Recent surveys by the NASD and others indicate that more than 75% of Americans own stock in a company, either directly or through ownership of mutual funds, which in turn own stocks.

When you buy the stock of a corporation, you have an ownership share — however small — in that corporation and are entitled to part of that corporation's earnings and assets. Stock investors — called shareholders or stockholders — make money when the stock increases in value or when the company that issued the stock pays dividends, or a portion of its profits, to its shareholders. Some companies are privately held, which means the shares are available to a limited number of people, such as the company's founders, its employees, and investors who fund its development. Other companies are publicly traded, which means their shares are available to any investor who wants to buy them. They are available for purchase on one or more of the stock "exchanges" where stocks are transacted. Examples of stock exchanges include the New York Stock Exchange, American Stock Exchange which are physical locations, or the Nasdaq which is a large network of computers and people operating them.

Why Would A Company Sell Shares Of Its Ownership?

A company may decide to sell stock to the public for a number of reasons such as providing liquidity for its original investors or raising money for acquisitions, product development or expansion. The first time a company issues stock is known as the initial public offering (IPO), and the company receives the proceeds from that sale. This process is called "Going public". After that, shares of the public stock are traded, or bought and sold on the securities markets among investors, but the corporation gets no additional income. The price of the stock moves up or down depending on how much investors are willing to pay for it. Occasionally, a company will issue additional shares of its stock, called a secondary offering, to raise additional capital.

Categories of stocks

Various "factors" are used to differentiate securities and portfolio styles, both with respect to developing investment strategy and explaining performance. These factors include price/earnings ratios, price/book ratios, dividend yield, market capitalization, earnings per share of growth, free cash flow, etc. The process that traditionally considered U.S. equities as a single asset class now has been enhanced to consider numerous sub-asset classes such as large-, mid- and small-cap growth, core or value. Other sub-asset classes exist as well, and a large part of my approach over the years has been to greatly expand from the traditional universe of stock classifications and focus on desired results. I believe this is superior to the commoditized, static approach that most of Wall Street uses to manage the assets of all but the most well-heeled investors.

Market capitalization of stocks.

One of the main ways to categorize stocks is by their market capitalization, sometimes known as market value. Market capitalization (market cap) is calculated by multiplying a company's current stock price by the number of its existing shares. For example, a stock with a current market value of $30 a share and a hundred million shares of existing stock would have a market cap of $3 billion.

Large vs. Small

Large and small refer to the company's capitalization, that is, the total market value of its outstanding equity (see above). In many categorizations, "large" capitalization U.S. equities are roughly coincident with portions of stocks contained in the Standard & Poor's 500 index. Large stocks, by this definition, comprise about 80% of the total U.S. equity market capitalization, and small stocks the remainder. Small companies are frequently assumed to be in earlier stages of their life cycles than large companies, and therefore are assumed to have more uncertain futures and more highly variable returns than large stocks. Additionally, small companies are typically not followed as closely by industry analysts. This suggests a greater inefficiency in pricing. To compensation for these higher risks, portfolios of smaller companies tend to have higher expected long-term returns.

Stocks are sometimes divided more finely into five or more categories by size (i.e., capitalization) ranges: large-cap, mid-cap, smid-cap, small-cap, and micro-cap. Large-cap stocks are currently defined as those with market capitalizations greater than $4.5 billion, mid-cap considers those with market capitalizations between $1 billion and $4.5 billion, and small-cap are those with market values between $50 million and $1 billion. Stocks with capitalizations under $50 million are sometimes called "micro-cap". Depending on the projected development of the company issuing the security, stocks falling anywhere between the small to mid cap range may be characterized as "smid cap". This category can be used to describe, for example, a small cap stock with a high rate of growth.

These designations are not standardized. Different practitioners define the dividing lines among these categories differently. In general, large-cap stocks tend to be less volatile than small-cap stocks. This is because small-cap stocks generally represent younger, less-established companies that do not have the financial resources of larger companies and are thus more vulnerable to a downturn in the economy. As you might expect, mid-cap stocks can offer a middle ground between the growth potential of small-caps and the reduced volatility of large-caps. Mid-caps typically cost less than large-cap stocks and are less vulnerable in economic downturns than small-caps.

Types of Stock

Common Stock

Common stockholders generally exercise greater control over the business, such as voting on important matters, including board members, and mergers or acquisitions. If there are other classes of stock, such as preferred stock, the common stock holders assume a greater risk, but generally have higher appreciation potential than other types. Common stock is the predominant stock found on the exchanges, and is the stock that is quoted when talking about a company's investment performance.

Preferred Stock

Preferred stock also represents an ownership interest, but the rights of the preferred stockholder are different from those of a common stockholder. Preferred stock has a claim on the company's earnings BEFORE payments to common stockholders (Which would be important in the event of liquidation). If the stock pays dividends, preferred stockholders are entitled to theirs at a pre-specified rate prior to any dividends paid on common stock. Preferred stockholders may not have any voting rights.

Blue Chip Stocks

Blue Chip stocks are those issued by companies well known for their high quality as an investment. These stocks will typically have wide acceptance of their products and services. The companies issuing the stocks are established as being consistent profit making, and the company's ability to pay dividends. There is no absolute, definitive, *quantitative* categorization for Blue Chip stocks.

Income Stocks

Income stocks pay higher dividends than the average stock, although they may vary in terms of their quality. For instance, a stock, such as a utility company stock, which pays an unusually high dividend may *have* to do so, in order to attract investors

Growth Stocks

Growth stocks represent companies that usually are growing their business at a rapid rate of growth in earnings. The stocks do not pay out more than nominal dividends to shareholders, but rather plow earnings back into the company to continue to grow. They may have high appreciation potential, but they also may exhibit wide volatility in stock price.

Value Stocks

Value stocks age generally issued by established companies, and usually pay at least a market dividend. They exhibit a ratio of price to earnings lower than the market, and may be less volatile than the average. Value stocks are those with lower than market (measured against the S&P 500 stock index) price/book ratios, price/earnings ratios, and higher than market dividend yields. As a consequence, value stocks usually have a lower earnings per share growth rate than growth stocks.

Growth vs. Value

Generally, growth stocks are those with higher than market (measured against the S&P 500 stock index) price/book value ratios, higher price/earnings ratios, and lower than market dividend yields. Consequently, these stocks represent a universe of companies that have high expected future earnings growth momentum.

Over the past 15 years, growth stocks have had a higher rate of return variability than value stocks. While we won't engage in the value vs. growth debate here, it is often assumed that the returns of value stocks are more stable than their growth counterparts due to the presumed reliability of the dividend yield. Growth stocks, however, are sometimes assumed to offer greater long-term rates of return due to the strong earnings rate associated with such companies. Of course, failure of a company to achieve high growth expectations creates greater variability and price risk.

Cyclical Stocks

A factor in stock performance is how closely a company's business success is tied to the condition of the economy. Cyclical stocks represent companies, which are strongly affected by the business cycle. Cyclical stocks, on the other hand, may flourish in good times and suffer when the economy dips. As the economy changes, some cyclical stocks will benefit; some will be hurt. Some examples of cyclical stocks include: auto, consumer-cyclicals, entertainment, steel, and paper. Cyclical stocks, may flourish in good times and suffer when the economy dips. Airlines, for example, tend to lose money when business and pleasure travel are cut back. When the economy slows down, cyclical stock prices typically fall, because company earnings are down as well. But when the economy recovers, the cycle may work in your favor: Earnings will probably rise and the stock price may go up.

Interest-Sensitive Stocks

Interest sensitive stocks fluctuate in value as interest rates change. As rates go up, their value goes down, and visa versa. Utility companies and financial institutions are generally interest rate sensitive. Interest-sensitive stocks generally have a positive correlation to the Bond market. That is, their behavior resembles bonds, going up and down the same time as Bonds.

Defensive Stocks

Defensive stocks are those, which exhibit price volatility lower than normal (or in other words, the market average). When the stock markets go down, defensive stocks should provide some cushion, and not decrease as much as the market. They will generally have a BETA lower than 1.00. Defensive stocks are concentrated in industries such as utilities, drugs, healthcare, and food, and are often more resilient in recessions and stock market slides— at least theoretically — because product demand continues. Many investors include them in their portfolios to offset more volatile stock investments.

221

Unfortunately, even defensive stocks are not as low risk as the name might imply. They are still stocks of course, and that means they can be caught up in the same wave of violence that can impact the market as a whole. Changes in an industry can have a great impact on how a class of stocks behaves. The prime example of this is U.S. telephone stocks following the government's deregulation of that industry in the early 1980's. At one time, there was only AT&T, which stock market participants simply referred to as "telephone". Then came the spinoffs of Bellsouth, Pacific Bell, etc. Later on, many of those companies merged, spun off their mobile phone divisions and made other corporate changes. A quarter-century later, what used to be considered a stock for "widows and orphans" (a Wall Street term used to imply safety), is anything but that. Well, at least we got competitive wireless phone rates out of all that.

Style Categories

Another method of categorizing equities is to divide them according to their economic characteristics, typically value and growth, then categorize them according to their capitalization. Thus you have, following the traditional approach, six fundamental categories:

1. Large-cap value

2. Mid-cap value

3. Small-cap value

4. Large-cap growth

5. Mid-cap growth

6. Small-cap growth

These categories are usually referred to as "style categories", and managers might characterize their investing styles as, for example, large-cap growth or small-cap value. Consultants frequently consider these sub-categories in developing investment policy, and direct specific assignments to managers specializing in these styles.

As their designation implies, growth stocks are typically differentiated from value stocks by the rate of expansion. However, these categories are not chiseled into stone, and there is some degree of overlap—growth stocks whose expansion has stabilized can become value stocks, and vice versa. Levels of capitalization also vary, with some experts adding "smid cap" to cover stocks which seem to straddle the boundary between small and mid cap, and others add a "micro-cap" category to quantify so-called "penny stocks" with especially attractive potential for future performance. Styles can thus be defined very broadly, or very narrowly depending on whom is doing the analysis.

Within the broad categories of growth and value, the numerous sub-strategies and style combinations offer different risk and return characteristics. These categories should not be oversimplified. For example, not only can the value style be further divided into yield strategies, interest-sensitive strategies, contrarian (out of favor), or distressed strategies, but managers may rotate within multiple styles or build portfolios that consist of multiple characteristics from each category, such as companies with low price earnings and high earnings growth rates. Each "sub-sub" style offers its own unique risk and return characteristics.

As investors have begun to understand the impact of investment style on return and risk, custom indexes have been developed that track these fundamental styles, e.g., a universe of stocks that represent only those securities that have the characteristics associated with the style being considered.

As you might expect from reading this book so far, I am not that concerned with trying to label stocks or the managers that buy them. If a money manager's style is likely to be successful in my estimation, that is far more important than what they call themselves. I guess you could say this is one area of investing where I choose not to be "politically correct". There are many others!

Events Which Impact Stock Values

Stock Splits

Stock splits occur when the Board, approved by shareholders elects to divide the number of shares outstanding into a greater number (i.e. a 2-for-1 split means that stockholders of record on a certain date. will now own 2 shares for every share they previously owned). When this occurs, the price of the stock in our example is halved. If a stock's price increases dramatically, the issuing company may split the stock to bring the price per share down to a level that stimulates more trading.

For example, a stock selling at $100 a share may be split 2-for-1, doubling the number of existing shares and cutting the price in half. The split doesn't change the value of an investment, at least initially. If you had 100 shares when the price was $100 a share, you'll have 200 shares worth $50 a share after the split. Either way, that's $10,000.

However, if the price per share moves back toward the pre-split price, as it may do, your investment will increase in value. For example, if the price goes up to $75 a share, your stock will be worth $15,000, a 50% increase. Investors who hold a stock over many years, through a number of splits, may end up with a substantial investment even if the price per share drops for a time A stock may be split 2-for-1, 3-for-1, or even 10-for-1, if the company wishes, though 2-for-1 is the most common. This is done for a number of reasons, including the desire to demonstrate a lower price in order to attract more potential shareholders, however, the net result to prior shareholders is even up at the end of the day.

A company can also reduce the number of shares in the market place and increase the price per share in what's known as a Reverse Split. The motive is frequently to prevent delisting from a stock exchange, which can happen if the share price falls below the exchange's minimum requirement.

Stock splits are not necessarily either good or bad. The impact of a split depends on the market conditions of that particular security. As discussed earlier in the book, while the number of shares an owner holds may change, the overall value of those shares typically does not.

Stock Dividends

A stock dividend is similar to a regular cash dividend (see above), but is an amount paid to shareholders in more stock, rather than cash. The dividend may be stock of the original company, an acquired company, or a subsidiary.

Warrants and Rights

A warrant gives the client the right to purchase securities at a pre-determined price at some point in the future. Ideally, the stock will be worth more that the price at the time to exercise the purchase. Warrants are often offered along with stocks as an incentive to purchase the stock..

Short Selling

A short sale is the sale of a security which you do not own. The process is heavily regulated, and at a point in time, the seller must "Cover" (purchase the stock sold). Ideally, at the point when the short sale is purchased, the price of the company will be lower than at the time it was sold, thus generating a profit for the investor. Short sales are done at brokerage firms by utilizing a margin account (The brokerage firm "Lends" the stock to the customer).

Short sellers are pessimists, expecting prices to go down. To profit from this anticipated drop as a short seller, you borrow shares of a stock from your broker, sell — or short — the shares, and pocket the money gained from the sale. If the price goes down — as you calculated it would — you buy back shares at the lower price and return the number of shares you borrowed to your broker. After you pay interest and commissions, you expect to have made more on the initial sale of the borrowed stock than it cost you to sell and repurchase the shares.

The strategy can backfire, however, if the stock price goes up rather than down, or even if the price is stable for an extended period. Interest charges mount, and you may decide to cover your short position by buying shares at a higher price than you realized when you sold them. That will leave you with a loss. And if the price continues to rise, your costs — and potential losses — will mount. My use of strategies that involve short selling is limited to situations where there is some stock owned in the same client portfolio (via individual shares or a mutual fund). Shorting on its own is risky. Shorting as part of an overall attempt to control volatility and smooth out returns is, in my opinion, a wise stop for many investors.

International and Global Equities

International equities (in the USA) are all stocks issued by countries other than the USA. In the US markets, they are most often represented by ADRs (American Depositary Receipts), which are essentially stock shares of non-U.S. companies that trade on U.S. stock exchanges. Global Equities include the US stocks discussed above along with the international stocks.

Risks Of Investing In Stocks

Investors buy a stock when they believe it's a good investment. More demand drives the stock price up. But if people think a company's outlook is poor, and either don't invest or sell shares they already own, the stock price will fall. In effect, investor expectations determine the price of a stock.

For example, if lots of investors buy Stock A, its price will be driven up. The stock will become more valuable because there is demand for it. But the reverse is also true. If a lot of investors sell Stock Z, its price will plummet. The further the stock price falls, the more investors sell it off, driving the price down even more. These conditions are not permanent; too much demand may cause a bubble, and lower prices make investment more attractive.

Investor enthusiasm for a stock can sometimes take on a momentum of its own, driving prices up independent of a company's actual financial outlook. Investor disinterest can drive prices down in a similar manner.

Many investors, however, disregard market trends and base their expectations on a company's sales and earnings, as quantifiable evidence of its current strength and future potential. When a company's earnings are up, investor confidence increases and the price of the stock usually rises. If the company is losing money— or not making as much as anticipated — the stock price usually falls, sometimes rapidly. The rising stock prices and regular dividends that reward investors and give them confidence are tied directly to the financial health of the company.

Dividends, like earnings, often have a direct influence on stock prices. When dividends are increased, the message is that the company is prospering. This in turn stimulates greater enthusiasm for the stock, encouraging more investors to buy, and driving the stock's price upward.

When dividends are cut, investors receive the opposite message and conclude that the company's future prospects have dimmed. One typical consequence is an immediate drop in the stock's price. Companies known as leaders in their industries with significant market share and name recognition tend to maintain more stable values than newer, younger, smaller, or regional competitors.

Rating systems and indices

There are a wide range of rating systems and indices to represent various components of the markets. Most financial service firms, especially brokerage houses, rate the stocks they follow independently. The most common rating system divides securities into "Buy", "Sell", or "Hold" categories (or some variation thereof). This has been a very contentious subject for Wall Street since 2002, when the public and the media finally noticed what many of us in the industry have been complaining about for years: brokerage analysts don't issue many "Sell" ratings. The main reason is that it would disrupt the highly incestuous relationship that existed between brokerages and the companies they report on. An analyst issuing a negative rating on a stock would practically ensure that firm's absence from any investment banking deals the company sought help with down the road. When I was at DLJ, I distinctly remember an analyst who, in a rare feat for that time, spoke his mind about a company in the industry he followed that was doing a lousy job of blending in the many companies they acquired. He called them a "serial diluter". He later stepped away from his position to start an independent operation, thus becoming one of the people I most admire in the business. Oh, Wall Street now issues more sell ratings than before the regulators came down on them. But I can't help but think they still have a lot of incentive to put a good face on all but the very worst companies. You might recall the commercial that showed a brokerage firm branch manager rallying his troops to get on the phones and sell a new IPO the company was doing. The famous line he used is one that originated on Wall Street—"Go out and put some lipstick on that pig". That's just one of the conflicted areas of the industry that unfortunately is not as "kosher" as we would like.

Index Use

Before the 1990's, tracking the performance of stock indexes was typically reserved for professional investors. The layperson might have heard of the Dow Jones Industrial Average, but probably didn't know much about the many ways that securities markets are benchmarked.

Today, the situation is different. Cable television, the Internet and an historic bull market have caused many people to want to learn more about how to track the success of their investments in the stock market. In some ways, this has gone too far. For instance, a notable percentage of the investing population refers to the Nasdaq as "the market," when in fact its simply an exchange where many current and former high-flyers list their shares.

227

Also, the Dow Jones index is still more familiar than the Standard and Poors (S&P) 500 Index, though the latter is a somewhat more representative index. Still, even many S&P 500 devotees don't realize that this index is largely dominated by the biggest companies in the U.S. stock market (i.e. it is weighted by the market capitalization of the 500 component stocks).

There is a version of the index that gives equal weighting to each of the 500 stocks but it is far less well-known than the "cap-weighted" index, which is the industry standard. Since many investors don't weight their portfolios by company size, tracking an equal-weighted index makes a lot of sense to us. In addition, many professional money managers have become slaves to the cap-weighted index – they base their decisions around the risk they take versus the index instead of the risk they are taking, period.

The other important issue with any index today is why use it at all? The majority of investors we encounter, having been through the index-crazed 1990's and the bursting of the bubble that followed, have sworn off indexes as a way to judge how they are performing. They tell us that their goal is to make money in most if not all market environments, and to proceed toward their long-term goals at a less volatile pace than an all-stock approach typically would. To many investors, the best index is whether there's a plus or minus sign in front of their returns. For the academically inclined, custom indexes can be created which reflect THEIR investment portfolio rather than measuring it against a "canned" benchmark.

Benchmarks are useful to investors. Artificial measurements are not. If your total portfolio is balanced (say 60% equities, 40% bonds) then you should not be comparing your results to the S&P 500. Indexing is only a tool—not a report card. Use them as the guideline for which they were intended, but use them wisely and accurately

FIXED INCOME

Bonds

Fixed income securities, commonly called "bonds", represent the debt of the issuer. Bonds are issued by the United States government, various governmental agencies, municipalities, and corporations. Bonds differ from stocks, which represent ownership. A bond is, in effect, a loan (US government bonds are loans to the US government and the "national debt" consists of outstanding government bonds).

A bond is a promise to repay a certain amount at a time in the future. This time period is the Bond's "Maturity". Until Maturity the purchaser of a Bond receives interest at a fixed rate. This rate is called the "coupon rate". Note that the interest amount does not change, but the bond's value or its price does go up or down. Accordingly, there are investment risks in bonds, just like in stocks. The Par Value is the face value of the bond (or any security). With bonds, it's typically $1000. When we use the term "ten bonds" we mean a set of bonds that will mature at some point for a value of $10,000.

Economic conditions affect the value of bond investments. Interest rates and inflation are two major economic factors that directly affect the worth and future of a bond. Changing interest rates represent a significant risk. If you own a bond that was issued before an interest rate increase, you may lose money if you sell the bond before maturity, since its price will probably be lower than par value. As interest rates fluctuate, the bonds you hold can become less attractive, as investors and traders seek other bonds that pay higher interest rates. Further, when interest rates are low, many investors put their money into stocks to get a higher return. Lack of interest in bonds can depress bond prices.

The other economic risk bondholders face is rising inflation. The risk of holding a bond to maturity is that rising inflation could erode the buying power of the interest payments as well as the value of the principal. The dollar amount or "face value" of the bond does not change, but the purchasing power of those dollars decreases at a predictable rate (with some exceptions, see "Inflation Protected Bonds" below). The longer you hold a fixed-income investment, the more likely it is that inflation will erode its value. The bond issuer may find itself in financial trouble. This risk, occurring most often with corporate bonds, can seriously diminish your return, or make it disappear completely.

Current Yield

Current Yield is the interest paid by a company expressed as a percentage of the purchase price. For example, a $1000 bond paying $40 interest annually, and currently selling for $1050 will have a yield to maturity of 3.8%. The current yield of this bond will be 4%. If the bond is selling at a discount it will have a yield to maturity greater than the current yield.

If you buy a 10-year $1,000 bond paying 6% and hold it until it matures, you'll earn $60 a year for ten years — an annual yield of 6%, which is the same as the interest rate. But if you buy in the secondary market, after the date of issue, the bond's yield may not be the same as its interest rate. That's because the price you pay affects the yield. For example, if a bond's current yield is 5%, it means your interest payments will be 5% of what you pay for the bond today — or 5% back on your investment annually. You can use the yield to compare the relative value of bonds. Return, on the other hand, is what you make on the investment when the par value of the bond, your profit or loss from trading it, and the yield, are computed. There's an even more precise measure of a bond's current value called the yield to maturity. It takes into account:

- The interest rate in relation to the price
- The purchase price in relation to the par value
- The years remaining until the bond matures

Yield to Maturity

Yield to maturity is a way to predict return over time, but it is calculated by a complicated formula — and it isn't often stated in newspaper bond tables. Advisors have access to the information, and it's available on websites that specialize in bond information or bond trading.

How Bonds Are Bought And Sold

New issues:

Just like a new issue of stock, the decision to issue debt begins with the Board of Directors of the entity. Corporations and municipalities undergo a comprehensive financial analysis to determine whether a Bond might be right for the financial purpose, such as to finance ongoing business, or the building of a bridge or hospital. Market considerations will help determine the terms of the issue, although, the yield most often is not determined until the issue is sold. The process follows stock issuance closely, with underwriters and investment bankers playing a significant role along with the lawyers. Investors purchase the issue from distributors, which hold an amount of the issue in inventory.

The Secondary Bond Market

Most already-issued corporate, municipal, and U.S. Treasury bonds are traded Over-The-Counter (OTC) in the bond trading rooms of U.S. exchanges and brokerage firms around the country. Bond brokers and dealers use electronic display terminals that give them the latest price information and handle the transactions by telephone. Typically, a buyer searches for a seller offering the best price for a particular issue and calls to negotiate the trade. Increasingly, this too is becoming a more automated process. Brokerage firms who make a market in particular bonds keep inventories on hand to sell to their own clients or to brokers from other firms who are trying to fill an order. At the same time, dealers working for the firm try to amass a supply of bonds at the lowest possible prices. In contrast, U.S. Treasury bills and notes are sold competitively in a Dutch auction. That means the bids offering to accept the lowest interest (which means they offer to pay the highest prices) are accepted first, and the auction continues at incrementally higher bids until the quota is filled. The final bid becomes the auction rate, and all lower bidders have their orders filled at that rate. Individual investors, who make noncompetitive offers, also get the auction rate.

Next we will look at the various types of bonds.

US Government Bonds

Government bonds are debt obligations of the US Government, and are considered the highest quality bonds. Short term Treasury Bills are considered the proxy for the risk-free rate of return. There are various types of government bonds, including:

Treasury Bills ("T-Bills"), Treasury Notes and Treasury Bonds

All three of these investments are fixed income securities issued by the United States Department of the Treasury. They constitute a significant source of income, commonly referred to as the "National Debt." Treasury Bills, Notes and Bonds differ in their maturities, but are otherwise similar.

T-Bills have short-term maturities—typically periods of 13 weeks, 26 weeks, or 52 weeks. They are purchased at a discount and mature at face value, with the difference considered interest. T-Notes have original maturities of between 1 and 10 years. They are issued in $1000 increments and pay interest semi-annually. T-Bonds are Notes with maturities of 10-30 years. Treasury Securities are taxable for federal income tax purposes, but are not taxable at the State income tax level.

Inflation Protected Bonds ("TIPS" and "STRIPS")

TIPS are inflation-protected Treasuries which pay a rate of interest plus an inflation "Kicker" tied to the Consumer Price Index (CPI). STRIPS are notes divided into principal and interest components, and are sold as Zero coupon Bonds. They are also known as CATS or TIGERS.

Agency Issues

Agency issues are government bonds issued by a governmental agency such and FNME or FMAC which is not the US Treasury. They are generally high quality, but nor as high as Treasuries. They also generally do not have the preferred state tax consideration of a Treasury Security.

Municipal Bonds

Municipal Bonds are issued by states, counties, cities or other municipal entities and their agencies. Generally, interest on Municipals are exempt from federal income tax, and state and local income tax within the state in which they are issued. There are various different types of municipal bonds:

GO

GO Bonds are general obligations of the Municipality, and not issued for a specific purpose such as a Bridge, Road or Hospital. They are subject to the credit quality of the municipality, and are repaid from the general treasury. Municipalities HAVE defaulted on their GO Bonds –ie: New York City in the 80s and Orange County, California in the 90s. However, these cases were rare.

Reserve Bonds

Reserve Bonds are generally issued for a specific purpose and have a "Reserve" of a certain percent established to make repayment of interest and principal.

Corporate Bonds

Corporate Bonds are issued by a legal, taxable entity and are subject to the credit worthiness of the company. Generally, lower quality issuers must pay higher rates of interest to attract investors. Corporate bonds are generally taxable at both the Federal and State levels. There are various ways to categorize corporate bonds:

Investment Grade

Investment Grade Bonds are those in the highest rating categories by ratings services (Moodys, Standard and Poors—see chart). They are generally qualified for purchase by Trusts and Pension Funds.

High Yield

High yield Bonds pay higher rates of interest than others, and are often called "Junk Bonds". The reason they pay higher interest is that the credit quality of the issuing company is below investment grade. When I do invest for a client in this asset class, I do so through a fund or managed account. It is a very tricky part of the industry for those who are not true experts. At the same time, High Yield has been a very helpful part of many portfolios, in my experience. The key I have found is to avoid getting lured by the very high returns of the true "junk". We tend to use portfolios that buy BB and B-rated bonds, the two highest categories below investment grade.

Zero coupon bonds

Zero coupon bonds do not pay interest, but are sold at a discount. For example, a bond maturing in 4 years at $1000, may be selling at $900, giving an effective yield of approximately 2.8%. Some bonds pay no interest while the loan is maturing. These bonds, called zero coupon bonds, are popular with some investors. Instead of separate fixed-interest payments, the interest of a zero coupon bond accrues, or builds up, and is paid in a lump sum at maturity. Corporate, municipal, and Treasury bonds are also available as zero coupon bonds. You buy zero-coupon bonds — or zeros — at a deep discount, far lower than par value. When the zero matures, the accrued interest and the original investment add up to the bond's par value.

The pros and cons of Zeros

Bond issuers like zeros because there's an extended period to use the money they have raised without paying periodic interest. Investors like zeros because the discounted price means you can buy more bonds with the money you have to invest, and you can buy bonds of different maturities, timed to coincide with anticipated expenses. Zeros have two potential drawbacks. They are extremely volatile in the secondary market, so you risk losing money if you need to sell before maturity. And, unless you buy tax-exempt municipal zeros, or buy zeros in a tax-free account, you have to pay taxes every year on the interest you would have received had the interest, in fact, been paid. I use zeroes quite a bit, and for a variety of reasons. However, I tend to use municipal issues if the account is taxable, and I have no intention or expectation that we will be selling prior to a bond's maturity. That keeps the risk/reward of using them at a very high level. It is my opinion that coupon bonds are overused by investors, and that more should use zeroes. This is especially true for those with specific cash flow objectives or those who are not likely to take out any income at all.

Convertible Bonds

Convertible Bonds may be exchanged under certain terms and conditions for the common or other stock of the issuer. They pay interest like a normal bond, but have the equity conversion feature.

Callable Bonds

A callable bond may be required to be redeemed by the issuer prior to maturity. If called, a bond MUST be sold back to the company. The terms of the call price (for instance, at PAR or the price paid) will be preset at the time of purchase. If a company, agency, or the government calls the bonds you own, it redeems your investment and pays back your principal. Issuers may call bonds if the interest rates drop and they have enough money on hand to pay back outstanding debt. By calling the bonds, they eliminate the expense of making further fixed-interest payments for the duration of the bond term, and can issue new bonds at a lower rate and save money. If your bond is called, you receive no more interest payments from the investment, forcing you to find another place to invest the money earlier than you anticipated. And if the company called your bonds due to an interest rate drop, you will find yourself reinvesting the money at a lower, less attractive interest rate. See the example using the Costanza Family earlier in the book for an example of this.

International and Global Fixed Income

International fixed income bears some of the general characteristics as domestic fixed income, but the additional risk of currency risk. The value of the issuing country's money to the domestic dollar may make the rate of interest more difficult to predict. Also, the traditional Bond rating services do not rate international Bonds, making them more difficult to evaluate.

Bond Risks: Maturity, Yield, Holding Period And Yield, Quality

A bond is a loan, repaid with interest. In some cases, such as with Treasury Bonds, this interest may be figured into the face value of the bond, or it may be added on top of the face value according to the principles of compounding as described above. Some bonds make payments on this interest over time, while others repay interest and principal at maturity or call.

Since value includes interest, changes in interest *rates* will produce similar changes in the total value of a bond. This is **Interest Rate Risk**. Interest rate risk is higher the longer the period of maturity, or the lower the coupon rate. As prices of Bonds go UP, yields go DOWN.

Interest rate risk is influenced by three main factors:

- **Holding Period**

  The longer the holding period of a bond is, the greater the interest rate risk. Likewise, the shorter the holding period, the lesser the expected impact of changes on interest rates is.

- **Maturity**

  The longer the period of maturity for a bond is, the greater the interest rate risk. Bonds with shorter periods of maturity are expected to be less subject to changes in value due to changes in interest rates.

- **Size And Timing Of Payment**

  The lower the coupon rate of a bond is, the greater the interest rate risk; more frequent payments decrease interest rate risk. Generally the higher the yield, the longer the maturity.

These factors indicate a definite (and frequently negatively correlated) relationship between interest rate, coupon rate, maturity, and bond value.

- As Coupon Rate decreases, interest rate risk increases.

- As maturity increases, interest rate risk also increases.

- Long-term zero coupon bonds have less value than short-term bonds.

- Current bond value is always higher with lower interest rates.

That "Price-Yield Thing"

One of the most misunderstood facts of life in investing is this: prices of high-quality bonds are determined largely by interest rates. If interest rates go up, bond prices go down. If rates go down, prices of bonds go up. Its not like the stock market where news on a particular company and buying and selling pressure are the main forces determining prices. With high-quality bonds, its about interest rates. That's it.

Just to be clear, when I say "high-quality" bonds, I'm talking about the types of bonds considered the least risky, as determined by the rating assigned to them by the bond rating agencies. That is, U.S. Treasury bonds and U.S. Government Agency Bonds (which both carry a AAA rating, the highest rating available), Corporate Bonds rated AA and AAA, Certificates of Deposit (CDs) and Municipal Bonds rated AA or AAA. Lower-rated bonds are a different story. News relating to the issuer of the bond is more important here.

For some reason, this inverse relationship between bond prices and bond yields is largely misunderstood by investors. I remember earlier in my career a bond manager I worked with was explaining to me that many of his clients did not understand this basic mathematic relationship. He referred to the problem as "that price-yield thing". Since he was a well-spoken and extremely intelligent man, I realized that he was being sarcastic. The problem is that not comprehending this basic fact about bond investing can lead to a lot of unnecessary stress for you as an investor.

Let's say that you own one AAA-rated municipal bond. You paid "par value" for it. That is, a bond is typically offered initially at $1000 per unit. This is also the amount that you will receive back from the issuer of the bond when it matures. In this case, let's assume that is in 5 years. Bond investing is simply lending your money to the issuer for a stated period of time. Let's also say that the bond pays you an interest rate of 4% per year, called the "coupon" – years ago, bonds were often held by the owner, not by a securities custodian. To get paid your interest every six months, you would send in a little coupon attached to the bond certificate in return for your money. Kind of like a cereal box top.

So a few months later you get your statement and that same bond shows a value of $970. What happened to this allegedly safe investment? Have you been hoodwinked? Has your advisor sold you a lemon? Has the world turned upside down? Most likely, market interest rates went up. That's it. When you bought your 5-year municipal bond, perhaps the going rate for such a bond was 4%. For whatever reason, interest rates for similar bonds today are 4.5%. Think of this from the side of someone who might want to buy your bond from you. How much would they pay to get a 4% bond when the going rate is 4.5%? Would they pay you $1000 for your bonds? No way. For $1000, they can buy a fresh, clean 4.5% bond from someone else. To sell yours, you'd have to give them a discount. But here's the good news: you are not selling your bond. You didn't buy it to trade it, you did so to get the 4% interest for 5 years, and then get your $1000 back at the end. The bond is basically a contract between you and the issuer. And if the issuer has given you no reason to be concerned about getting your $1000 back in 5 years, who cares what influences of the market do to the price of the bond before then? YOU SHOULD NOT CARE. I don't either. Because in 5 years, you'll get that $1000 they promised you. And even if the price of your bond drops further, if the drop is simply related to rising interest rates, ignore the price fluctuation. It really doesn't matter.

The same holds true if your high-quality bond went up a bit in value because rates fell. It's not a gift; you should not sell it out if your objective was income and stability. Why not? If you sell that bond and try to buy another 5-year bond, you'll get a lower interest rate. In other words, you will be no better off swapping one bond for a similar one. Like many areas of investing, there are exceptions to this. But they don't come up very often if you are a buy-and-hold-to-maturity bond investor.

I have seen confusion about the price-yield thing lead to big problems when someone comes to me with a portfolio of high-quality bond mutual funds. These funds have performed very well over the past quarter-century thanks to consistently falling interest rates. This has lulled many into thinking that bond funds are as safe as individual bonds. Oh, Wall Street would like you to think that! They make plenty of money hawking many varieties of bond funds. But there's a big difference. Most bond funds are actively managed. They have professional managers whose job is to make you money beyond what the bonds pay you in interest. They also have to overcome the fees they charge. When interest rates go up for a while, these funds will not perform well. From reading this appendix, you now know why. The bonds went down in price. While this does not impact you, it does make life difficult for an active bond manager. That manager does not buy bonds to hold them to maturity. They buy them to make a profit. When rates rise, it's like hitting a golf ball into a stiff wind, only worse. At least the golf ball still moves in a positive direction. Your bond fund won't.

Downgrading

One additional danger bondholders face—and one than cannot be effectively anticipated—is that a rating service may downgrade its rating of a company or municipal government during the life of a bond, creating a "fallen angel". That happens if the issuer's financial condition deteriorates, or if the rating service feels a business decision might have poor results. If downgrading occurs, investors instantly demand a higher yield for the existing bonds. That means the price of the bond falls in the secondary market. It also means that if the issuer wants to float new bonds, the bonds will have to be offered at a higher interest rate to attract buyers.

The greatest risk the investor faces is default, which occurs when the issuer doesn't live up to its promise to pay. Issuers who default on their loans can default on interest — which means you receive your principal but the interest is not paid. An issuer can also default on repayment, which means you receive some of your interest but lose your principal. Bankruptcy typically results in total default, making your client's bonds worthless. Thoroughly researching bonds can help you protect your clients from some risk, but sometimes even the best-looking investments can, in time, turn out to be troublesome.

Bond Prices And Rating Systems

There are several firms, which rate bonds (not including brokerage firms, who generally perform their own independent internal research). The most commonly known are Moody's, Standard and Poor's, Duff and Phelps, and Fitch. Note that each rating service may rate the same bond differently (see the chart provided below). However, a bond which is rated (for example) investment grade by one rating system will usually be rated similarly by the other rating systems.

While most bonds have a par value of $1,000, the prices of different types of bonds are quoted in slightly different ways. Prices of corporate and municipal bonds are quoted in points and 8ths of a point, and each point is a unit of $10. You can multiply the listed price by 10 to get the actual price. For example, if a bond's price is quoted as 96 1/2, it's selling at $965 (96.5 x 10 = 965). Prices of Treasury bills and notes are quoted in units of 100 and 32nds of 100 (rather than 8ths) to permit subtler price differences. As with corporate and municipal bonds, you multiply the number by 10 to get the actual price. Let's say a T-bond's price is 100 and 9/32 (sometimes abbreviated as 100:09). To get the actual price you convert the fraction to a decimal (9/32 = 9 x 0.3125 = 2.8125). Then you attach it to the end of the whole number. So a bond quoted as 100 and 9/32 is selling for $1,002.81. A bond quoted at 100 is trading at its exact par value ($1,000). A bond quoted over 100 is trading at a premium. And, a bond quoted under 100 is trading at a discount. However, don't assume that the price in the paper or even the online version of the newspaper is 100% accurate. The bond market changes constantly, and an active off-hours market exists.

Rating services consider many key issues in rating a bond, including:

- The bond issuer's overall financial condition
- The issuer's debt profile
- How fast the company's revenues and profits are growing
- The state of the economy
- How well similar corporations or governments are doing given the current economic environment

The primary concern of these rating services is to alert investors to the risks of a particular issue, and to continue evaluating the financial condition of the bond's issuer until the bond reaches maturity. Depending on the issuer's current and ongoing financial condition, a bond's rating may rise or fall in quality. A drop in a bond's rating is one of the risks you face as a bond investor. If an issuer's financial condition deteriorates, rating services may downgrade the rating of a corporate or municipal bond. In the worst case scenario, the bond goes into default. Default occurs when the bond issuer fails to pay interest as it comes due and/or fails to repay the par value of the bond at maturity.

The bond quality rating systems of the two major services are similar, but not identical. Both services also make distinctions within categories Aa/AA and lower. Moody's uses a numerical system (1,2,3,) and Standard & Poor's uses a + or −.Investment-grade generally refers to any bonds rated Baa or higher by Moody's, or BBB or higher by Standard & Poor's. Junk bonds are the lowest-rated corporate and municipal bonds —meaning there's a greater-than-average chance that the issuer will fail to repay its debt. But investors may be willing to take the risk of buying these low-rated bonds because the yields are often much higher than on other, safer investments. However, the prices are volatile as well, exposing investors to additional risk if they have to sell before maturity. On the following page is a chart describing the classifications used by the various bond rating agencies which explains this point in more detail.

Fig. 21: Bond Rating Systems Used by Different Rating Agencies

Level of Credit Risk	Moody's	S&P	Fitch	Duff & Phelps
INVESTMENT GRADE				
Highest Quality	Aaa	AAA	AAA	AAA
Very Strong	Aa	AA	AA	AA
Strong	A	A	A	A
Medium Grade	Baa	BBB	BBB	BBB
NOT INVESTMENT GRADE				
Somewhat Speculative	Ba	BB	BB	BB
Speculative	B	B	B	B
Possibility of Default	Caa	CCC	CCC	CCC
Most Speculative	Ca	CC	CC	CC
Interest Unpaid or Bankruptcy Filed	C	C	C	C
In Current Default	D	D	D	D

Source: Lohr

Other Traditional Investments and Strategies

There are a vast variety of investment vehicles to choose from today, and the options grow almost daily. We will discuss some of these traditional styles and strategies next.

Cash Equivalents

While there are many investment vehicles considered to be cash equivalents, we will consider four common equivalents, while noting that T-Bills, often considered a cash equivalent, are discussed above.

Certificate of Deposit

Certificates of Deposit are issued by Banks and Savings institutions such as credit unions. They are usually insured by a governmental agency (like FDIC, the Federal Deposit Insurance Corporation) up to $100,000 per owner. Thus a married couple can deposit $400,000 in insured CDs ($100,000 in each partner's name only, and $200,000 jointly held). CDs pay interest, which can be paid out or capitalized until maturity. Rates are generally comparable to T-Bill, Note rates (See the Section on the Federal Reserve System earlier in the book).

Money Market

Money Market funds are mutual funds, which invest in very short term issues, and offer liquidity (often limited monthly) in the form of checking accounts. They generally pay a higher rate of interest than regular interest bearing checking accounts. They are issued by Banks, Brokerage Firms and other financial institutions.

Commercial Paper

Commercial Paper is unsecured debt securities issued by companies for short-terms, with a maximum of 270 days. They are generally high quality.

Repurchase Agreements

REPOs are generally offered by the Federal Open Market Committee (FOMC). FOMC buys T-Bills from a dealer, who agrees to repurchase them a short time later at a prior agreed-upon price. The Dealer can pass them along to institutional customers. They are often cash management tools for short-term investments.

Derivatives

Once a lowly step-child of the investment industry, Derivatives have taken on new meaning as more and more creative investment products have been packaged. They are securities created by Dealers or Financial Institutions to meet certain market needs. The popular ETFs and I-Shares are derivatives, as are options and futures. Some of the more common types encountered are options, commodities, and futures.

Options

Options are rights to buy or sell a certain amount of stock at a specified price at a specified time in the future. Investors may write (sell) options or buy them. The theory is that the company stock price will have moved favorably in the future so that the investor can profit.

Puts and Calls

A put is the right (and obligation) to sell a stock at a price in the future. The investor who purchases a put will hope the stock price will go down, so that it is sold for more than the price of the stock.

A call is the right to purchase a stock at a price in the future. The investor who purchases a call hopes the price will go up, so that it is higher than the stipulated price in the option. In both cases, the investors will have made a profit.

Buying and Selling options

There are various option exchanges, which are supervised by the Options Clearing Corporation (OCC) which supervises, lists and guarantees performance on option contracts. They are only sold through Brokerage Firms.

In and Out of the Money

An option, which has value currently is said to be In The Money. For instance, a call with the security selling for more that the strike price, and a put with the security selling for less than the strike price are examples of In The Money Options. An Out-of-the-Money Option is currently priced unfavorably to the investor (NOTE: It may change, prior to the expiration date).

Strike Price and Expiration Date

Strike price is the price at which the security would be bought or sold at the end of the term of the option. The expiration date is the end of the term of the option.

Intrinsic value and Time value

The intrinsic value is the amount by which the option is In The Money. The time value is the total amount of the option when due.

Commodities

Commodities are hard goods such as grain, oil, currencies, ore, timber, minerals, etc. They are generally, but not always, purchased in the Futures Market, in which contracts for purchase and sale at a time in the future are sold.

Futures

Futures specify a forward date of delivery or receipt of an amount of a tangible product. Futures are often used as a hedge against price changes, and as speculation vehicles. In general I am not a huge fan of futures trading for individual investors (again, using a mutual fund run by an expert is OK). I have just witnessed too many times that anyone without a clear expertise in this area can get slaughtered. That doesn't mean one can't learn. Just be prepared for the education to take a long time.

Alternative Investments And Strategies

Managed Futures

Managed Futures offer a money manager specializing in Futures which purchases and sells contracts for the client with discretion. Managed Futures are often used as a diversification tool, offsetting stocks, bonds and traditional securities. However, I think that in most cases, these strategies have been offered to the retail investor with layers of fees attached, and with limited liquidity. I just think there are more efficient, simpler ways to capitalize on the trends that managed futures seek to gain from.

Mortgage Backed Securities (MBS's)

Mortgage backed securities are secured by mortgages on commercial and individual properties. They are generally bonds of medium quality, buy higher yield. Again, this is an area where you had better be an expert or be prepared for some surprises. Even with all the reputable people that exist in this segment of the market, I have witnessed some of most incredibly hard sales pitches from so-called "advisors" offering MBS's, CMO's and other asset-backed bonds. One in particular took place at my office, by a fellow who was escorted to our place in a limousine. We had been urged by a friend to hear about how he generated incredible returns of 15% and higher with no risk, and that his clients had never lost any principal or interest. To me, this is the industry equivalent of a UFO, but we entertained the meeting as a favor and with a very slight degree of curiosity. That curiosity escaped out the window of our conference room long before I was able to.

When I finally interrupted his attempt at intimidating us into believing him, I asked him to take me through an example of a CMO transaction. I suggested we start with a mythical $100 investment in a single security. He continued by saying that bond would pay about $13 a year in interest with no risk (this was in 2005, not 1978 so that's a huge premium over what "safe" bonds were paying at the time). I asked him what would happen if interest rates went up, since I assumed that the bond price would go down. Specifically, I asked what would happen if the price of the bond fell to $90. At this point he confidently looked at the rest of us in the room and said "I'd just sell it and buy another bond, probably one that yielded more than 13%".

That story is probably the best way to test yourself on the basic bond knowledge covered in this Appendix. As you know, there is no guarantee whatsoever that the new bond will EVER recover the lost principal from the sale of the first bond. Remember this example the next time interest rates rise for a few years in a row. And warn your friends not to fall for salesmanship that preys on investors' lack of understanding of the basic relationship between bonds and interest rates. This guy and others like him may have made tons of money for people over the years, but that's just not a pitch I'm going to swing at!

Oh, by the way, my darling wife looked his name up on the NASD broker-check site (pretty good for someone not in the industry!). He's been with more second-rate brokerage firms than anyone I've ever seen! Knowledge of that fact alone prior to the meeting could have saved us from sitting through it.

Real Estate Investment Trusts (REITS)

REITS are packages of properties, or a fund of such packages (such as shopping centers, commercial developments, etc.) which pay a relatively high rate of interest. They are often limited partnerships, and have tax considerations, which may or may not be favorable.

American Depositary Receipts

ADRs are domestic securities tied to foreign stocks and sold on US exchanges in dollar denominated forms. They offer investors a convenient and understandable way to invest in foreign companies. Although dollar denominated, they still bear the currency risk of the home country as they mirror what impacts the stock there.

Direct Investments/Private Placements

A Private Placement is a security sold to a limited number of qualified investors, and may have any of the investment vehicles discussed in this section as the underlying securities. Partners are limited as to their liability in the venture, and the placement will be managed by a general partner who takes more risk, but is paid a management fee, as well as their share. Many Hedge Funds operate as Private Placements. Direct Investments are sold as limited partnerships and pass through income and tax losses directly to investors.

Investment Companies (Open End/Closed End)

An Open-End Investment Company is a mutual fund, which is not listed and traded on an exchange, but is sold directly to investors. When the investor sells, the fund is the purchaser. They can issue as many shares as people want to buy. These are the common mutual funds and there are thousands of them. Closed-End Funds are listed on exchanges and are bought and sold like stocks. The number of shares in a Closed-End Fund is fixed.

Hedge Funds

Hedge Funds were unregulated investments until the SEC required Hedge Fund managers to meet their registration requirements in February, 2006. Of course, some firms found have ways to delay the process by extending the time in which their investors could access their capital (called the "lockup period"). If there's a loophole in the rules, they'll find it. Unlike traditional Managed Accounts, the investor does not know what the Manager is buying, selling, shorting or optioning. They are offered as direct private placements or as Fund of Funds, which is a package of several hedge funds collectively offered by a specialist. Hedge funds and fund-of-funds are discussed in more detail in chapter 10. Hybrid Strategies are discussed in detail in Chapters 2 and 10.